T0297646

Data Architecture

Data Architecture

A Primer for the Data Scientist

Second Edition

W.H. Inmon
Daniel Linstedt
Mary Levins

Academic Press is an imprint of Elsevier
125 London Wall, London EC2Y 5AS, United Kingdom
525 B Street, Suite 1650, San Diego, CA 92101, United States
50 Hampshire Street, 5th Floor, Cambridge, MA 02139, United States
The Boulevard, Langford Lane, Kidlington, Oxford OX5 1GB, United Kingdom

© 2019 Elsevier Inc. All rights reserved.

No part of this publication may be reproduced or transmitted in any form or by any means, electronic
or mechanical, including photocopying, recording, or any information storage and retrieval system, without
permission in writing from the publisher. Details on how to seek permission, further information about
the Publisher's permissions policies and our arrangements with organizations such as the Copyright
Clearance Center and the Copyright Licensing Agency, can be found at our website: www.elsevier.com/
permissions.

This book and the individual contributions contained in it are protected under copyright by the
Publisher (other than as may be noted herein).

Notices
Knowledge and best practice in this field are constantly changing. As new research and experience
broaden our understanding, changes in research methods, professional practices, or medical treatment
may become necessary.

Practitioners and researchers must always rely on their own experience and knowledge in evaluating and
using any information, methods, compounds, or experiments described herein. In using such information
or methods they should be mindful of their own safety and the safety of others, including parties for
whom they have a professional responsibility.

To the fullest extent of the law, neither the Publisher nor the authors, contributors, or editors, assume
any liability for any injury and/or damage to persons or property as a matter of products liability, negligence
or otherwise, or from any use or operation of any methods, products, instructions, or ideas contained in
the material herein.

Library of Congress Cataloging-in-Publication Data
A catalog record for this book is available from the Library of Congress

British Library Cataloguing-in-Publication Data
A catalogue record for this book is available from the British Library

ISBN 978-0-12-816916-2

For information on all Academic Press publications
visit our website at https://www.elsevier.com/books-and-journals

Working together
to grow libraries in
developing countries

www.elsevier.com • www.bookaid.org

Publisher: Mara Conner
Acquisition Editor: Mara Conner
Editorial Project Manager: Thomas Van Der Ploeg
Production Project Manager: Punithavathy Govindaradjane
Cover Designer: Mark Rogers

Typeset by SPi Global, India

Dedication

This book is dedicated to the doctors and the hospitals who literally saved my life. This book would have never been written without the doctors and the hospital and their fine care:

Rose Hospital, Denver, Colorado
National Jewish Hospital, Denver, Colorado
Dr Christopher Stees, Rose Hospital
Dr Peder Horner, Rose Hospital
Dr Michael Firstenberg, Rose Hospital
Ryan Tobin, Rose Hospital
Dr Susan Kotake, National Jewish Hospital
Dr Ellen Volker, National Jewish Hospital

and to all the nurses and other staff who are too many to mention.

Thank you, thank you, thank you
WHI Feb 2019.

Contents

An Introduction to Data Architecture

Data architecture is about the larger picture of data and how it fits together in a typical organization. The natural starting point for looking at the big picture of how data fit together in a corporation begins naturally enough with *all* the data in the corporation.

Fig. 1.1.1 depicts symbolically *all* the data—of every kind—in the corporation.

Fig. 1.1.1 depicts every kind of data found in the corporation. It depicts data generated by running transactions. It depicts e-mail. It depicts telephone conversations. It depicts data found in personal computers. It depicts metering data. It depicts office memos. It depicts contracts, safety reports, and time sheets. It depicts pay ledgers.

In a word, if it is data and it is in the corporation, it is depicted by the bar shown in Fig. 1.1.1.

SUBDIVIDING DATA

There are many ways to subdivide the data shown in Fig. 1.1.1. The way that is shown is only one of many ways data can be understood.

One way to understand the data found in the corporation is to look at structured data and nonstructured data. Fig. 1.1.2 shows this subdivision of data.

Structured data are data that are well defined. Structured data are typically repetitive. The same structure of data recurs repeatedly. The only difference between one occurrence of data and another is in the contents of the data. As a simple example of structured data, there are records of the sale of a good—an "SKU"—made by a retailer. Each time Walmart makes a sale the item sold, the amount of the sale, the tax paid, and the date and location of the sale are recorded. In a day's time, Walmart will create many records of the sale of many items. From a structural standpoint, the sale of one item will be identical to the sale of another item. The data are called "structured" because of the similarity of the structure of the records.

1

Data Architecture. https://doi.org/10.1016/B978-0-12-816916-2.00001-2

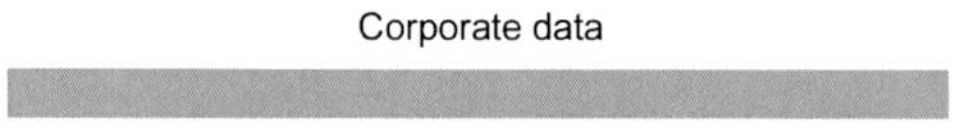

Corporate data

FIG. 1.1.1
The totality of corporate data.

Structured
data

FIG. 1.1.2
Structured data is only a small part of corporate data.

The high degree of structure and definition of the records make the records easy to handle inside a database management system.

However, structured records are hardly the only kind of data in the corporation. In fact, structured data typically represent only a small fraction of the data found in the corporation. The other kind of data found in the corporation is called unstructured data.

It has been conjectured as to how much data in the corporation are structured and how much are unstructured. There are estimates as low as 2% and as high as 20%. The estimate really depends on the nature of the business of the corporation and the nature of what data are used in the calculation of the equation.

REPETITIVE/NONREPETITIVE UNSTRUCTURED DATA

There are two basic kinds of unstructured data in the corporation—repetitive unstructured data and nonrepetitive unstructured data.

Fig. 1.1.3 depicts the different kinds of unstructured data in the corporation.

A typical form of repetitive unstructured data in the corporation might be the data generated by an analog machine. For example, a farmer has a machine that reads the identification of railroad cars as the railroad cars pass through the farmer's property. Trains pass through the property night and day. The electronic eye reads and records the passage of each car on the track.

Nonrepetitive unstructured data are data that are nonrepetitive, such as e-mails. Each e-mail can be long or short. The e-mail can be in English or Spanish (or some other languages.) The author of the e-mail can say anything that he/she

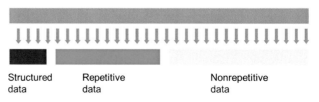

Structured
data

Repetitive
data

Nonrepetitive
data

FIG. 1.1.3
Repetitive data and nonrepetitive data.

pleases. It is only a pure accident if the contents of any e-mail are identical to the contents of any other e-mail. And there are *many* forms of nonrepetitive unstructured data. There are voice recordings, there are contracts, there are customer feedback messages, etc.

Because of its irregular form, unstructured data do not fit well with standard database management systems.

THE GREAT DIVIDE OF DATA

It is not obvious at all, but the dividing line in unstructured data between unstructured repetitive data and unstructured nonrepetitive data is very significant. In fact, the dividing line between unstructured repetitive data and unstructured nonrepetitive data is so important that the division can be called the "great divide" of data.

Fig. 1.1.4 shows the great divide of data.

It is hardly obvious why there should be this great divide of data. But there are some very good reasons for the divide:

Repetitive data usually have very limited business value, while nonrepetitive data are rich in business value.
Repetitive data can be handled one way; nonrepetitive data are handled very differently.
Repetitive data can be analyzed one way, while nonrepetitive data can be analyzed in a very different manner.
And so forth.

The two worlds—of repetitive data and of nonrepetitive data—are as different as chalk and cheese. Tools and techniques that work in one world simply are not applicable to the other world and vice versa.

In many ways, the great divide of data is as profound as the continental divide. In the continental divide, snow that falls on one side of the divide ends up as

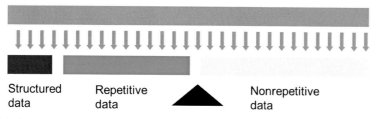

Structured data   Repetitive data   Nonrepetitive data

FIG. 1.1.4
The great divide.

FIG. 1.1.5
The great divide.

water that flows to the Pacific Ocean, whereas snow that falls on the other side of the divide ends up heading for the Atlantic Ocean.

Fig. 1.1.5 shows the continental divide.

TEXTUAL/NONTEXTUAL DATA

The unstructured nonrepetitive data can be further subdivided. Nonrepetitive unstructured data can be divided into textual and nontextual data.

Fig. 1.1.6 shows this further subdivision of data.

Textual data are that data that are embodied in the form of text. An obvious example is e-mail or contract data. An e-mail is nothing but text, and a contract is nothing but text. Nonrepetitive nontextual data might be the picture an insurance adjuster takes of a car after it has been in an accident. Or the real estate agent may make a video tape of a house that is for sale.

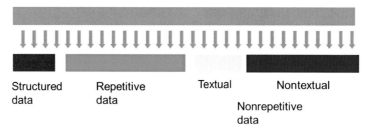

FIG. 1.1.6
Textual and nontextual nonrepetitive data.

THE DIFFERENT FORMS OF DATA

The basic divisions of data that are shown in Fig. 1.1.6 are important for a lot of reasons. Each of the divisions of data requires their own infrastructure, their own technology, and their own treatment. Even though all forms of data exist in the same corporation, each of the forms of data may as well exist on different planets. They simply require their own treatment and their own unique infrastructure.

BUSINESS VALUE

There are then many reasons for the different treatment of the different forms of data. But perhaps the most salient reason for the difference in the forms of data is the relationship to business value.

Fig. 1.1.7 shows that there is a very different relationship to business value across the different forms of data.

Fig. 1.1.7 shows that there is a very high degree of business value for structured data. As an example of the value of structured data, it is really important to the business to have the correct bank account balance, both to the bank and to the customer.

Textual data contain even more highly valued business data. When customers talk to an agent of the company through a call center, everything the customer says is valuable.

And there is significantly less business value for nonrepetitive nontextual data and unstructured repetitive data.

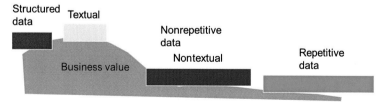

The business value of different types of data is very different

FIG. 1.1.7
Business value varies dramatically across different types of data.

The Data Infrastructure

If there is any secret to data management and data architecture, it is understanding data in terms of its infrastructure. Stated differently, trying to understand the larger architecture under which data are managed and operate is almost impossible without understanding the underlying infrastructure, which surrounds data. Therefore, we shall spend some time understanding infrastructure.

TWO TYPES OF REPETITIVE DATA

A good starting point for understanding infrastructure is to start with the observation that there are two types of repetitive data found in corporate data. In the structured side of corporate data, repetitive data are found. In the unstructured big data side of corporate data, repetitive data are also found. Despite the fact that the types of data sound the same, there are significant differences between the different types of repetitive data. When it comes to structured repetitive data, it is normal to have transactions as part of the repetitive data. There are sales transactions, stocking of SKU transactions, inventory replenishment transactions, payment transactions, and so forth. In the structured world, there are many of these transactions that find their way into the repetitive structured world.

The other kind of repetitive data is the repetitive data found in the unstructured big data world. In the unstructured big data world, we might have metering data, analog data, manufacturing data, clickstream data, and so forth.

There is the question then—are these types of repetitive data the same? They certainly are repetitive. But these different types of repetitive data are not the same. What is the difference then between these two types of repetitive data? Fig. 1.2.1 shows (symbolically) these two types of repetitive data.

REPETITIVE STRUCTURED DATA

In order to understand the differences between these two types of repetitive data, it is necessary to understand each type of data individually. Let's start with

7

Data Architecture. https://doi.org/10.1016/B978-0-12-816916-2.00002-4

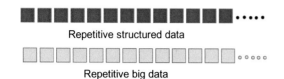
Repetitive structured data

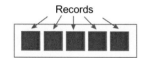
Repetitive big data

FIG. 1.2.1
Two types of repetitive data.

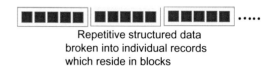
Repetitive structured data
broken into individual records
which reside in blocks

FIG. 1.2.2
Repetitive data broken into blocks.

Records

FIG. 1.2.3
Records inside a block.

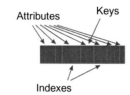
Attributes   Keys

Indexes

FIG. 1.2.4
Attributes, keys, and indexes.

repetitive structured data. Fig. 1.2.2 shows the repetitive structured data are broken into records and blocks.

The most basic unit of information in the repetitive structured environment is a block of data. Inside each block of data are records of data.

Fig. 1.2.3 shows a simple record of data.

Each record of data is (normally!) representative of a transaction. For example, there are records of data representing the sale of a product. Each record is representative of a single sale.

Inside each record are keys, attributes, and indexes. Fig. 1.2.4 shows the anatomy of a record.

If a record is representative of a sale, the attributes might be information about the date of the sale, the item sold, the cost of the item, any tax on the item, who bought the item, and so forth. The key of the record is one or more attributes that uniquely define the record. The key for a sale might be the date of sale, item sold, and location of the sale.

The indexes that are attached to the record are on the attributes that are needed when there is a desire to have quick access to the record.

The infrastructure that is attached to structured repetitive data managed under a DBMS is seen in Fig. 1.2.5.

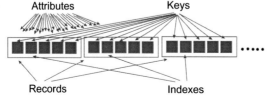
Attributes   Keys

Records   Indexes

FIG. 1.2.5
A standard DBMS.

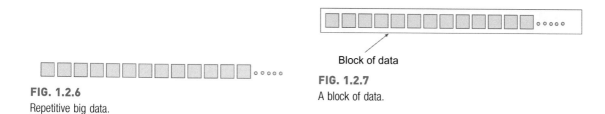

Block of data

FIG. 1.2.7
A block of data.

FIG. 1.2.6
Repetitive big data.

REPETITIVE BIG DATA

The other type of repetitive data is repetitive data found in big data. Fig. 1.2.6 depicts the repetitive data found in big data.

At first glance, there are just a lot of repetitive records seen in Fig. 1.2.6. But upon closer examination, it is seen that all of those repetitive big data records are packed away into a string of data and that string of data is stored inside a block of data, as seen in Fig. 1.2.7.

The structured infrastructure seen in Fig. 1.2.7 is typical of an infrastructure managed under one of several DBMS such as Oracle, SQL Server, and DB2.

The infrastructure for big data is quite different than the infrastructure found in a standard DBMS. In the infrastructure for big data, there is a block. And in the block are found many repetitive records. Each record is merely concatenated to each other record. Fig. 1.2.8 is representative of a record that might be found in big data.

In Fig. 1.2.8, it is seen that there is merely a long string of data, with records stacked one against the other. The system only sees the block and the long string of data. In order to find a record, the system needs to "parse" the string, as seen in Fig. 1.2.9.

Suppose the system wants to find a given record. The system needs to sequentially read the string of data until it recognizes that there is a record. Then, the system needs to go into the record and determine whether it is record "B." This is how a search is conducted in the most primitive state in big data.

It doesn't take much of an imagination to see that a lot of machine cycles are chewed up looking for data in big data. To this end, the big data environment employs a means of processing referred to as the "Roman census" approach. More will be described about the Roman census approach in the chapter on big data.

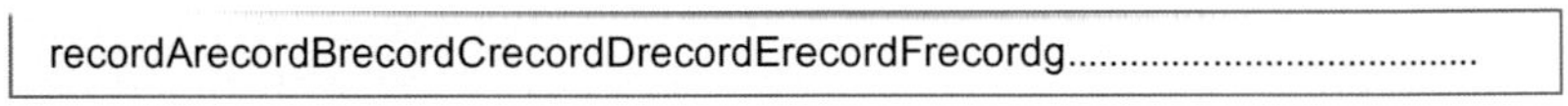

recordArecordBrecordCrecordDrecordErecordFrecordg..

FIG. 1.2.8
Records inside the block.

FIG. 1.2.9
Parsing records inside the block.

THE TWO INFRASTRUCTURES

The two different infrastructures are contrasted in Fig. 1.2.10.

Without much effort, it is seen that the infrastructures surrounding big data and structured data are quite different. The infrastructure surrounding big data is quite simple and streamlined. The infrastructure surrounding structured DBMS data is elaborate and anything but streamlined.

There is then no argument as to the fact that there are significant differences between the infrastructure of repetitive structured data and repetitive big data.

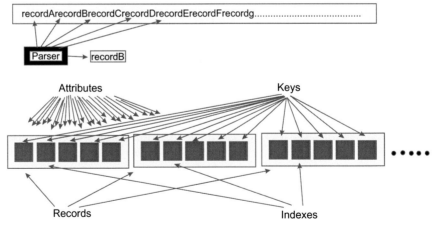

FIG. 1.2.10
Two different infrastructures.

WHAT'S BEING OPTIMIZED?

When looking at the two infrastructures, it is natural to ask—what is being optimized by the different infrastructures. In the case of big data, the optimization of the infrastructure is on the ability of the system to manage almost unlimited

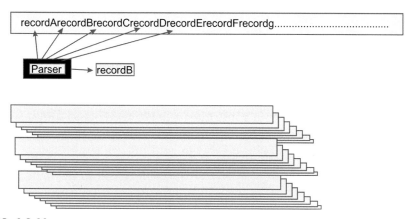

FIG. 1.2.11
Optimal for storing massive amounts of data.

amounts of data. Fig. 1.2.11 shows that with the infrastructure of big data, adding new data is a very easy and streamlined thing to do.

But the infrastructure behind a structured DBMS is optimized for something quite different than managing huge amounts of data. In the case of the structured DBMS environment, the optimization is on the ability to find any one given unit of data quickly and efficiently.

Fig. 1.2.12 shows the optimization of the infrastructure of a standard structured DBMS.

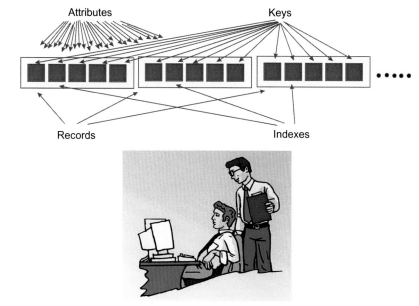

FIG. 1.2.12
Optimal for direct online access of data.

COMPARING THE TWO INFRASTRUCTURES

Another way to think of the different infrastructures is in terms of the amount of data and overhead required to find a given unit of data. In order to find a given unit of data, the big data environment has to search through a whole host of data. Many input/output operations (I/Os) have got to be done to find a given item. To find that same item in a structured DBMS environment, only a few I/Os need to be done. So if you want to optimize on the speed of access of data, the standard structured DBMS is the way to go.

On the other hand, in order to achieve the speed of access, an elaborate infrastructure for data is required by the standard structured DBMS. An infrastructure must be both built and maintained over time, as data change. A considerable amount of system resources is required for the building and maintenance of this infrastructure. But when it comes to big data, the infrastructure required to be built and maintained is nil. The big data infrastructure is built easily and maintained very easily.

This section began with the proposition that repetitive data can be found in both the structured and big data environment. At first glance, the repetitive data are the same or are very similar. But when you look at the infrastructure and the mechanics implied in the infrastructure, it is seen that the repetitive data in each of the environments are indeed very different.

The "Great Divide"

CLASSIFYING CORPORATE DATA

Corporate data can be classified in many different ways. One of the major classifications is by structured versus unstructured data. And unstructured data can be further broken into two categories—repetitive unstructured data and nonrepetitive unstructured data. This division of data is shown in Fig. 1.3.1.

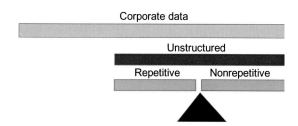

FIG. 1.3.1
The great divide.

Repetitive unstructured data are data that occur very often and whose records are almost identical in terms of structure and content. There are many examples of repetitive unstructured data—telephone call records, metered data, analog data, and so forth.

Nonrepetitive unstructured data are data that consist of records of data where the records are not similar, in terms of either structure or content. There are many examples of nonrepetitive unstructured data—e-mails, call center conversations, warranty claims, and so forth.

Data Architecture. https://doi.org/10.1016/B978-0-12-816916-2.00003-6

THE "GREAT DIVIDE"

Between the two types of unstructured data is what can be termed the "great divide."

The "great divide" is the demarcation of repetitive and nonrepetitive records, as seen in the figure. At first glance, it does not appear that there should be a massive difference between repetitive unstructured records and nonrepetitive unstructured records of data. But such is not the case at all. There indeed is a HUGE difference between repetitive unstructured data and nonrepetitive unstructured data.

The primary distinction between the two types of unstructured data is that repetitive unstructured data focus its attention on the management of data in the Hadoop/big data environment, whereas the attention of nonrepetitive unstructured data focuses its attention on textual disambiguation of data. And as shall be seen, this difference in focus makes a huge difference in how the data are perceived, how the data are used, and how the data are managed.

This difference—the "great divide"—is shown in Fig. 1.3.2.

It is seen then that there is a very different focus between the two types of unstructured data.

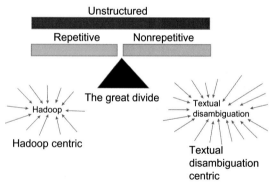

FIG. 1.3.2
Different types of unstructured data.

REPETITIVE UNSTRUCTURED DATA

The repetitive unstructured data are said to be "Hadoop" centric. Being "Hadoop" centric means that processing of repetitive unstructured data revolves around processing and managing the Hadoop/big data environment. The centricity of the repetitive unstructured data is seen in Fig. 1.3.3.

The center of the Hadoop environment naturally enough is Hadoop. Hadoop is one of the technologies by which data can be managed over very large amounts of data. Hadoop/big data is at the center of what is known as "big data."

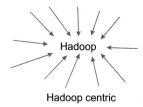

FIG. 1.3.3
Hadoop centric unstructured data.

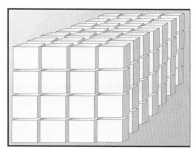

FIG. 1.3.4
Hadoop.

FIG. 1.3.5
Services needed by big data.

Hadoop is one of the primary storage mechanism for big data. The essential characteristics of Hadoop are that Hadoop

- is capable of managing very large volumes of data,
- manages data on less expensive storage,
- manages data by the "Roman census" method,
- stores data in an unstructured manner.

Because of these operating characteristics of Hadoop, very large volumes of data can be managed. Hadoop is capable of managing volumes of data significantly larger than standard relational database management systems.

The big data technology of Hadoop is depicted in Fig. 1.3.4.

But Hadoop/big data is a raw technology. In order to be useful, Hadoop/big data requires its own unique infrastructure.

The technologies that surround Hadoop/big data serve to manage the data and to access and analyze the data found in Hadoop. The infrastructure services that surround Hadoop are seen in Fig. 1.3.5.

The services that surround Hadoop/big data are familiar to anyone that has ever used a standard DBMS. The difference is that in a standard DBMS, the services are found in the DBMS itself, while in Hadoop, many of the services have to be done externally. A second major difference is that throughout the Hadoop/big data environment, there is the need to service huge volumes of data. The developer in the Hadoop/big data environment must be prepared to manage and handle extremely large volumes of data. This means that many infrastructure tasks can be handled only in the Hadoop/big data environment itself.

Indeed, the Hadoop environment is permeated by the need to be able to handle extraordinarily large amounts of data. The need to handle large amounts of data—indeed, almost unlimited amounts of data—is seen in Fig. 1.3.6

There is then an emphasis on doing the normal tasks of data management in the Hadoop environment where the process must be able to handle very large amounts of data.

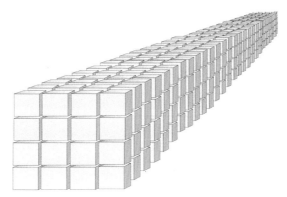

FIG. 1.3.6
An infinite amount of data.

NONREPETITIVE UNSTRUCTURED DATA

The emphasis in the nonrepetitive unstructured environment is quite different than the emphasis on the management of the Hadoop big data technology. In the nonrepetitive unstructured environment, there is an emphasis on "textual disambiguation" (or on "textual ETL"). This emphasis is shown in Fig. 1.3.7.

Textual disambiguation is the process of taking nonrepetitive unstructured data and manipulating it into a format that can be analyzed by standard analytic software. There are many facets to textual disambiguation, but perhaps the most important functionality is one that can be called "contextualization." Contextualization is the process by which text is read and analyzed and the context of the text is derived. Once the context of the text is derived, the text is then reformatted into a standard database format where the text can be read and analyzed by standard "business intelligence" software.

The process of textual disambiguation is shown in Fig. 1.3.8.

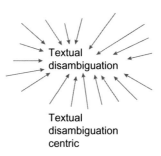

FIG. 1.3.7
Textual disambiguation centric unstructured data.

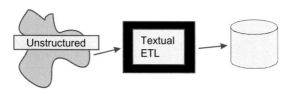

FIG. 1.3.8
From unstructured to structured data.

There are many facets to textual disambiguation. Textual disambiguation is completely free from the limitations of natural language processing (NLP). In textual disambiguation, there is a multifaceted approach to the identification of and derivation of context.

Some of the techniques used to derive context include the following:

- The integration of external taxonomies and ontologies
- Proximity analysis
- Homographic resolution
- Subdocument processing
- Associative text resolution
- Acronym resolution
- Simple stop word processing
- Simple word stemming
- Inline pattern recognition

In truth, there are many more facets to the process of textual disambiguation than those shown. Some of the more important facets of textual disambiguation are shown in Fig. 1.3.9.

There is a concern regarding the volume of data that is managed by textual disambiguation. But the volume of data that can be processed is secondary to the

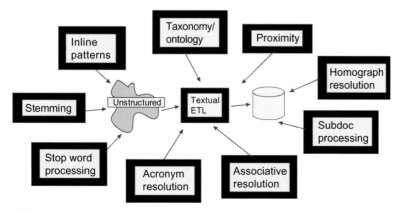

FIG. 1.3.9
Some of the services needed to turn unstructured into structured data.

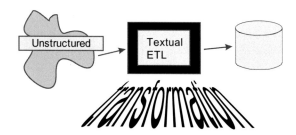

FIG. 1.3.10
Transformation.

transformation of data that occurs during the transformation process. Simply stated, it doesn't matter how fast you can process data if you cannot understand what it is that you are processing. The fact that textual disambiguation is dominated by transformation is depicted in Fig. 1.3.10.

There is then a completely different emphasis on the processing that occurs in the repetitive unstructured world versus the processing that occurs in the nonrepetitive unstructured world.

DIFFERENT WORLDS

This difference is seen in Fig. 1.3.11.

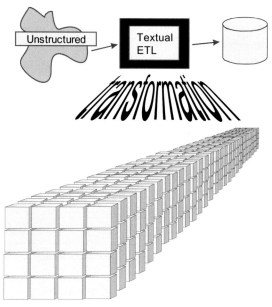

FIG. 1.3.11
Transforming big data.

Part of the reason for the difference between repetitive unstructured data and nonrepetitive unstructured data lies in the very data themselves. With repetitive unstructured data, there is not much of a need to discover the context of the data. With repetitive unstructured data, data occur so frequently and so repeatedly that the context of that data is fairly obvious or fairly easy to ascertain. In addition, there typically are not much contextual data to begin with when it comes to repetitive unstructured data. Therefore, the emphasis is almost entirely on the need to manage volumes of data.

But with nonrepetitive unstructured data, there is a great need to derive the context of the data. Before the data can be used analytically, the data need to be contextualized. And with nonrepetitive unstructured data, deriving the context of the data is a very complex thing to do. For sure, there is a need to manage volumes of data when it comes to nonrepetitive unstructured data. But the primary need is the need to contextualize the data in the first place.

For these reasons, there is a "great divide" when it comes to managing and dealing with the different forms of unstructured data.

Demographics of Corporate Data

It is one thing to understand that corporate data can be divided up into different categories. It is another thing to understand those categories in depth.

Fig. 1.4.1 shows one way how corporate data can be divided.

In Fig. 1.4.1, it is seen that all data in big data are unstructured and that big data can be divided up into two major categories—repetitive unstructured data and nonrepetitive unstructured data. The diagram in Fig. 1.4.1 shows the major categorization of corporate data. But the diagram can be very misleading. Some corporations have a tremendous amount of repetitive unstructured data, and other corporations have no repetitive unstructured data at all.

A more realistic representation of the demographics of repetitive unstructured data is shown by Fig. 1.4.2.

In Fig. 1.4.2, it is seen that there is a wide spectrum of ratios of repetitive data to other types of data. From a demographic standpoint, some corporations have a preponderance of repetitive unstructured data, and other corporations have no repetitive unstructured whatsoever. And other corporations are somewhere between the two extremes.

The type of business has a great deal to do with exactly how much repetitive unstructured data there are (or are not). A typical scattering of repetitive ratios by type of business is shown in Fig. 1.4.3.

In Fig 1.4.3, it is seen that certain industries have a lot of repetitive unstructured data. Weather services, manufacturing, and public utilities are at the top of the list. These types of corporations have activities that generate a huge amount of repetitive unstructured data. On the other hand, small retailing organizations may have no repetitive unstructured data at all.

There is then a spectrum of ratios of repetitive unstructured data to other types of data depending on the business.

Another way to look at the same thing is to look at types of data. The spectrum of ratios is seen in Fig. 1.4.4.

Data Architecture. https://doi.org/10.1016/B978-0-12-816916-2.00004-8

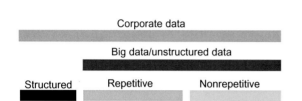

FIG. 1.4.1
One way to look at corporate data.

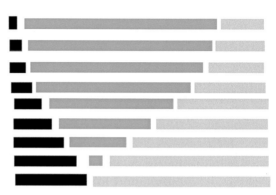

FIG. 1.4.2
The spectrum of ratios of data types.

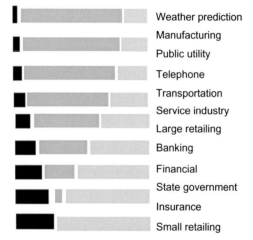

FIG. 1.4.3
Different environments.

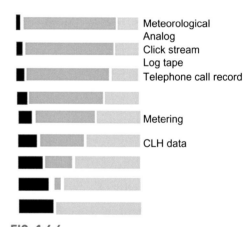

FIG. 1.4.4
Some other environments.

In Fig. 1.4.4, it is seen that when it comes to repetitive unstructured data, there are a lot of meteorologic data, a lot of analog data, and a lot of click stream data for some corporations.

While the demographics of repetitive unstructured data are an interesting way to view corporate data, there are other interesting perspectives as well. Another interesting perspective is from the perspective of business relevancy. Business relevancy refers to the usefulness of data in the decision-making process. Some corporate data are highly business-relevant, and other corporate data are not really relevant to the decision-making in the corporation at all.

How business relevancy relates to corporate data is seen in Fig. 1.4.5.

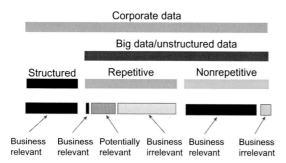

FIG. 1.4.5
Business value across the different types of data.

In Fig. 1.4.5, it is seen that there really are three classes of business relevancy—business-relevant data, business-irrelevant data, and potentially business-relevant data.

Each of these categories of data deserves their own explanation.

The first category of data is that of structured data. Structured data are typically managed by a DBMS. Fig. 1.4.6 shows that all structured data are (at least potentially) business-relevant.

Much of structured data are available for online processing. And all elements of data in the structured environment are able to be located and accessed for processing. For this reason, all structured data are categorized as business-relevant data.

Consider an example. A customer walks into the bank and asks for a withdrawal of $500. The bank teller accesses the customers' account and sees that there is a sufficient balance in the account. The bank teller then authorizes the withdrawal for $500. The data regarding the customers' account have been used and are certainly business-relevant.

Now, consider the data in the structured database of the bank that are not being accessed by a bank teller. Are these data still business-relevant even though they are not being used? The answer is that the data are still business-relevant even though they are not being used. They are still business-relevant if they *might* be used.

That is why all structured data are considered to be business-relevant. Its actual usage has little to do with its business value. The data still have business value and relevancy even if they are not being actively used.

Now, consider the business relevancy of repetitive unstructured data. Fig. 1.4.7 shows that only a tiny fraction of repetitive unstructured data are business-relevant. A larger percentage of repetitive unstructured data are potentially business-relevant. And a significant portion of repetitive unstructured data are not business-relevant.

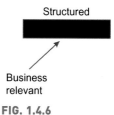

FIG. 1.4.6
Business relevant data.

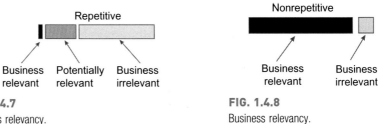

FIG. 1.4.7
Business relevancy.

FIG. 1.4.8
Business relevancy.

In order to understand the business relevancy of repetitive unstructured data, look at one of the many examples of repetitive unstructured data. Consider log tapes. When looking at a log tape, nearly, all the records on the log tape are meaningless to the business user. Only a few important records on the log tape may have direct business relevancy.

Or consider telephone call detail records. In a days' time, many, many records will be created. And suppose you are looking for phone calls relating to terrorism. Out of the millions and millions of phone calls made, only a handful will relate to activities of terrorism.

The same phenomenon is true of click stream data, analog data, metering data, and so forth. There do exist however records that are not directly business-relevant but are *potentially* business-relevant. These potentially business-relevant records are records that are not immediately useful to the business but are potentially useful under other circumstances.

Now, let's consider the business relevancy of nonrepetitive unstructured data. Nonrepetitive unstructured data are made up of records such as e-mail, call center data, conversations, and insurance claims. Fig. 1.4.8 depicts nonrepetitive unstructured data.

In nonrepetitive unstructured data, there are data such as spam, blather, and stop words. These types of data are not business-relevant. But much of the data found in the nonrepetitive unstructured category are business-relevant (or are at least *potentially* business-relevant).

Now, let's stop and take a look at the demographics of business relevancy as they relate to unstructured data (big data). Fig. 1.4.9 shows where business relevancy lies.

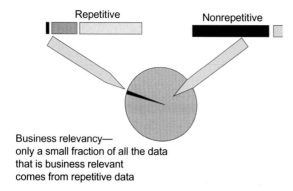

Business relevancy—
only a small fraction of all the data
that is business relevant
comes from repetitive data

FIG. 1.4.9
Business relevancy.

Fig. 1.4.9 shows that the vast majority of the business relevancy of big data lies in the realm of nonrepetitive unstructured data. There simply is relatively little business relevancy found in repetitive unstructured data.

This graphic perhaps explains why the early proponents of big data that focused almost entirely on repetitive unstructured data had such a difficult time establishing business relevancy for big data.

Corporate Data Analysis

Data are fairly worthless unless it can be analyzed. So, the data architect must always keep in mind that ultimately, the purpose of data is to support analysis.

The analysis of corporate data is pretty much like the analysis of other kinds of data with one exception. And that exception is that most of the time, corporate data come from multiple sources and multiple types of data. The fact that the origins of corporate data are multifaceted colors all of the analysis of corporate data. Fig. 1.5.1 depicts the need to analyze corporate data.

As is the case with all data analysis, the first consideration of analysis is whether the analysis will be a formal analysis or an informal analysis. A formal analysis is one with corporate or even legal consequences. Occasionally, an organization has to do an analysis that is governed under rules of compliance. Typical governing bodies are Sarbanes-Oxley or HIPAA. And there are plenty other types of compliance, such as audit compliance. When a formal analysis is occurring, the analyst has to concern himself/herself with the validity and the lineage of the data. If incorrect data are used for a formal analysis, the consequences can be dire. Therefore, if a formal analysis is to occur, then veracity and the lineage of the data are very important. In the case of public corporations, an external public accounting firm must sign off on the quality and accuracy of the data.

The other type of analysis to be done is an informal analysis. An informal analysis is done really quickly and can use any available numbers. While it is nice if the data used for an informal analysis is accurate, the consequences of using less than accurate information for an informal analysis are not severe.

When doing data analysis, constant awareness must be made as to whether the analysis is formal or informal.

The first step in doing corporate data analysis is physically gathering the data to be analyzed. Fig. 1.5.2 shows there are usually many diverse sources of corporate data.

In many cases, the sources of data are automated, so physically gathering data is not much of a problem. But in some cases, the data exist on a physical medium such as paper, and the data must pass through technology such as optical

27

Data Architecture. https://doi.org/10.1016/B978-0-12-816916-2.00005-X

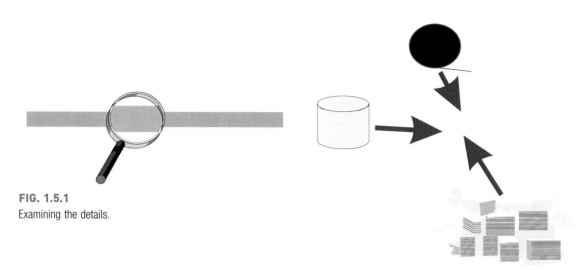

FIG. 1.5.1
Examining the details.

FIG. 1.5.2
Diverse sources of textual data.

character recognition (OCR) software. Or in other cases, the data exist as conversations and must pass through voice recognition/transcription technology.

Usually, the physical gathering of data is the easiest part of doing analysis across the corporation. Much more challenging is the logical resolution problem. The logical resolution aspect of corporate data management addresses the issue of bringing together many disparate sources of data and reading and processing the data seamlessly. There are MANY problems with the logical resolution of corporate data. Some of the many problems are as follows:

Resolving key structures—a key in one part of the corporation is different from a similar key in another part of the corporation.
Resolving definitions—data defined one way in the corporation are defined another way in a different part of the corporation.
Resolving calculations—a calculation made one way in the corporation is made using a different formula in another part of the corporation.
Resolving data structures—data structured one way in the corporation are structured differently in another part of the corporation.

And the list goes on.

In many cases, the difficulties of resolution are so difficult and so ingrained in the data that resolution cannot be satisfactorily done. In this case, the corporation ends up having different analyses being done by different organizations in the corporation. The problem with different organizations doing their own separate analysis and calculation is that the result is parochial among the different organizations. No one at the corporate level is able to see what is going on at the highest level of the corporation.

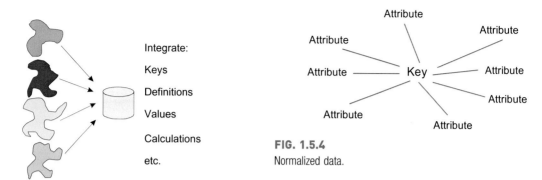

Integrate:

Keys

Definitions

Values

Calculations

etc.

FIG. 1.5.3
Integration of data.

FIG. 1.5.4
Normalized data.

The problem of resolution of data is magnified with corporate data when data cross the boundary of structured data and big data. And even within big data, when data cross the boundary between repetitive unstructured data and non-repetitive unstructured data, there is a challenge.

There are then serious challenges when the corporation attempts to create a cohesive, holistic view of data across the entire corporation. If there is to be a true corporate foundation of data, it is necessary to integrate data, as seen in Fig. 1.5.3.

Once data are integrated (or at least once as much data as can be integrated are in fact integrated), it is then reformatted into a normalized fashion. There is nothing particularly magical about a normalized structuring of data other than

- normalization is a logical way to organize data,
- tools that do much of analytic processing operate best on normalized data.

Fig. 1.5.4 shows that once data are normalized, it is easy to analyze.

The result of normalization is that data can be placed into flat file records. Once data are placed into normalized, flat file records, the data can be easily calculated and compared and all the other aspects of normalization.

Normalization is an optimal state for data to be analyzed because in a normalized state, the data are at a very low point of granularity. Because the data are at a very low point of granularity, it can be categorized and calculated in many different ways. From an analogical standpoint, data in a normalized state are similar to grains of silicon. Raw grains of silicon can be recombined and remanufactured into many different forms—glass, computer chips, body implants, and so forth. By the same token, normalized data can be reworked into many different forms of analysis.

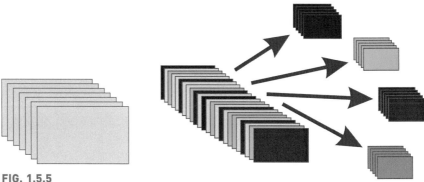

FIG. 1.5.5
Normalized records of data.

FIG. 1.5.6
Categorization of data.

(As a side note, normalizing data does not necessarily mean that data will be placed into a relational structure. Most of the time, the normalized data are placed into a relational structure. But it is entirely possible to place normalized data in a structure other than a relational structure if that makes sense.)

Whatever structuring of data is used, the result is that normalized data are placed into records of data that may or may not have a relational foundation, as seen in Fig. 1.5.5.

Once the data are structured into a granular state, the data can then be analyzed in many different ways. In truth, once corporate data are integrated and placed into a granular state, the analysis of corporate data is not very different than the analysis of any other kind of data.

Typically, the first step of analysis is categorization of data. Fig. 1.5.6 suggests the categorization of data.

Once data are categorized, many sorts of analysis can ensue. One of the typical forms of analysis is the identification of exceptional data. For example, the analyst may wish to find all customers who have spent more than $1,000 in the past year. Or the analyst may want to find days when production peaked over 25 units a day. Or the analyst may want to find what products were painted red that weighed more than 50 pounds. Fig. 1.5.7 depicts an exception analysis.

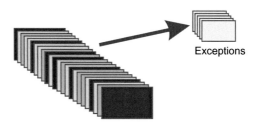

Exceptions

FIG. 1.5.7
Exceptions analysis.

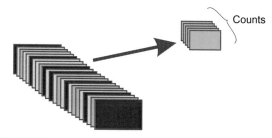

FIG. 1.5.8
Simple counts of records.

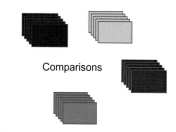

FIG. 1.5.9
Comparisons of different records.

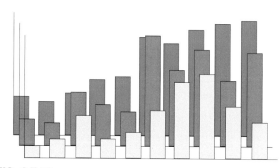

FIG. 1.5.10
Comparing information over time.

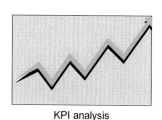

KPI analysis

FIG. 1.5.11
Key performance indicators (KPIs).

Another simple form of analysis is that of categorizing data and counting the data. Fig. 1.5.8 shows a simple categorization and count.

And of course, once counts by category can be done, comparisons across categories can be done as well, as seen in Fig. 1.5.9.

Another typical form of analysis is that of comparing information over time, as seen in Fig. 1.5.10.

And finally, there are key performance indicators (KPIs). Fig. 1.5.11 shows the calculation and tracking of a KPI over time.

The Life Cycle of Data: Understanding Data Over Time

Data in the corporation have a predictable life cycle. The life cycle applies to most data. There are however a few exceptions. Some data do not follow the life cycle that will be described (but most does). The life cycle of data looks like the diagram shown in Figs. 1.6.1 and 1.6.2.

The life cycle of data shows that raw data enter the corporate information systems. The entry of raw data can be made in many ways. The customer may do a transaction, and the data are captured as a by-product of the transaction. An analog computer may make a reading, and the data are entered as part of the analog processing. A customer may initiate an activity (such as make a phone call), and a computer captures that information. There are many ways that data can enter the information systems of the corporation.

After the raw detailed data have entered the system, the next step is that the raw detailed data pass through a capture/edit process. In the capture/edit process, the raw detailed data pass through a basic edit process. In the edit process, the raw detailed data can be adjusted (or even rejected). In general, the data that enter the information systems of the corporation are at the most detailed level.

After the raw detailed data have passed through the edit/capture process, the raw detailed data then go through an organization process. The organization process can be as simple as simple indexing the data. Or the raw detailed data may be subjected to an elaborate filtering/calculation/merging process. At this point, the raw detailed data are like putty that can be shaped in many ways by the system designer.

Once the raw detailed data have passed through the organization process, the data are then fit to be stored. The data can be stored in a standard DBMS or in big data (or in other forms of storage). After the data are stored, before the data are fit for analysis, it typically passes through an integration process. The

⇨ Entry ⇨ Capture ⇨ Organize ⇨ Store ⇨
Life cycle of data (1)

FIG. 1.6.1
The life cycle of data.

⇨Integration ⇨Usefulness ⇨Archive⇨ Discard
Life cycle of data (2)

FIG. 1.6.2
The life cycle of data.

33

Data Architecture. https://doi.org/10.1016/B978-0-12-816916-2.00006-1

purpose of the integration process is to restructure the data so that they are fit to be combined with other types of data.

It is at this point that the data enter the cycle of usefulness. The cycle of usefulness will be discussed at length later. After the data have fulfilled its usefulness, the data can be either archived or discarded.

The life cycle of data that has been described is for raw detailed data. There is a slightly different life cycle of data for summarized or aggregated data.

The life cycle of summarized or aggregated data is seen in Fig. 1.6.3.

The life cycle for most summarized or aggregated data begins the same way that raw detailed data begin. Raw data are ingested into the corporation. But once that raw data become a part of the infrastructure, the raw data are accessed, categorized, and calculated. The calculation is then saves as part of the information infrastructure, as seen in Fig. 1.6.3.

Once raw and summarized become part of the information infrastructure, the data are then subject to the "curve of usefulness." The curve of usefulness states that the longer data remain in the infrastructure, the less likely it is that the data will be used in analysis.

Fig. 1.6.4 illustrates that when looked at from the standpoint of age, the fresher the data are, the greater the chances are that the data will be accessed. This phenomenon applies to most types of data found in the corporate information infrastructure.

As data age in the corporate information infrastructure, the probability of access drops. The older data—for all practical purposes—become "dormant."

The phenomenon of data becoming dormant is not quite as true for structured online data.

There are certain types of business where the phenomenon of data aging is not as true, as well. One type of industry is the life insurance industry, where actuaries are regularly looking at data that are over 100 years old. And in certain scientific and manufacturing research organizations, there may be great interest in results that were generated over 50 years ago. But most organizations do not

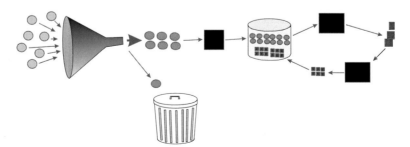

FIG. 1.6.3
From raw data to summarized data.

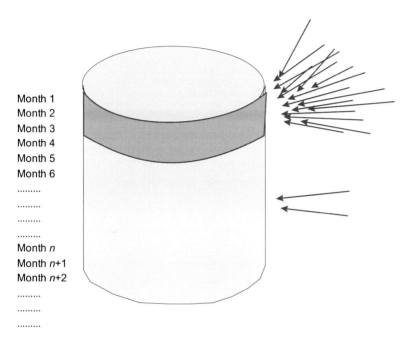

Month 1
Month 2
Month 3
Month 4
Month 5
Month 6
....
....
....
....
Month *n*
Month *n*+1
Month *n*+2
....
....
....

FIG. 1.6.4
Distinctive pattern of usage of data.

have an actuary or a scientific research facility. For those more ordinary organizations, the focus is almost always on the most current data.

The declining curve of usefulness can be expressed by a curve, as seen in Fig. 1.6.5.

The declining curve of usefulness states that over time, the value of data decreases, at least insofar as the probability of access is concerned. Note that the value never actually gets to zero. But after a while, the value *nearly* approaches zero. At some point in time, the value is so low that for all practical purposes, it might as well be zero.

The curve is a rather sharp curve—a classical Poisson distribution.

An interesting aspect of the curve is that the curve is actually different for summary and detailed data. Fig. 1.6.6 shows the difference in the curve for detailed data and summary data.

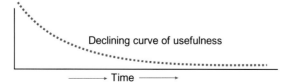

Declining curve of usefulness

Time

FIG. 1.6.5
The declining curve of usefulness of data.

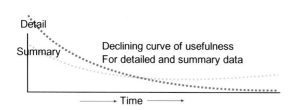

FIG. 1.6.6
The declining curve of usefulness for detailed data and summary data.

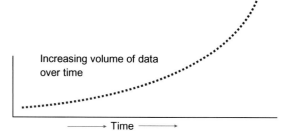

FIG. 1.6.7
The increasing volume of data over time.

Fig. 1.6.6 shows that the declining curve of usefulness for data is much steeper for detailed data than it is for summary data. Furthermore, over time, the usefulness of summary data goes flat but does not approach zero, whereas the curve for detailed data indeed does approach zero. And in some cases, the curve for summarized data over time starts to actually grow, although at a very incremental rate.

There is another way to look at the dormancy of data over time. Consider the curve that expresses the accumulation of data over time. This curve is shown in Fig. 1.6.7.

Fig. 1.6.7 shows that over time, the volume of data that accumulates in the corporation accelerates. This phenomenon is pretty much true for every organization.

Another way to look at this accumulation curve is shown in Fig. 1.6.8.

Fig. 1.6.8 shows that as data accumulate over time in the corporation, there are different and dynamic bands of usage of data. There is one band of data that shows that some data are heavily used over time. There is another band of data for lightly used data. And there is yet another band of data for data that are not used at all.

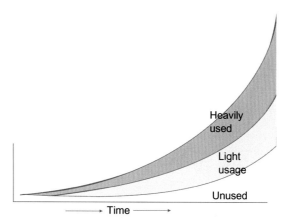

FIG. 1.6.8
Different and dynamic bands of usefulness of data over time.

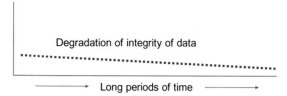

FIG. 1.6.9
The degradation of data over time.

As time passes, these bands of data expand.

Usually, the bands of data relate to the age of the data. The younger the data are, the more relevant the data are to the current business of the corporation. And the younger the data are, the more the data are accessed and analyzed.

When it comes to looking at data over time, there is another interesting phenomenon that occurs. That phenomenon is that over long periods of time, the integrity of data "degrades." Perhaps, the term degrades is not appropriate because there is a pejorative sense to "degrades." And—as used here—the term "degrades" has no such pejorative connotations. Instead, as used here, the term "degrades" simply means that there is a natural and normal decay of meaning of data over time.

Fig. 1.6.9 shows the degradation of integrity of data over time.

In order to understand the degradation of integrity over time, let's look at some examples. Let's consider the price of meat—say hamburger—over time. In 1850, hamburger was 0.05 cents a pound. In 1950, the price of hamburger was 0.95 cents a pound. And in 2015, the price of hamburger is $2.75 a pound. Does this comparison of the price of hamburger over time make sense? The answer is it *sort of* makes sense. The problem is not in the measurement of the price of hamburger. The problem is in the currency by which hamburger is measured. Even the meaning of what is a dollar is different in 1850 than what a dollar is in 2015.

Now, let's consider another example. The stock price of one share of International Business Machines (IBM) was $35 in 1950, and the price of that same share of stock in 2015 is $200 a share. Is the comparison of a stock price over time a valid comparison? The answer is *sort of*. IBM in 2015 is not the same company as it was in 1950, in terms of products, in terms of customers and revenues, and in terms of the value of the dollar. In a hundred ways, doing the examination of IBM in 1950 compared with IBM in 2015, there simply is no comparison. Over time, the very definition of the data has changed. So while a comparison of IBM's stock price in 1950 versus the stock price in 2015 is an interesting number, it is a completely relative number, because the very meaning of the number has drastically changed.

Given enough time, the very definition of values and data changes. That is why degradation of the definition of data is simply a fact of life.

A Brief History of Data

No book on data architecture would be complete without a narrative regarding the advances made in the technology of data.

In the beginning were wired boards. These hand-wired boards were "plug-ins" to an early rendition of the computer. The hardwired connections directed the computer as to how data were to be treated.

PAPER TAPE AND PUNCH CARDS

But wired boards were clumsy and error prone and could handle only small volumes of data (very small volumes of data!). Soon, an alternative was paper tape and punched cards. Paper tape and punched cards were able to handle larger volumes of data. And there was a greater range of functions that could be handled with punched cards and paper tape. But there were problems with paper tape and punched cards. When a programmer dropped a deck of cards, it was a very laborious activity to reconstruct the sequence of the cards. And once a card was punched, it was next to impossible to make a change to the card (although in theory it could be done).

Another shortcoming was that a relatively small amount of data could be held in this media.

Fig. 1.7.1 depicts the media of cards and paper tape.

Cards/paper tape

FIG. 1.7.1
Punched cards and paper tape.

Data Architecture. https://doi.org/10.1016/B978-0-12-816916-2.00007-3

MAGNETIC TAPES

Quickly replacing paper tape and punched cards was the magnetic tape. The magnetic tape was an improvement over the paper tape and punched cards. With a magnetic tape, a much larger volume of data could be stored. And the record size that could be stored on a magnetic tape was variable. (Previously, the record size stored on a punched card was fixed.) So, there were some important improvements made by magnetic tape.

But there were limitations that came with magnetic tapes. One limitation was that the magnetic tape file had to be accessed sequentially. This meant that the analyst had to sequentially search through the entire file when looking for a single record. Another limitation of the magnetic tape file was that over time, the oxide on the tape stripped away. And once the oxide was gone, the data on the tape were irretrievable.

Despite the limitations of the magnetic tape file, the magnetic tape file was an improvement over punched cards and paper tape.

Fig. 1.7.2 shows a magnetic tape file.

FIG. 1.7.2
Magnetic tape.

DISK STORAGE

The limitations of the magnetic tape file were such that soon there was an alternative medium. That alternative medium was called disk storage (or *direct access storage*). Direct access storage held the great advantage that data could be accessed directly. No longer was it necessary to read an entire file in order to access just one record. With disk storage, it was possible to go directly to a unit of data.

Fig. 1.7.3 shows disk storage.

FIG. 1.7.3
Disk storage.

At first, disk storage was expensive, and there wasn't all that much capacity that was available. But the hardware vendors quickly improved on the speed, the capacity, and the cost of disk storage. And the improvements have continued until today.

DATA BASE MANAGEMENT SYSTEM (DBMS)

Along with the advent of disk storage came the appearance of the database management system (DBMS). The database management system controlled the placement, access, update, and deletion of data on disk storage. The DBMS saved the programmer from doing repetitive and complex work.

With the appearance of the DBMS came the ability to tie processors to the database (and disk). Fig. 1.7.4 shows the advent of the DBMS and the close coupling of the database with the computer.

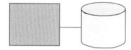

FIG. 1.7.4
Uniprocessor architecture.

At first, a simple uniprocessor architecture sufficed. In a uniprocessor architecture, there was an operating system, the DBMS, and an application. The early computers managed all these components. But in short order, the capacity of the processor was stretched. It was at this point that the capacity considerations of storage switched from improvements on the storage technology to improvements on the management of the storage technology. Prior to this point in time, the great leaps forward in data had been made by improving the storage media. But after this point in time, the great leaps forward were made architecturally, at the processor level.

Soon, the uniprocessor simply ran out of capacity. The consumer could always buy a bigger faster processor, but soon, the consumer was surpassing the capacity of the largest uniprocessor.

COUPLED PROCESSORS

The next major advance was the tight coupling together of multiple processors. Fig. 1.7.5 shows the coupling together of multiple processors.

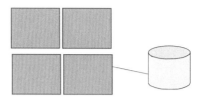

FIG. 1.7.5
Multiplexed architecture.

By coupling together multiple processors, the processing capacity automatically increased. The ability to couple the processors together was made possible by the sharing of memory across the different processors.

ONLINE TRANSACTION PROCESSING

With the advent of greater processing power and the control of a DBMS, it was now possible to create a new kind of system. The new kind of system was called the online real-time system. The processing done by this type of system was called *OLTP*, or *online transaction processing*.

Fig. 1.7.6 shows an online real-time system.

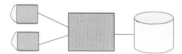

FIG. 1.7.6
Online real time architecture.

With online real-time processing, it was now possible to use the computer in a manner that had not before been possible. With the online real-time processing system, the computer could now be used interactively. The business could now be engaged with the usage of the computer in a manner not before possible. Suddenly, there were airline reservation systems, bank teller systems, ATM systems, inventory management systems, car reservation systems, and many, many more systems. Once real-time online processing became a reality, the computer was used in business as never before.

And with the explosive growth in the usage of the computer, there was an explosive growth in amount of data and types of data that were being created. With the flood of data came the desire to have *integrated* data. No longer was it sufficient to merely have data from an application. With the flood of data came the need to look at data in a cohesive manner.

DATA WAREHOUSE

Thus, born was the data warehouse, as seen in Fig. 1.7.7.

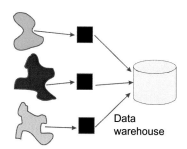

FIG. 1.7.7
Data warehouse architecture.

With the data warehouse came what was called the *single version of the truth* or the *system of record*. With the single version of the truth, the organization now had a foundation of data that the organization could turn to with confidence.

The volumes of data continued to explode with the advent to the data warehouse. Prior to the data warehouse, there was no convenient place to store historical data. But with data warehouse, for the first time, there was a convenient and natural place for historical data.

PARALLEL DATA MANAGEMENT

It is normal and natural that with the ability to store large amounts of data, the demand for data management products and technology skyrocketed. Soon, there emerged an architectural approach called the *parallel* approach to data management.

Fig. 1.7.8 illustrates the parallel approach to data management.

With the parallel approach to data management, a huge amount of data could be accommodated. Far more data could be managed in parallel than was ever possible with nonparallel techniques. With the parallel approach, the limiting factor as to how much data could be managed was an economic limitation, not a technical limitation.

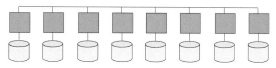

FIG. 1.7.8
Parallel architecture.

DATA VAULT

As data warehouses grew, it was realized that there needed to be flexibility in the design of the data warehouse and in the improvement in the integrity of data. Thus, born was the *data vault*, as seen in Fig. 1.7.9.

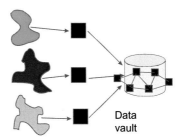

FIG. 1.7.9
Data vault architecture.

With data vault, the data warehouse now enjoyed the ultimate in design and integrity.

BIG DATA

But volumes of data continued to increase. Soon, there were systems that went beyond the capacity of even the largest parallel database. A new technology known as *big data* evolved in which the optimization of the data management software was on the volumes of data to be managed, not on the ability to access data in an online manner.

Fig. 1.7.10 depicts the arrival of big data.

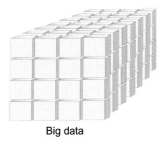

Big data

FIG. 1.7.10
Big data architecture.

With big data came the advent of the ability to capture and store an almost unlimited amount of data. The arrival of the ability to handle massive amounts of data brought with it the need for a completely new infrastructure.

THE GREAT DIVIDE

And with the recognition of the need for a new infrastructure came the recognition that there were two distinctly different types of big data. There is repetitive big data, and there is nonrepetitive big data. And both repetitive big data and nonrepetitive big data required dramatically different infrastructure.

Fig. 1.7.11 shows the recognition of the difference between repetitive big data and nonrepetitive big data.

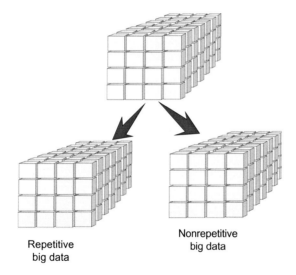

Repetitive
big data

Nonrepetitive
big data

FIG. 1.7.11
The great divide.

The End-State Architecture—The "World Map"

There is a data architecture to which corporations are evolving. That data architecture can be called the "end state" data architecture or the "world map" of data.

ARCHITECTURAL COMPONENTS

Fig. 2.1.1 depicts the "end state" data architecture.

The different components of the end-state data architecture are as follows:

Text—the text that belongs to the corporation that is worthy of inclusion into the end state

Textual ETL—the process that transforms text into a standard database format

The data warehouse—the place where the corporate single version of the truth resides

The data vault—the component of the data warehouse where rigorous data governance can be done

Data marts—the place where individual departments have their customized analytic data

Applications—the operational applications where day-to-day transactions are run

ETL—the process by which application data are transformed into corporate data

ODS—operational data store—a hybrid structure where integrated data can be quickly accessed online

The archival facility—the process by which older data are removed from active analysis

The refine process—the process by which bulk data are processed and entered into active analysis

Bulk data warehouse—the data warehouse where the single version of the truth data with a low probability of access is stored

The bulk data vault—the data vault where data with a low probability of access are stored where rigorous data governance can be done

Data Architecture. https://doi.org/10.1016/B978-0-12-816916-2.00008-5

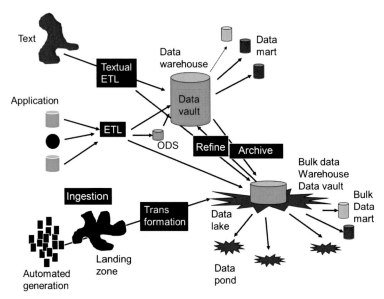

FIG. 2.1.1
The end state architecture. *Copyright Bill Inmon, 2018.*

The data lake—the place where very large volumes of data are stored
The bulk data mart—the data mart built to manage large volumes of data
The data pond—the place where selective subsets of data are stored
Automated generation of data—the mechanism by which large volumes of data are generated
The landing zone—the place where large volumes of data are first touched by the system and are available for processing
Data lake transformation—the process by which large volumes of data are edited and manipulated

Each of these components will be defined and discussed throughout this book. Each of these components has their own properties. There is a distinct value to each of these components.

DIFFERENT KINDS OF DATA IN THE END STATE ARCHITECTURE

There are many ways to understand the end-state architecture. One of the easiest ways to understand the architecture is to examine the different kinds of data that are found in different places.

Fig. 2.1.2 describes some of the different kinds of data found throughout the architecture.

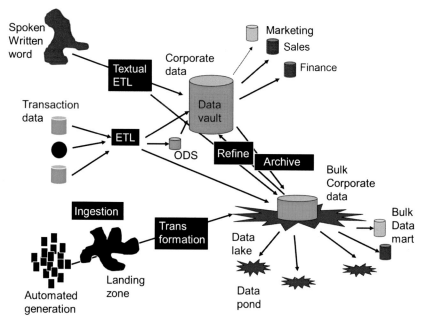

FIG. 2.1.2
Different kinds of data throughout the end state architecture. *Copyright Bill Inmon, 2018.*

Text can be either spoken or written. Text can be transformed through the auspices of voice to text transcription. Written text—if it is not already in the form of electronic text—can be captured and transformed by optical character recognition, OCR. However, the text exists; it is prepared into the form of electronic text.

Transaction data are data that have been captured as the by-product of the execution of a transaction. There are many kinds of transactions. There are bank teller transactions, ATM transactions, airline reservations, retail purchases, credit card activity, inventory management transactions, payment ledger transactions, and many more. These transactions are usually run by applications. As a rule, applications are developed and built in a "siloed" fashion. This means that when one application is built, it does not take into consideration the other applications with which it must interact. Corporations end up with a whole collection of applications, each one of which acts independently. The result is unintegrated application data.

Corporate data are data that have entered the system and then have been transformed into an integrated corporate state. The transformation moves the data from being application-oriented data to a data warehouse where the data are integrated into a corporate state. As a simple example of corporate integration, application A has gender as male/female, application B has gender designated as x/y, and application C has gender designated as 1/0. The corporate standard for the designation of gender is m/f. The application data are converted as they were moved into the data warehouse from the application.

The data marts contain data that are customized for the different groups that will be analytically using the data. Typically, there are data marts for marketing, sales, finance, and others. The source of data for the data marts is the data warehouse.

The data lake contains a variety of data. Some of the data found in the data lake are archival data. Other data in the data lake are simply bulk data. And it is possible to build a bulk data warehouse in the data lake. In addition, the bulk data warehouse may contain a bulk data vault. The bulk data warehouse is the single version of the truth for bulk amounts of data.

The data ponds are the subsets of the data lake that are set aside for different purposes. There may be an archival data pond, a litigation support data pond, a general purpose data pond, a manufacturing data pond, an analog data pond, and so forth.

SHAPING THE DATA THROUGH MODELS

Each of the different types of data in the end-state architecture is shaped by different types of data models. There are different kinds of data models that are suited to the different environments. The data model that is found in the many places where data are shaped throughout the architecture serves as an intellectual information paradigm for the building of applications, data warehouses, data marts, etc.

Fig. 2.1.3 shows the different kinds of data models that are found in the end-state architecture.

Applications are typically shaped by functional decompositions and data flow diagrams. The data found in text are shaped by taxonomies. The data warehouse is shaped by the corporate data model, usually consisting of an entity relationship diagram (ERD), a data item set (dis), and a physical model. The data marts are shaped by the dimensional model, consisting of star joins, fact tables, and dimensions. The data vault is shaped by the data vault data model.

The data lake is shaped by the selective subdivision of data.

WHERE IS THE DATA WAREHOUSE?

One of the important questions that quickly arises is are there two data warehouses—a standard data warehouse and a bulk data warehouse? Fig. 2.1.4 outlines this question.

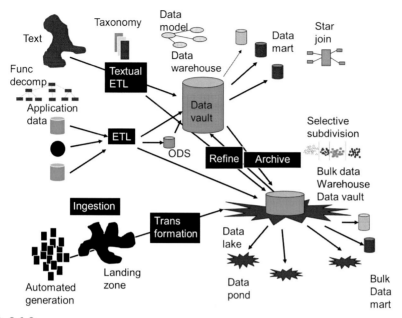

FIG. 2.1.3
Different data modelling techniques throughout the end state architecture. *Copyright Bill Inmon, 2018.*

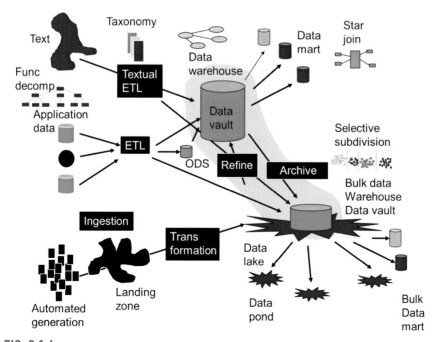

FIG. 2.1.4
A physical data warehouse and a logical data warehouse. *Copyright Bill Inmon, 2018.*

The answer to that question is a little less than straightforward. From a physical standpoint, there are indeed two data warehouses—a standard data warehouse and a bulk data warehouse. But from a logical standpoint, there is only one data warehouse. The physical possibilities for a data warehouse are the following:

A standard data warehouse
A bulk data warehouse
A standard data warehouse and a bulk data warehouse

The confusion arises when a data warehouse is built inside a data lake, as is certainly a possibility. The data lake resides on physically different technology (i.e., big data) than the standard data warehouse (which typically resides on relational technology).

However, even though there are physically two different data warehouses, there should never be any overlap of data from the standard data warehouse to the bulk data warehouse. Therefore, there is logically one data warehouse that is physically implemented over two environments.

There are several advantages to this "duplexed" approach. One advantage is that the data warehouse can grow to any size. Another advantage is that the data warehouse infrastructure cost is minimized. Both of these advantages are quite attractive to most organizations.

WHERE DIFFERENT TYPES OF QUESTIONS ARE ANSWERED ACROSS THE END STATE ARCHITECTURE

Yet, another way to understand the end-state architecture is to look at the different types of questions that are answered in different places in the end-state architecture.

Fig. 2.1.5 shows the possibilities.

The raw text is captured and analyzed when someone asks the question—"can I get a loan?" The question itself becomes the basic data that go into the database.

Operational transaction questions relate to specific instances and values of data. When you say "what is my account balance?" you want to know exactly how much money you have in your account right now. You want the correct answer, and you want the answer very quickly.

Now, suppose you want to know your average monthly account balance for the past 5 years. That data will not be in the online application database. Instead, you need to look for specific data over time. The place to find that data is the data warehouse.

Suppose you want to examine the spending habits of all customers who deposit more than $1000 a month in their account. You need to look at all of that data

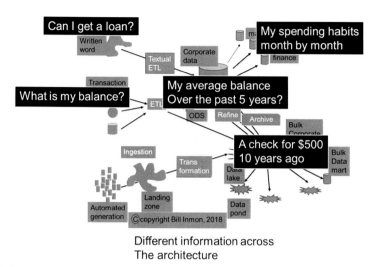

Different information across
The architecture

FIG. 2.1.5
Different information across the end state architecture.

in order to satisfy a special study. You might look for these data in a data mart. The processing you do here is of an analytic nature.

Now, suppose you are being audited by the IRS. You need to go back 10 years to show that a check was written a decade ago. You would go to your bulk data warehouse in the data lake.

The factors that determine where data are placed include the following:

How much data are there?
How old are the data?
How quickly do the data have to be retrieved?
Can the data be updated?

Data in different places have different properties. And those properties affect their usage.

DATA IN THE DATA LAKE

There can exist different kinds of data in the data lake. There are several reasons why data are placed in a data lake:

The probability of access of the data has dropped significantly.
There are so much data that there is no better place to put the data.
The data have aged.
The usage of the data does not warrant being placed elsewhere.

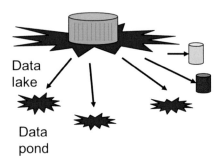

FIG. 2.1.6
Data in the data lake. *Copyright Bill Inmon, 2018.*

Accordingly, data are placed in the data lake.

However, just because data have been placed in a data lake does not mean that the data are (or are not) in a data warehouse. It is entirely possible that the data warehouse has been extended into the data lake.

Fig. 2.1.6 shows the data in the data lake.

METADATA IN THE END STATE ARCHITECTURE

It is not obvious when looking at the end-state architecture, but there is another important part of the architecture that is transparent. That part of the architecture is the metadata infrastructure that overlays each component of the end-state architecture.

The metadata are descriptive of the data that lie within the end-state architecture. The metadata are useful to designers, programmers, and end users. In a word, anyone who must find their way around the architecture needs to use the metadata.

It is noteworthy that each component has its own metadata and that both the component and the metadata for that component are different from one component to the next. In other words, the metadata for text look different than the metadata for applications, which also are different from the metadata for the data warehouse, and so on.

Fig. 2.1.7 shows the metadata infrastructure associated with the end-state architecture.

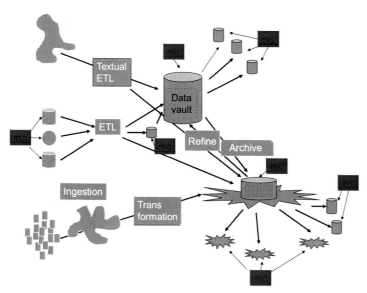

FIG. 2.1.7

The metadata infrastructure. *Copyright Bill Inmon, 2018.*

NETWORKED METADATA

Another feature of the metadata infrastructure is that the metadata infrastructure is networked. A person looking at one collection of metadata can easily traverse to another collection of metadata. And—if desired—the analyst can exchange metadata from one metadata collection to the next.

Fig. 2.1.8 shows the ability to network the metadata across the architecture.

AN EVOLUTIONARY EXPERIENCE

Another typical question that arises with the end-state architecture is how it is built. In a word, arriving at the end-state architecture is an evolutionary experience. No one sits down and builds all of the end-state architecture at once. Such an undertaking is too large, too complex, and too expensive. Instead, the end-state architecture grows over time.

Some organizations start building one direction. Other organizations start building another direction. Some organizations build part of the end-state architecture and never build other parts.

There is no one "correct" path to the evolution of the architecture.

Fig. 2.1.9 shows that there are many paths to the building of the end-state architecture.

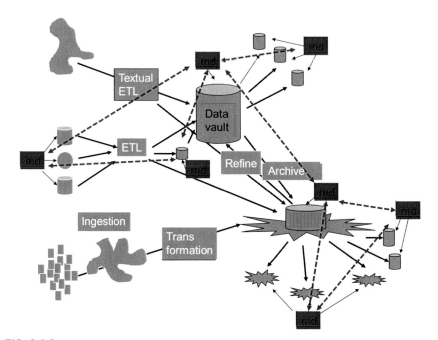

FIG. 2.1.8

Networked metadata. *Copyright Bill Inmon, 2018.*

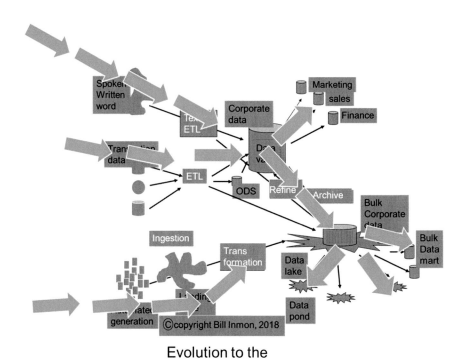

Evolution to the architecture

FIG. 2.1.9

The evolving architecture.

THE DATA LAKE ARCHITECTURE

The architecture component surrounding the data lake deserves a deeper explanation. In front of the data lake is a mechanism for capturing and prepping the data about to enter the data lake from external sources of data. There are several reasons for the need for an elaborate interface. The primary reasons for the need for an ingestion interface are the following:

> Data arrive so fast that the data lake cannot ingest the data as rapidly as it is generated.
> There are so much data that some sort of landing zone is appropriate.
> Raw editing of data needs to be employed before the data arrive in the data lake. In some cases, data are discarded. In other cases, data are categorized. In yet other cases, data are refurbished before their entry into the data lake.

Fig. 2.1.10 shows the data lake infrastructure.

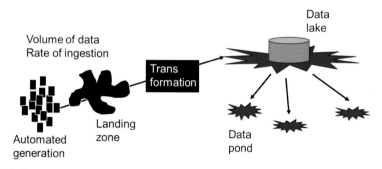

FIG. 2.1.10
The data lake infrastructure. *Copyright Bill Inmon, 2018.*

Transformations in the End-State Architecture

When you take your first glance at the end-state data architecture, several things jump out at you. One of those things is the need for transformation processes. There are a variety of transformations that occur. There is textual ETL. There is ETL. There are data marts that are created by using the techniques of dimensional data modeling. There is refinement of bulk data, and so forth.

REDUNDANT DATA

One of the apparent by products of this transformation process is the creation (or proliferation) of redundant data. A superficial glance at the end-state architecture produces the conclusion that redundancy of data is to be found everywhere in the architecture.

Fig. 3.1.1 shows the apparent proliferation of redundant data in the end-state data architecture.

When you look at the simple example shown in Fig. 3.1.1, it is hard to argue that there is no redundancy of data found in the end-state architecture. The example proves that—in fact—there is redundancy of data. However, there is more to the example than meets the eye. The redundancy of data found in the end-state architecture deserves a more careful scrutiny.

While it is true that there is redundancy of data in the end-state data architecture, there are some very good and very powerful reasons for the redundancy.

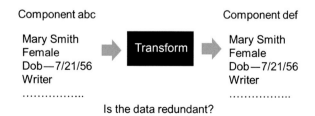

FIG. 3.1.1
The proliferation of data.

59

Data Architecture. https://doi.org/10.1016/B978-0-12-816916-2.00009-7

TRANSFORMATIONS

In order to understand the role that redundancy of data plays, it is necessary to understand the transformations of data found in the end-state data architecture. There are several major transformations of data found in the end-state data architecture. Those transformations are the following:

> The transformation of text into a database format—textual ETL
> The transformation of application data into corporate data—ETL
> The transformation of corporate data into customized analytic data—dimensional modeling
> The transformation of corporate data into bulk corporate data
> The transformation of automatically generated data into a data lake
> The refinement of bulk data into corporate analytic data

There is a good reason for each of these transformations.

When you look at the larger picture of what is going on, the creation and proliferation of redundancy is not nearly as simple and straightforward as it at first seems.

Consider the transformation shown in Fig. 3.1.2.

Fig. 3.1.2 shows that application data are transformed into corporate data. As a simple example of the transformation, all corporate designations of gender are

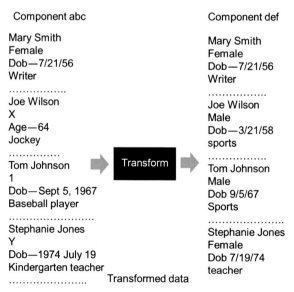

FIG. 3.1.2
Transforming data.

converted to either male or female. It just so happens that in the application state, the data for Mary Smith just happen to be female. So no conversion is done for Mary's record. And indeed, the record for Mary Smith in the applications is redundant with the record for Mary Smith in the corporation. But conversions from other application data are made. So, looking at just one record of data may lead to the incorrect conclusion about the issue of the redundancy of data.

CUSTOMIZING DATA

There are many reasons why data need to be transformed. Turning data into corporate data is only one of the many reasons. Another reason data need to be transformed is to customize data for the purpose of analytic processing.

Fig. 3.1.3 shows that records are edited and collected so that a customized analysis can be done.

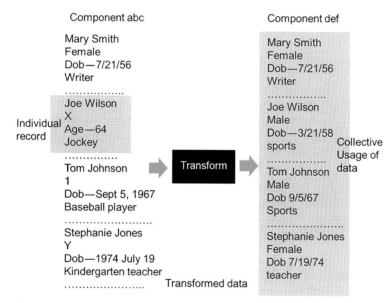

FIG. 3.1.3
Once transformed, data can be used collectively.

In order to do customized analysis, it is necessary to use data collectively. And data need to be integrated before they can be used collectively.

TRANSFORMING TEXT

One of the most obvious transformations is that of the reading of raw text and the conversion of the raw text into a standard database format. A lot of work

"She ate her hot dog with mustard. She spilled some on her
Dress. She was angry when the mustard left a stain…."

Tramsform

Doc abc, byte 12, word—hot dog, context—food
Doc abc, byte 24, word—mustard, context—condiment
Doc abc, byte 37, word—spilled, context—accident
Doc abc, byte 54, word—dress, context—clothing

FIG. 3.1.4
A textual transformation.

goes into the creation of the database because of the need to determine both the
value of text and the context of text. The database that is created contains both
the text and the context of the text.

Fig. 3.1.4 shows the transformation of text into the format of a database.

Once you see the transformation found in Fig. 3.1.4, it is obvious why there is
value in transformation. You cannot effectively do analytic processing on raw
text. Instead, the raw text must be read; the text must be analyzed and converted
into the form of a database. Once the text is converted into the form of a database, it can then be used for analytic processing. As long as the text is still in the
form of text, it cannot be meaningfully used as part of analytic processing.

TRANSFORMING APPLICATION DATA

Another common form of transformation is that of converting data from application data into corporate data.

Fig. 3.1.5 shows this transformation.

In Fig. 3.1.5, application data are seen in its raw state. Data are unintegrated. In
one record, male is designated as 1, and female is designated as a Y. In another
record, male is an X, and female is 0. And other elements of data are similarly
unintegrated.

Trying to look at the application data from a corporate perspective is very difficult to do. A transformation of data occurs as data are put into a corporate
format. Data are converted into a common format and placed into a data warehouse. Now, the data warehouse can be read and analyzed corporately.

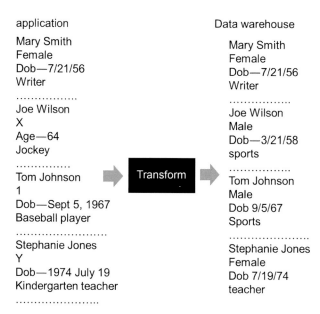

application

Mary Smith
Female
Dob—7/21/56
Writer
....
Joe Wilson
X
Age—64
Jockey
....
Tom Johnson
1
Dob—Sept 5, 1967
Baseball player
....
Stephanie Jones
Y
Dob—1974 July 19
Kindergarten teacher
....

Transform

Data warehouse

Mary Smith
Female
Dob—7/21/56
Writer
....
Joe Wilson
Male
Dob—3/21/58
sports
....
Tom Johnson
Male
Dob 9/5/67
Sports
....
Stephanie Jones
Female
Dob 7/19/74
teacher

FIG. 3.1.5
A data warehouse transformation.

TRANSFORMING DATA INTO A CUSTOMIZED STATE

Yet, another type of transformation occurs when data need to be customized for the purpose of analytic processing.

Fig. 3.1.6 shows this kind of transformation.

In this transformation, raw, detailed data are read. The data are then summarized and put into a data mart for further analysis.

The customization is typically done for marketing, sales, or finance. However, there are other organizations who occasionally need to do such a transformation.

Typically, the analysis that is done on the customized data is done in the fashion of establishing and measuring key performance indicators—KPIs. Typically, KPIs are calculated on a periodic basis—monthly, weekly, quarterly, etc.

TRANSFORMING DATA INTO BULK STORAGE

Another form of transformation is the movement of data from an active component to a less active component. The movement is done when the probability of access for a given unit of data drops. A typical strategy is to move the data as

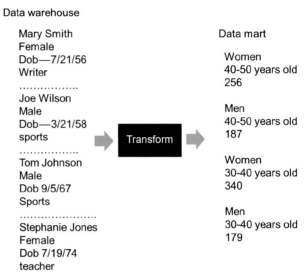

Data warehouse

Mary Smith
Female
Dob—7/21/56
Writer
....
Joe Wilson
Male
Dob—3/21/58
sports
....
Tom Johnson
Male
Dob 9/5/67
Sports
....
Stephanie Jones
Female
Dob 7/19/74
teacher

Transform

Data mart

Women
40-50 years old
256

Men
40-50 years old
187

Women
30-40 years old
340

Men
30-40 years old
179

FIG. 3.1.6
A data mart transformation.

they age based on the assumption that older data are accessed less frequently than current data.

There are however other occasions where the probability of access of data drops other than through aging.

The movement of data from active storage to less active storage is seen in Fig. 3.1.7.

TRANSFORMING DATA GENERATED AUTOMATICALLY

Another important transformation of data occurs as automatically generated data enter the data lake.

Fig. 3.1.8 shows that data are automatically generated (often times by a machine).

In Fig. 3.1.8, data are generated quickly and in great volumes. Several things happen to the data that are generated automatically. Not all data are selected for movement into the data lake. Some data are selected randomly. Other data are selected because they are outside a preset threshold of boundaries. Other data are selected because of the time of day they were generated. There are many criteria that can be applied to the selection of data that have been automatically generated.

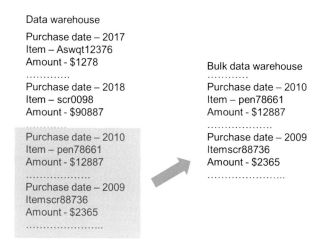

FIG. 3.1.7
A transformation from actively used storage to inactively used storage.

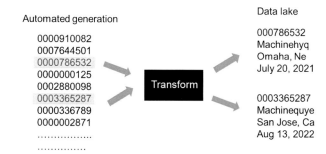

FIG. 3.1.8
Data generated automatically.

After the data for movement are selected, other data are typically added. Typical data that are added are the date and time of the generation, the location of the data, the machine identification of the data generated, and so forth.

After the data have been selected and modified, it is placed in the data lake.

TRANSFORMING BULK DATA

One of the more interesting transformations occurs when data go from the data lake back to the corporate data warehouse. In this case, mass amounts of data are read and filtered. The results of the filtering are sent to the data warehouse where the data can be actively analyzed. In addition, the filtered data can be combined with existing active data.

Fig. 3.1.9 shows the refinement of bulk data.

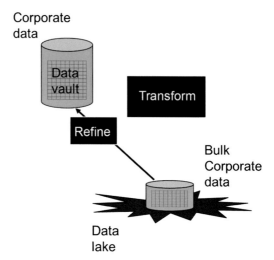

FIG. 3.1.9
The refinement of bulk data.

TRANSFORMATION AND REDUNDANCY

There are then a number of good reasons for the transformation of data throughout the end-state architecture. There is no question that there is some degree of redundancy of data that occurs. But as data move across the architecture, they move for very valid reasons.

Fig. 3.1.10 shows some of the major reasons why there is transformation inside the end-state architecture.

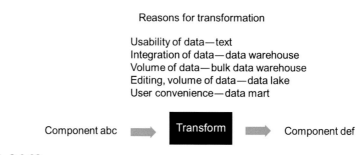

FIG. 3.1.10
Going to the end state architecture.

A Brief History of Big Data

There are many ways to describe history. When it comes to describing parts of the history of computer science, one way to describe it is in terms of technology. Another way to describe it is in terms of organizations.

The way that we will describe a brief history of big data is from a marketing standpoint.

AN ANALOGY—TAKING THE HIGH GROUND

Using an analogy to describe the history of big data and how things came to be is useful. The analogy that will be used is the military tactic of taking the high ground.

Fig. 4.1.1 shows that military tacticians have long known that taking the high ground was important in any military conflict.

In Fig. 4.1.1, we see that an army has placed a cannon on top of a ridge, thus taking a position of command.

In many ways, the maneuvering of database technology has been the moral equivalent of taking the high ground. Whatever company has the DBMS that serves the largest amount of data is the company that enjoys a commanding advantage in the battlefield. In this case, the battlefield is the database marketplace, and the battle is over market share. How many customers have signed up for and are using the DBMS is the measurement of success in the battlefield.

There are other DBMS that do not use the volume of data that can be managed as their distinctive criteria. These DBMS have their own battlefield and their own criteria of success in the battlefield. The battlefield for big data however is a battle field whose hallmark is the management of the largest amount of data.

TAKING THE HIGH GROUND

The progression of events that has led up to big data is seen in Fig. 4.1.2.

67

Data Architecture. https://doi.org/10.1016/B978-0-12-816916-2.00010-3
© 2019 Elsevier Inc. All rights reserved.

FIG. 4.1.1
The battlefield.

A brief marketing history of big data

1. Early systems—chaos (pre 1960)
2. IBM system 360—IMS data base (1960–1970)
3. IBM Online transaction processing (1970–1990)
4. Teradata—MPP parallel processing (1990–2010)
5. Hadoop—Big Data technology (2000–2005)
6. IBM/Hadoop Big Data marketing (2005–present)

FIG. 4.1.2
A brief marketing history of big data.

In the early dawn of the computer industry, there were many computer systems, many applications, and many operating systems. There were many vendors, and choosing technology was a risky and painful task. There were many problems with the early systems. One of the primary problems was that there was no standardization—no standardization of languages, no standardization of operating systems, and no standardization of applications. Because there was no standardization of anything, everything had to be made on a customized basis. Furthermore, all that custom code had to be maintained on a custom code basis.

In short, in the early days, there was chaos.

STANDARDIZATION WITH THE 360

Then, IBM introduced the 360 line of processors. The IBM 360 was the first broad-scale successful attempt at standardization. With the IBM 360 when you wrote code, that code could be upgraded to a larger processor in the 360 line of products with little or no alteration of the code. Today, we take the interchangeability of software and systems for granted. But there once was a day when upgrading software and systems was a real headache.

Shortly after the IBM 360 was introduced, IBM introduced the information management system—IMS. IMS ran on the IBM 360 line of products. IMS was not the first DBMS. But IMS was the first DBMS that could run on standardized software. In addition, IMS was able to manage a large amount of data. (Note: large is an entirely relative number. The amount of data that IMS could process in its early years is miniscule to what can be processed today. But the volume of data that IMS could handle was significant for the day and age.)

IBM had recognized and had taken the high ground for large-scale, standardized database management with IMS. From a military standpoint, IBM enjoyed the high ground.

ONLINE TRANSACTION PROCESSING

But in short order, it was discovered that other things than database management could be done with IMS. Not only could IMS manage databases, but also when you coupled a data communications (DC) component into the mix, that IMS coupled with a data communication monitor could do what is termed online transaction processing.

Now, IBM and IMS were positioned to do something that was dramatic. Now, IBM and IMS were positioned to start to engage in online transaction processing.

The dramatic thing about online transaction processing was that with online transaction processing, the computer could be ingrained very deeply into the fabric of the business. Prior to online transaction processing, the computer was able to enhance many business processes. But with the advent of online transaction processing, the computer could be woven into the day-to-day fabric of the operations of the corporation. Never before had the computer been an essential ingredient to the running of the business. With online transaction processing, the computer took on a role of importance never before envisioned.

With online transaction processing, the organization was able to build reservation systems—airline, car rental, and other reservation systems. With online transaction processing, there appeared online bank teller systems and ATMs. In a word, online transaction processing systems enabled a business to do what had heretofore been impossible.

At this point, IBM had a firm grip on the high ground of corporate processing.

ENTER TERADATA AND MPP PROCESSING

Enter the mix a company called Teradata. Teradata featured a database technology called *massively parallel processing* (MPP). With MPP database technology, Teradata could process significantly more data than IBM. The architecture of MPP technology was such that IBM's IMS-based technology simply could not keep pace when it came to processing volumes of data. Suddenly, Teradata took the high ground.

But Teradata's entrance into the marketplace was not an immediate and resounding success. IBM had very good account control and was able to resist Teradata's intrusion for a long time. But Teradata persevered, and after much marketing, much sales effort, and much technology advancement, Teradata began to win over clients. Now, Teradata was beginning to capitalize on the holding of the high ground.

THEN CAME HADOOP AND BIG DATA

Almost innocently into the fray came Hadoop technology. Hadoop was a response to the need to handle even more data than Teradata. In actuality, the limit to Teradata's management of data was an economic limitation more than a technological limitation. But Hadoop was addressing the problem of optimizing a database management system on management of volumes of data, not on the ability to manage every field of data. There was a change in emphasis on the management of volumes of data from the management of units of data within the environment.

Hadoop was the heart of big data. With Hadoop's technology, big data went from a dream to a reality.

Hadoop catered to just a few large-scale clients with specialized needs. Hadoop and its associated vendors were satisfied with being a niche player in the marketplace even though Hadoop had entered into even higher ground than Teradata.

IBM AND HADOOP

After Hadoop proved that it was a viable commodity, IBM recognized that by partnering with Hadoop, it could "piggyback" its way back to the higher ground. With the advent of big data, IBM has once again achieved the high ground of large-scale database management systems.

HOLDING THE HIGH GROUND

The advantage of holding the high ground is of inestimable importance. So many opportunities fall open when the vendor has the high ground. The vendor is free to exploit hardware, software, consulting opportunities, and more.

What Is Big Data?

The definition of big data as defined by Gartner Group is

volume,
velocity,
variety.

While this definition is often quoted and used on a widespread basis, it is not a definition at all. The load handled by a semitruck going down the highway fits this definition and the cargo of an ocean liner. In fact, there are many things that fit this definition other than big data.

ANOTHER DEFINITION

The problem with the Gartner definition is that it describes some of the characteristics of big data, but it does not disclose the *identifying* characteristics.

The definition of big data that we will use for this book is as follows:

Big data is
data that is stored in very large volumes,
data that is stored on inexpensive storage,
data that is managed by the "Roman census" method,
data that is stored and managed in an unstructured format.
These then are the defining characteristics of big data that will be used in this book.

Each of these characteristics deserves a more elucidating explanation.

LARGE VOLUMES

Most organizations already have an adequate amount of data to run day-to-day business. But some organizations have an extraordinary amount of data. Some organizations have a need to look at such things as the following:

All the data on the Internet
Meteorologic data sent down by a satellite

73

Data Architecture. https://doi.org/10.1016/B978-0-12-816916-2.00011-5

All of the e-mails in the world
Manufacturing data generated by an analog computer
Railroad cars as they traverse tracks
Many more applications

For these organizations, there is no good and inexpensive way to store and manage data. Even if the data could be stored in a standard DBMS, the cost of storage would be exorbitantly high. So for some organizations, there is a need to store and manage very large amounts of data.

When facing the issue of managing very large amounts of data, there is the issue of business value that arises. The fundamental question of "what business value is there in being able to look at massive volumes of data?" needs to be addressed. The old saw of "build it and they will come" does not apply to large amounts of data. Before the organization sets out to store massive amounts of data, there needs to be a good understanding of what business value of data lies in the data itself.

INEXPENSIVE STORAGE

Even if big data were able to store and manage massive amounts of data, it would not be practical to create huge stores if the storage medium that was used was expensive storage. Stated another way, if big data stored data on only expensive high-performance storage, the cost of big data would be prohibitive. In order to be a practical and useful solution, big data, of necessity, must be able to use inexpensive storage.

THE ROMAN CENSUS APPROACH

One of the cornerstones of big data architecture is processing referred to as the "Roman census approach." By using the Roman census approach, a big data architecture can accommodate the processing of almost unlimited amounts of data.

When people first hear the "Roman census approach," it appears to be counterintuitive and unfamiliar. The reaction most people have is "and just exactly what is a Roman census approach?" Yet, the approach—architecturally—is at the core of the functioning of big data. And—surprisingly—it turns out that many people are much more familiar with the Roman census approach than they ever realized.

Once upon a time—about 2000 years ago—the Romans decided that they wanted to tax everyone in the Roman empire. But in order to tax the citizens of the Roman empire, the Romans first had to have a census. The Romans quickly figured out that trying to get every person in the Roman empire to march through the gates of Rome in order to be counted was an impossibility. There were people in North Africa, in Spain, in Germany, in Greece, in Persia, in Israel, in England, and so forth. Not only were there a lot of people in faraway places; trying to transport everyone on ships and carts and donkeys to and from the city of Rome was simply an impossibility.

So, the Romans realized that creating a census where the processing (i.e., the counting and the taking of the census) was done centrally was not going to work. The Romans solved the problem by creating a body of "census takers." The census takers were organized in Rome and then were sent all over the Roman empire, and on the appointed day, a census was taken. Then, after taking the census, the census takers headed back to Rome where the results were tabulated centrally.

In such a fashion, the work being done was sent to the data, rather than trying to send the data to a central location and doing the work in one place. By distributing the processing, the Romans solved the problem of creating a census over a large diverse population.

Many people don't realize that they are very familiar with the Roman census method and don't know it. You see, there once was a story about two people—Mary and Joseph—who had to travel to a small city, Bethlehem, for the taking of a Roman census. On the way there, Mary had a little baby boy—named Jesus—in a manger. And the shepherds flocked to see this baby boy. And Magi came and delivered gifts. Thus, born was the religion many people are familiar with—Christianity. The Roman census approach is intimately entwined with the birth of Christianity.

The Roman census method then says that you don't centralize processing if you have a large amount of data to process. Instead, you send the processing to the data. You distribute the processing. In doing so, you can service the processing over an effectively unlimited amount of data.

UNSTRUCTURED DATA

Another issue related to big data is that of whether big data is structured or unstructured. In many circles, it is said that all big data is unstructured. In other circles, it is said that big data is structured.

So who is right? As we shall see, the answer lies entirely in how you define the term "structured" and "unstructured."

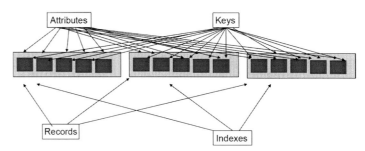

FIG. 4.2.1
A standard data base structure.

So what does "structured" mean? One widely used definition of structured is that anything managed by a standard DBMS is structured. Fig. 4.2.1 shows some data managed by a standard database management system.

In order to load the data into the DBMS, there needs to be a careful definition of the logical and the physical characteristics of the system. All data—attributes, keys, indexes, etc.—need to be defined before the data can be loaded into the system.

The notion of structure meaning "able to be managed under a standard DBMS" is a very widely used understanding of what is meant by structured. The meaning has been around for a long time and is widely understood by a large body of people.

DATA IN BIG DATA

Now, consider what data looks like when it is stored in big data. There is none of the definitional infrastructure that is found in a standard DBMS. All sorts of data are stored in big data, and they are stored with no notion of what the structure of the data looks like.

Fig. 4.2.2 shows data stored in big data.

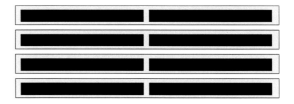

FIG. 4.2.2
Big data.

FIG. 4.2.3
Different types of data.

If the definition of structured is taken to mean "managed by a standard DBMS," then the data stored in big data is definitely unstructured.

However, there are different interpretations of what is meant by the term "structured." Consider the (very normal) circumstance of big data consisting of many repetitive records. Fig. 4.2.3 shows that big data can certainly contain blocks of data that are made up of many repetitive records. There are many instances where big data contains just this sort of information. Some of the many instances include the following:

 Click stream data
 Metered data
 Telephone call record data
 Analog data
 Many more types of repetitive records

When there are repetitive records, the same structure of data is repeated over and over, from one record to the next. And often times, the same value of data is repeated as well.

When repetitive records are found in big data, there is no index facility as there is in a standard DBMS. But there still is indicative data in big data even if it is not managed by an index.

CONTEXT IN REPETITIVE DATA

Fig. 4.2.4 shows that inside the repetitive record inside big data, there is information that can be used to identify the record. Sometimes, this information is known as context.

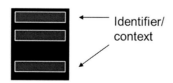

Identifier/
context

FIG. 4.2.4
Context.

FIG. 4.2.5
Repetitive records have the same context.

In order to find this information in the record, the record must be *parsed* in order to determine its value. But the fact is that the information is there, inside the record.

And when you look at all of the repetitive records inside the big data storage blocks, the same type of data is in each record, in precisely the same format. Fig. 4.2.5 shows that the repetitive records have the same identifying information in exactly the same structure.

From the standpoint of repetitiveness and predictability, big data indeed has very structured data inside it.

So in answer to the question does big data have structure?—if you look at the question from the standpoint of structure meaning a structured DBMS infrastructure, then big data does not contain structured data. But if you look at big data from the standpoint of containing repetitive data with predictable context, then big data can be said to be structured.

The answer to the question then is neither yes nor no. The answer to the question depends entirely on the definition of what is meant by structured and unstructured.

NONREPETITIVE DATA

Even if big data can contain structured data, big data can also contain what is called "nonrepetitive" data as well. Nonrepetitive records of data are records where the structure and content of the records are entirely independent of each other. Where there is nonrepetitive data, it is entirely an accident if any two records resemble each other, either in content or structure.

There are many examples of nonrepetitive data. Some examples of nonrepetitive data include the following:

E-mails
Call center information
Health-care records
Insurance claim information
Warranty claim information

Nonrepetitive information contains indicative information. But the indicative information found in nonrepetitive records is very erose. There simply is no pattern to the contextual information found in nonrepetitive data.

CONTEXT IN NONREPETITIVE DATA

Fig. 4.2.6 shows that the blocks of data found in the big data environment that are nonrepetitive are very irregular in shape, shape, and structure.

There is contextual data found in the nonrepetitive records of data. But the contextual data must be extracted in a very customized manner (Fig. 4.2.7).

Context is found in nonrepetitive data. However, context is not found in the same manner and in the same way that it is found in using repetitive data or classical structured data found in a standard DBMS.

In later chapters, the subject of textual disambiguation will be addressed. It is through textual disambiguation that context in nonrepetitive data is achieved.

There is another way to look at the repetitive and the nonrepetitive data found in big data. That perspective is shown in Fig. 4.2.8.

In Fig. 4.2.8, it is seen that the vast majority of the volume of data found in big data is typically repetitive data. Fig. 4.2.8 shows that nonrepetitive makes up only a fraction of the data found in big data, when examined from the perspective of volume of data.

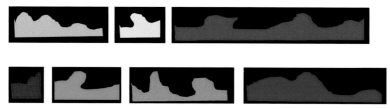

FIG. 4.2.6
Nonrepetitive data.

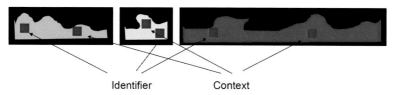

Identifier   Context

FIG. 4.2.7
Context—found in different places and in different ways.

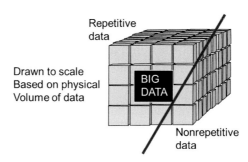

FIG. 4.2.8
Repetitive data and nonrepetitive data in big data.

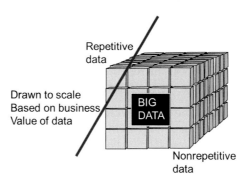

FIG. 4.2.9
A different perspective.

However, Fig. 4.2.9 shows a very different perspective.

Fig. 4.2.9 shows that from the perspective of business value that the vast majority of value found in big data lies in nonrepetitive data.

There is then a real mismatch between the volume of data and the business value of data. For people that are examining repetitive data and hoping to find massive business value there, there is most likely disappointment in their future. But for people looking for business value in nonrepetitive data, there is a lot to look forward to.

When you compare looking for business value in repetitive and nonrepetitive data, there is an old adage that applies here. That adage is that "90% of the fishermen fish where there are 10% of the fish." The converse of the adage is that "10% of the fishermen fish where 90% of the fish are."

Parallel Processing

The very essence of big data is the ability to handle very large volumes of data. Fig. 4.3.1 symbolically depicts a lot of data.

There are so much data that need to be handled by big data that trying to load, access, and manipulate the data is a real challenge. It is safe to say that no computer is capable of handling all the data that can be accumulated in the big data environment.

The only possible strategy is to use multiple processors to handle the volume of data found in big data. In order to understand why it is mandatory to use multiple processors, consider the (old) story about the farmer that drives his crop to the marketplace in a wagon. When the farmer is first starting out, he doesn't have much of a crop. He uses a donkey to pull the wagon. But as the years pass by, the farmer raises bigger crops. Soon, he needs a bigger wagon. And he needs a horse to pull the wagon. Then, one day, the crop that is put in the wagon becomes immense, and the farmer doesn't just need a horse. The farmer needs a large Clydesdale horse.

Time passes, and the farmer prospers even more, and the crop continues to grow. One day, even a Clydesdale horse is not large enough to pull the wagon. The day comes where multiple horses are required to pull the wagon. Now, the farmer has a whole new set of problems. A new rigging is required. A trained driver is required to coordinate the team of horses that pull the wagon.

The same phenomenon occurs where there are lots of data. Multiple processors are required to load and manipulate the volumes of data found in big data.

In a previous chapter, there was a discussion of the "Roman census" method. The Roman census method is one of the ways in which parallelization of processing for the management of large amounts of data can occur.

Fig. 4.3.2 depicts the parallelization that occurs in the Roman census approach.

Fig. 4.3.2 shows that multiple processors are linked together to operate in a coordinated manner. Each processor controls and manages its own data. Collectively, the data that are managed constitute the volumes of data known as "big data."

Note that the network is irregular in terms of its shape. Note that new nodes can be easily added to the network. Also note that the processing that occurs in one node is

81

Data Architecture. https://doi.org/10.1016/B978-0-12-816916-2.00012-7

FIG. 4.3.1
A lot of data.

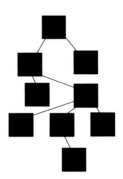

Processors linked together to operate
in parallel

FIG. 4.3.2
Processors linked together to provide parallel
processing.

entirely independent of the processing that occurs in another node. Fig. 4.3.3 shows that several nodes can be processed at the same time as other nodes.

An interesting thing about parallelization is that the total number of machine cycles required to process big data is not reduced by parallelization. In fact, the total number of machine cycles required is actually raised by parallelization, due to the fact that coordination of processing across different nodes is now required. Instead, the total elapsed time is what is reduced by introducing parallelization. The more parallelization there is, the less elapsed time there is to manage the data found in big data.

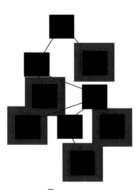

Processors
executing in
parallel
independently

FIG. 4.3.3
Processors executing independently.

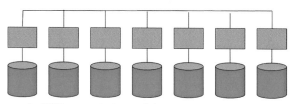

An MPP—massively parallel processor—architecture

FIG. 4.3.4
An MPP—massively parallel processor.

There are different forms of parallelization. The Roman census method is not the only form of parallelization. Another classical form of parallelization is that seen in Fig. 4.3.4.

The form of parallelization seen in Fig. 4.3.4 is called the "massively parallel processing" (MPP) approach to the management of data. In the MPP form of parallelization, each processor controls its own data (as is the case where the Roman census approach is used.) But in the MPP approach, there is a tight coordination of processing across the nodes. The tight control of the nodes can be accomplished by the fact that before the data are loaded, they are parsed and defined to fit the MPP data structure. Fig. 4.3.5 shows the parsing and fitting of the data to the MPP structure.

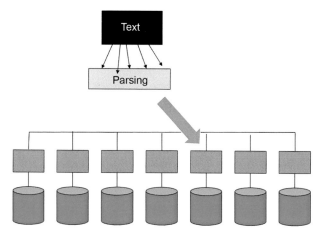

FIG. 4.3.5
Text is parsed then placed in the appropriate processor.

Fig. 4.3.5 shows that in the MPP architecture, the parsing of the data greatly affects the placement of the data. One record is placed on one node. Another record is placed on another node.

The great benefit of parsing the data and using the parsing information as the basis for the placement of data is that the data are efficient to locate. When an analyst wishes to locate a unit of data, the analyst specifies the value of data that is of interest to the system. The system uses the algorithm that was used to place the data into the database (typically a hashing algorithm), and the system locates the data very efficiently.

In the Roman census approach to parallelization, the sequence of events is different from the MPP approach. In the Roman census approach, query is sent to the system to search for some data. The data managed by a node are searched and then parsed. Upon parsing, the system knows it has found the data that were being sought.

Fig. 4.3.6 shows the parsing that occurs.

It is seen from Fig. 4.3.6 that in order to find a single instance of data, quite a bit of work has to be done by the system. But, given that there are lots of processors,

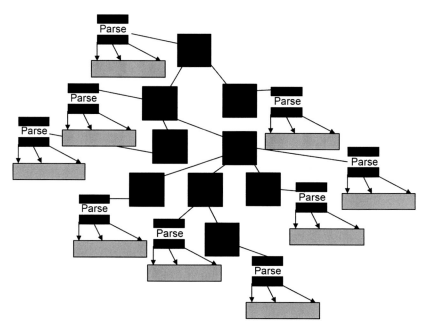

FIG. 4.3.6
Parsing is done in parallel.

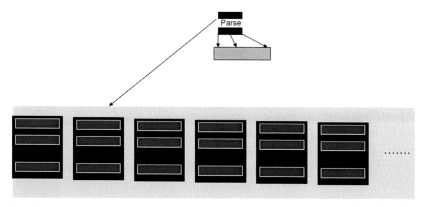

FIG. 4.3.7
Parsing repetitive data.

the elapsed time to do the search can be cut into a reasonable amount of time. If it were not for parallelism, the amount of time to do a search would be abhorrent.

There is some good news however. The good news is that parsing repetitive data is a fairly straightforward exercise. Fig. 4.3.7 shows the parsing of repetitive data.

Fig. 4.3.7 shows that in the case of repetitive data in big data, the parsing algorithm is fairly straightforward. Relative to other data found in the repetitive record, there is very little contextual information, and where there is contextual information, it is found easily. This means that the work done by the parser is fairly simple work. (Note: the term "simple" here is entirely relative to the work that must be done by the parser elsewhere.)

Contract the parsing of repetitive data versus the parsing of nonrepetitive data.

Fig. 4.3.8 shows the parsing of nonrepetitive data.

The parsing of nonrepetitive is an entirely different matter than the parsing of repetitive data. In fact, the term—"parsing of nonrepetitive data"—is often

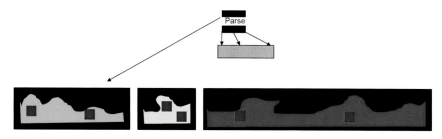

FIG. 4.3.8
Parsing nonrepetitive data.

referred to as textual disambiguation. There is much more to the reading of nonrepetitive data than merely parsing it.

However it is done, nonrepetitive data are read and turned into a form that can be managed by a database management system.

There is a very good reason why nonrepetitive data require well beyond a parsing algorithm. The reason is that context in nonrepetitive data hides in many and complex forms. For that reason, textual disambiguation is usually done external to the nonrepetitive data in big data. (In other words, because of the inherent complexity of nonrepetitive data, textual disambiguation is done outside of the database system that manages big data.)

A related issue to parallel processing in the big data environment is that of the efficiency of queries. As seen in Fig. 4.3.6, when a simple query is done against big data, the parsing of the entire set of data contained in big data must be parsed. Even though the data are managed in parallel, such a full database scan of data causes many machine resources to be used.

An alternate approach is to scan the data once and create a separate index. This approach works only for repetitive data, not nonrepetitive data. Once the index for the repetitive data is created, it can be scanned much more efficiently than doing a full table scan. Once the index is created, there no longer is a need to do a full table scan every time big data needs to be searched.

Of course, the index must be maintained. Every time data are added to the big data collection of repetitive data, an update to the index is required.

In addition, the designer must know what contextual information is available at the moment of the building of the index.

Fig. 4.3.9 shows the building on an index from the contextual data found on repetitive data.

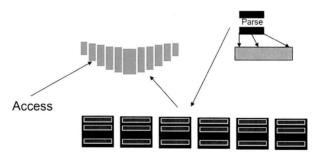

FIG. 4.3.9
Building an index on repetitive data.

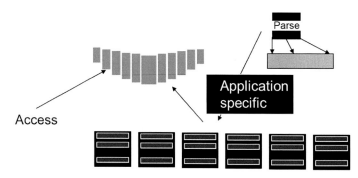

FIG. 4.3.10
The application nature of building an index on repetitive data.

One of the issues of creating a separate index on data found in repetitive data is that the index that is created is application-specific. The designer must know what data to look for before the index is built.

Fig. 4.3.10 displays the application-specific nature of building an index for repetitive data in big data.

Unstructured Data

It is estimated that over 80% of the data in the corporation are unstructured information. There are many different forms of unstructured information. There is video. There is audio. There are images. But far and away the most interesting and useful for unstructured data is textual information.

TEXTUAL INFORMATION—EVERYWHERE

Textual information is found everywhere in the corporation. Text is found in contracts, in e-mail, in reports, in memorandum, in human resource evaluations, and so forth. In a word, textual information makes up the fabric of corporate life, and that is true for every corporation.

Unstructured information can be broken into two major categories—repetitive unstructured data and nonrepetitive unstructured data. Fig. 4.4.1 shows the categories that describe all corporate data.

DECISIONS BASED ON STRUCTURED DATA

For a variety of reasons, the vast majority of corporate decisions are made based on structured data. There are several reasons for this. The primary reason is that structured information is easy to automate. Structured data fit naturally and normally on standard database technology. And once on database technology, the data can easily be analyzed inside the corporation. It is easy to read and

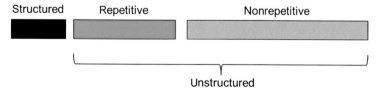

FIG. 4.4.1
Unstructured data can be repetitive or nonrepetitive.

Data Architecture. https://doi.org/10.1016/B978-0-12-816916-2.00013-9

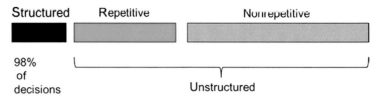

FIG. 4.4.2

In most organizations the vast majority of decisions are made on the basis of structured data.

analyze 100,000 records of structured information. There are plenty of analytic tools that can handle the analysis of standard database records.

Fig. 4.4.2 shows that most corporate decisions are made based on structured data.

Despite the fact that most corporate decisions are made on the basis of structured information, there is a wealth of untapped potential in the unstructured information of the corporation. The challenge then is unlocking that potential.

THE BUSINESS VALUE PROPOSITION

Fig. 4.4.3 shows that there is a different business value proposition for the different types of unstructured data. Repetitive unstructured data have business value. But the business value in repetitive unstructured data is hard to find and hard to unlock. And in many cases, there simply is no business value whatsoever in repetitive unstructured data.

However, it is in nonrepetitive unstructured data where there is huge business value. There are many, many cases where the business value in nonrepetitive unstructured data is very high.

Some of the more obvious cases where there is business value in nonrepetitive unstructured data include the following:

E-mails, where customers express their opinions
Call center information, where customers have a direct line to the corporation

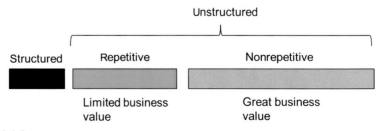

FIG. 4.4.3

Business value varies depending on whether data is repetitive or nonrepetitive.

Corporate contracts, where corporate obligations are disclosed

Warranty claims, where the manufacturer can find out where the weak points of the manufacturing process are

Insurance claims, where the insurance company can assess where profitable business lies

Marketing analysis companies, where direct customer feedback can be analyzed

These cases represent merely the most obvious tip of the iceberg for finding and using nonrepetitive unstructured information.

REPETITIVE AND NONREPETITIVE UNSTRUCTURED INFORMATION

Fig. 4.4.4 illustrates the visceral differences between the repetitive and the non-repetitive unstructured environments.

As has been discussed in conversations on the "great divide," there are many differences between the repetitive and the nonrepetitive environments. But perhaps the most poignant, most relevant difference between the two environments is that of the ease with which analytic processing can be done.

Fig. 4.4.5 shows that analytic processing is quite easy to do when it comes to working with repetitive unstructured data. But when it comes to doing analysis on nonrepetitive unstructured data, analysis is awkward and difficult to do.

EASE OF ANALYSIS

Fig. 4.4.5 shows that analysis in the repetitive unstructured environment is as easy as putting a square peg in a square hole whereas analysis in the nonrepetitive unstructured environment is as awkward and as difficult as placing a square peg in a round hole.

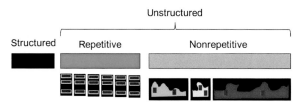

FIG. 4.4.4
Representations of repetitive and nonrepetitive data.

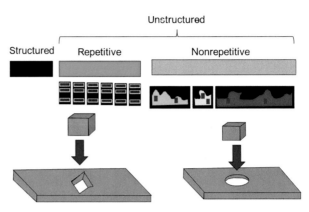

FIG. 4.4.5
Analysis on nonrepetitive data is like fitting a square peg in a round hole.

There are lots of reasons for this major difference between repetitive and non-repetitive unstructured data. Repetitive unstructured data are easy to analyze because of the following:

The records are uniform in shape.
The records are usually small and compact.
The records are easy to parse because the contextual information in the record is easy to find.

Pretty much the opposite is true of the nonrepetitive unstructured records. Nonrepetitive unstructured records are the following:

Very nonuniform in shape.
Sometimes small, sometimes large, and sometimes very large.
The records are quite difficult to parse because the records are made up of text and text requires an entirely different approach than simple parsing.

There are probably more differences between these two types of data. But these differences alone warrant the recognition of the "great divide" between the types of unstructured data.

So, what is so difficult about going in and working with text? Fig. 4.4.6 shows some typical text.

There are many reasons why text is so difficult to work with.

First off, there is the discussion of whether text is actually unstructured at all. An English teacher might argue that text is anything but unstructured. There are rules that govern the structure of all text. Some of the rules include the following:

Account 123887-12 was closed on July 12, 2016 by John Crumley. On Aug 15, 2016 Mrs Gabrielle Crumley produced c court order mandating that the account be opened. The clerk at the ban honored the court order and shows the Account balance to Mrs Crumley.
Then the lawyer for Mr Crumley appeared and the money was withdrawn from the account and assigned to the lawyer. Mrs Crumley objected and demanded that the money be given to Her.
At this moment a sheriff appeared and commenced to take the money form the lawyer. The lawyer ....

FIG. 4.4.6
Some typical text.

Spelling
Punctuation
Grammar
Proper sentence construction

It cannot be argued that there are no rules that govern the creation of proper text. But those rules are so complex that the rules are not obvious and apparent to the computer. From the computer's perspective, text is unstructured simply because the computer cannot understand all the rules of proper textual construction.

CONTEXTUALIZATION

There are many parts of text that must be managed if text is to be turned into a form that is useful to the computer. But easily, the most important and the most complex aspect of text that must be mastered is that of finding and determining the context of text. Stated differently, if you do not understand the context of text, you cannot use text for any form of useful decision-making.

Contextualization of text then is the single largest challenge facing the analyst who wishes to use nonrepetitive unstructured text in the decision-making process.

Fig. 4.4.7 shows an example of the importance of understanding context.

Two gentlemen are standing on a corner, and one gentleman says to the next as a young lady passes by—"She's hot."

Now, what is being said here?

FIG. 4.4.7
Text makes no sense without understanding context.

FIG. 4.4.8
Finding context.

One interpretation is that the gentleman finds the young lady to be attractive and he would like to have a date with her.

Another interpretation is that it is Houston, Texas, on a July day and it is 98 degrees and 100% humidity. The lady is wet from pouring sweat. She's hot.

Another interpretation is that the two gentlemen are in a hospital and they are doctors. One doctor has just taken the lady's temperature, and she has a temperature of 104 degrees. She is burning up with fever, and she's hot.

These then are three very different meanings of the words—"She's hot." Trying to use and interpret these words without understanding the context could lead to disaster and embarrassment.

The need to find and understand context is hardly limited to the words—"She's hot." The need to find and understand context is true for *all* words.

The largest challenge facing the analyst who wishes to make sense of nonrepetitive unstructured data then is that of understanding how to *contextualize* text.

It is noteworthy that there are other challenges as well. As important as contextualization is, it is hardly the only challenge when it comes to doing analysis.

Fig. 4.4.8 shows that finding context in nonrepetitive unstructured data is a major challenge.

SOME APPROACHES TO CONTEXTUALIZATION

The notion that finding context in nonrepetitive unstructured data is a challenge is not a new idea. Indeed, people have been attempting to contextualize text for a long time. The earliest attempt to trying to contextualize text is a technology called "NLP." NLP stands for natural language processing (or sometimes "natural language programming.")

NLP has been around a long time and has met with modest success. There are several inherent limitations to NLP. The first limitation is that NLP makes the assumption that context of text can be derived from text itself. The problem is that only a small amount of context comes from text itself. In the case of the two gentlemen standing around and saying—"She's hot"—the vast majority of the context comes from external sources, not textual sources. Is the lady young and attractive? Is it Houston, Texas, in the summertime? Is the conversation taking place in a hospital? All of these circumstances that provide context are external to the words that are being spoken.

The second limitation of NLP is that NLP does not account for emphasis. Suppose the words are spoken—"I love you." How are these words to be interpreted?

If you say "I love you" where the emphasis is on "I," the meaning is that it is me and not someone else who loves you. If the emphasis is on the word "love," the meaning is that the emotion I feel is strong, one of love. I don't like you—I actually love you. If the emphasis is on the word "you," the meaning is that it is you and not someone else that I love.

So, the same words can have very different meaning based on the way the words are said.

But there is a very different reason why NLP has had a hard time showing concrete results. That reason is that NLP—in order to be implemented effectively—must understand the logic behind words. The problem is that the English language has evolved over many years and many circumstances, and at the end of the day, the logic behind the English language is very complex. Trying to map out the logic of the English language is very difficult to do. It is tortuous.

For these reasons (and probably more), NLP processing has met with modest success.

A much more practical approach is that of textual disambiguation.

Fig. 4.4.9 shows the two approaches toward contextualization of text.

In later chapters, much more will be said about textual disambiguation.

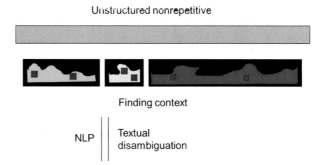

FIG. 4.4.9
NLP does not do a good job of finding and managing context of text.

MAP REDUCE

Another approach to contextualization that is found in big data is that of a technology called MapReduce. Fig. 4.4.10 shows MapReduce.

MapReduce is a language for the technician that can be used to do all sorts of useful things in big data. However, the number of lines of code that must be written and maintained and the sheer complexity of contextualizing nonrepetitive unstructured data limits the usefulness of MapReduce for the purpose of contextualizing nonrepetitive unstructured data.

MANUAL ANALYSIS

There is one other time-honored approach to analyzing nonrepetitive unstructured data. That approach is to do things manually. Fig. 4.4.11 shows that nonrepetitive unstructured data can be analyzed manually.

The great appeal of doing analysis manually is that no infrastructure is required. The only thing that is required is a human being that is capable of reading and

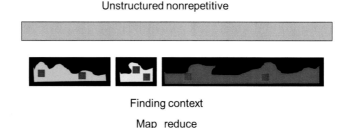

FIG. 4.4.10
Map reduce can be used to address text.

Unstructured nonrepetitive

FIG. 4.4.11
Manual analysis is appealing for small, one time only projects.

Unstructured nonrepetitive

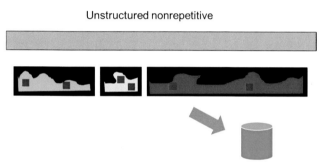

FIG. 4.4.12
In order to do analytical processing, text needs to be placed in a data base.

analyzing information. So, a person can start right away to doing analysis of nonrepetitive unstructured information.

The great drawback of doing analysis like this manually is that the human brain can only absorb so much information. There is no contest between the amount of information a computer can absorb and digest versus what a human can absorb and digest.

Fig. 4.4.12 shows that when it comes to reading and storing information in a database, a computer far outstrips even the brightest of human beings.

It simply is no contest.

Contextualizing Repetitive Unstructured Data

In order to be used for analysis, all unstructured data need to be contextualized. This is as true for repetitive unstructured data as it is for nonrepetitive unstructured data. But there is a big difference between contextualizing repetitive unstructured data and nonrepetitive unstructured data. That difference is that contextualizing repetitive unstructured data is easy and straightforward to do, whereas contextualizing nonrepetitive unstructured data is anything but easy to do.

PARSING REPETITIVE UNSTRUCTURED DATA

In the case of repetitive unstructured data, the data are read, usually in Hadoop. After the block of data is read, the data are then parsed. Given the repetitive nature of the data, parsing the data is straightforward. The record is small, and the context of the record is easy to find.

The process of parsing and contextualizing the data found in big data can be done with a commercial utility or can be a custom-written program.

Once the parsing takes place, the output can be placed in any one of many formats. One format the output data can be placed in is in the form of selected records. The parsing takes place. If the selection criteria are met, the data—record at a time—are gathered.

A variation of the record selection process occurs when only the context is selected, not the entire record.

Yet, another variation occurs when the record—once selected—is merged on output with another record.

There are undoubtedly many other variations other than the ones that are suggested here.

Fig. 4.5.1 shows the possibilities that have been discussed.

Data Architecture. https://doi.org/10.1016/B978-0-12-816916-2.00014-0

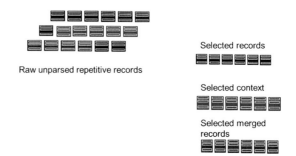

FIG. 4.5.1
Two database alternatives.

RECASTING THE OUTPUT DATA

Once the parse and selection process has been completed, the next step is to physically recast the data. There are many factors that determine how the output data are to be physically recast. One of the factors is how much output data are there. Another factor is what the data will be used for. And there are undoubtedly many other factors as well.

Some of the possibilities for that recasting of the output data include placing the output data back into big data. Another possibility is to place the output data into an index. Yet, another possibility is to send the output data to a standard database management system.

Fig. 4.5.2 shows the output recasting possibilities.

In the final analysis, even though repetitive unstructured data have to be contextualized, the process of contextualizing repetitive unstructured data is a straightforward process.

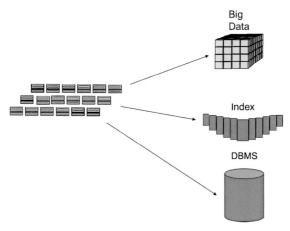

FIG. 4.5.2
Data recast according to its content.

Textual Disambiguation

The process of contextualizing nonrepetitive unstructured data is accomplished by technology known as "textual disambiguation" (or "textual ETL"). The process of textual disambiguation has an analogous process in structured processing known as "ETL"—"extract/transform/load." The difference between ETL and textual ETL is that ETL transforms old legacy system data and textual ETL transforms text. At a very high level, they are analogous, but in terms of the actual details of processing, they are very different.

FROM NARRATIVE INTO AN ANALYTICAL DATA BASE

The purpose of textual disambiguation is to read raw text—narrative—and to turn that text into an analytic database. Fig. 4.6.1 shows the general flow of data in textual disambiguation.

Once raw text is transformed, it arrives in the analytic database in a normalized form. The analytic database looks like any other analytic database. Typically, the analytic data are "normalized," where there is a unique key with dependent elements of data. The analytic database can be joined with other analytic databases to achieve the effect of being able to analyze structured data and unstructured data in the same query.

Each element in the analytic database can be tied back directly to the originating source document. This feature is needed if there ever is any question to the accuracy of the processing that has occurred in textual disambiguation. In addition, if there ever is any question as to the context of the data found in the analytic database, it can be easily and quickly verified.

Note that the originating source document is not touched or altered in any way.

Fig. 4.6.2 shows that each element of data in the analytic database can be tied back to originating source.

Data Architecture. https://doi.org/10.1016/B978-0-12-816916-2.00015-2

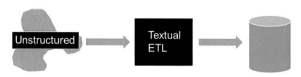

FIG. 4.6.1
Transformation of text into a standard database.

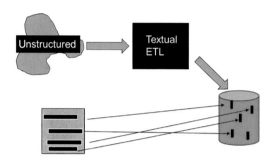

Tying the output data base back to the original source document
Is easy and straightforward to do

FIG. 4.6.2
Tying the text to the database.

INPUT INTO TEXTUAL DISAMBIGUATION

The input into textual disambiguation comes from many different places. The most obvious source of input is the electronic-based text that represents the document that is to be disambiguated. Another important source of data is taxonomies. Taxonomies are essential to the process of disambiguation. There will be an entire chapter on taxonomies. And there are many other types of parameters based on the document being disambiguated.

Fig. 4.6.3 shows some of the typical input into the process of textual disambiguation.

MAPPING

In order to execute textual disambiguation, it is necessary to "map" a document to the appropriate parameters that can be specified inside textual disambiguation. The mapping directs textual disambiguation as to how the document needs to be interpreted. The mapping process is akin to the process of designing how a system will operate. Each document has its own mapping process.

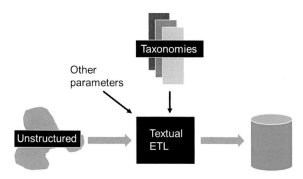

FIG. 4.6.3
Raw text, taxonomies and other parameters are input into textual ETL.

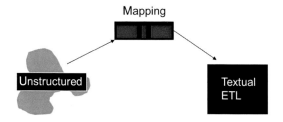

It is through mapping that textual ETL knows how to interpret
the raw text that is input to it

FIG. 4.6.4
Mapping.

The mapping parameters are specified, and upon completion of the mapping process, a document can then be executed. All documents of the same type can be served by the same mapping. For example, there may be one mapping for oil and gas contracts, another mapping for human resource resume management, and another mapping for call center analysis.

Fig. 4.6.4 shows the mapping process.

In almost every case, the mapping process is done in an iterative manner. The first mapping of a document is created. A few documents are processed, and the analyst sees the results. The analyst decides to make a few changes and reruns the document through textual disambiguation with the new mapping specifications. The process of gradually refining the mapping continues until the analyst is satisfied.

The iterative approach to the creation of a mapping is used because documents are notoriously complex and there are many nuances to a document that are

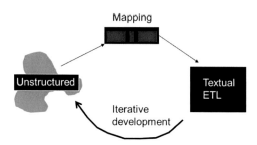

FIG. 4.6.5
Iterative development.

not immediately apparent. For even an experienced analyst, the creation of the mapping is an iterative process.

Because of the iterative nature of the creation of the mapping, it NEVER makes sense to create a mapping and then process thousands of documents using the initial mapping. Such a practice is wasteful because it is almost guaranteed that the initial mapping will need to be refined.

Fig. 4.6.5 shows the iterative nature of the mapping process.

INPUT/OUTPUT

The input to the process of textual disambiguation is electronic text. There are *MANY* forms of electronic text. Indeed, electronic text can come from almost anywhere. The electronic text can be in the form of proper language, slang, shorthand, comments, database entries, and many other forms. Textual disambiguation needs to be able to handle all the forms of electronic text. In addition, electronic text can be in different languages.

Textual disambiguation can handle nonelectronic text after the nonelectronic text passes through an automated capture mechanism such as optical character recognition (OCR) processing.

The output of textual disambiguation can take many forms. The output of textual disambiguation is output that is created in a "flat file format." As such, the output can be sent to any standard DBMS or to Hadoop.

Fig. 4.6.6 shows the types of output that can be created from textual disambiguation.

The output from textual disambiguation is placed into a work table area. From the work table area, the data can be loaded into a standard DBMS using the load utility of the DBMS.

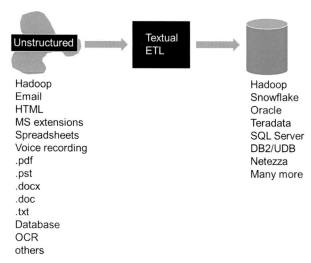

Hadoop
Email
HTML
MS extensions
Spreadsheets
Voice recording
.pdf
.pst
.docx
.doc
.txt
Database
OCR
others

Hadoop
Snowflake
Oracle
Teradata
SQL Server
DB2/UDB
Netezza
Many more

FIG. 4.6.6
Input and output passing through textual ETL.

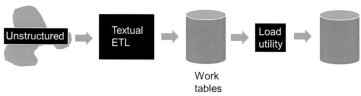

Work tables

Once the output work tables are created, the data is loaded into
the final data base format by means of a load utility

FIG. 4.6.7
A load utility.

Fig. 4.6.7 shows that data are loaded into the DBMS load utility from the work area created and managed by textual disambiguation.

DOCUMENT FRACTURING/NAMED VALUE PROCESSING

There are many features to the actual processing done by textual disambiguation. But there are two primary paths of processing a document. These paths are called *document fracturing* and *named value processing*.

Document fracturing is the process by which a document is processed—word by word—doing such processing as stop word processing, alternate spelling and acronym resolution, and homographic resolution. The effect of document fracturing is that upon processing, the document still has a recognizable shape, albeit in a modified form. For all practical purposes, it appears as if the document has been fractured.

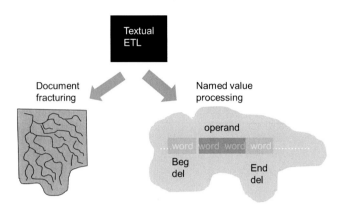

FIG. 4.6.8
The two main processing components of textual ETL.

The second major type of processing that occurs is named value processing. Named value processing occurs when inline contextualization needs to be done. Inline contextualization is done where the text is repetitive, as sometimes occurs. When text is repetitive, it can be processed by looking for unique beginning delimiters and ending delimiters.

There are other types of processing that can be done by textual disambiguation, but document fracturing and named value processing are the two primary analytic processing paths.

Fig. 4.6.8 depicts the two primary forms of processing that occur in textual disambiguation.

PREPROCESSING A DOCUMENT

On occasion, it is necessary to preprocess a document. On occasion, the text of a document cannot be processed in a standard fashion by textual disambiguation. In these circumstances, it is necessary to pass the text through a preprocessor. In the preprocessor, the text can be edited to alter the text to the point that the text can be processed in a normal manner by textual disambiguation.

As a rule, you don't want to preprocess text unless you absolutely have to. The reason why you don't want to have to preprocess text is that by preprocessing text, you automatically double (or more!) the machine cycles that are required to process the text.

Fig. 4.6.9 shows that—if necessary—electronic text can be preprocessed.

On occasion it is necessary to preprocess text before it passes to Textual ETL

FIG. 4.6.9
Preprocessing text.

E-MAILS—A SPECIAL CASE

E-mails are a special case of nonrepetitive unstructured data. E-mails are special because everybody has them and because there are so many of them. Another reason why e-mails are special is that e-mails carry with them an enormous amount of system overhead that is useful to the system and no one else. Also, e-mails carry a lot of valuable information when it comes to customer's attitudes and activities.

It is possible to simply send e-mails into textual disambiguation. But such an exercise is fruitless because of the spam and blather that are found in e-mails. Spam is the nonbusiness relevant information that is generated outside the corporation. Blather is the internally generated correspondence that is nonbusiness related. For example, blather contains the jokes that are sent throughout the corporation.

In order to use textual disambiguation effectively, the spam, blather, and system information need to be filtered out. Otherwise, the system becomes overwhelmed meaningless information.

Fig. 4.6.10 shows that there is a filter to remove unnecessary information from the stream of e-mails before the e-mails are processed by textual disambiguation.

SPREADSHEETS

Another special case is the case of spreadsheets. Spreadsheets are ubiquitous. Sometimes, the information on the spreadsheet is purely numerical. But on

FIG. 4.6.10
Filtering emails.

You need to reformat spreadsheet data before it can be passed to Textual ETL

FIG. 4.6.11
Reformatting spreadsheet data.

other occasions, there is character-based information on a spreadsheet. As a rule, textual disambiguation does not process numerical information from a spreadsheet. That is because there are no metadata to accurately describe numeric values on a spreadsheet. (Note: there is formulaic information for the numbers found on a spreadsheet, but the spreadsheet formulas are almost worthless as metadata descriptions of the meaning of the numbers.) For this reason, the only data that are found on the spreadsheet that make its way into textual ETL are the character-based descriptive data.

To this end, there is an interface that allows the data on the spreadsheet that are useful to be formatted from the spreadsheet into a working database. From the working database, the data are then sent into textual disambiguation, as seen in Fig. 4.6.11.

REPORT DECOMPILATION

Most textual information is found in the form of a document. And when text is on a document, it is processed linearly by textual disambiguation. Fig. 4.6.12 shows that textual disambiguation operates in a linear fashion.

But text on a document is not the only form of nonrepetitive unstructured data. Another common form of nonrepetitive unstructured data is that of a table. Tables are found everywhere—in bank statements, in research papers, in corporate invoices, and so forth.

Word1 word2 word3 word4 word5 word6 word7 word8 word9 ....

FIG. 4.6.12
Linear processing of text.

On some occasions, it is necessary to read the table in as input, just as text is read in on a document. To this end, a specialized form of textual disambiguation is required. This form of textual disambiguation is called *report decomposition*.

In report decomposition, the contents of the report are handled very differently than the contents of text. The reason why reports are handled differently from text is that in a report, the information cannot be handled in a linear format.

Fig. 4.6.13 shows that there are different elements of a report that must be brought together in a normalized format. The problem is that those elements appear is a decidedly nonlinear format.

Therefore, an entirely different form of textual disambiguation is required.

Fig. 4.6.14 shows that reports can be sent to spreadsheet report decompilation for reduction to a normalized format.

The end result of report decompilation is exactly the same as the end result of textual disambiguation. But the processing and the logic that arrive at the end result are very different in content and substance.

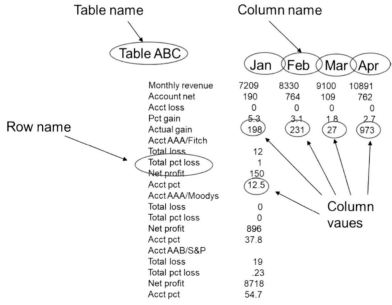

FIG. 4.6.13
An entirely different form of textual disambiguation.

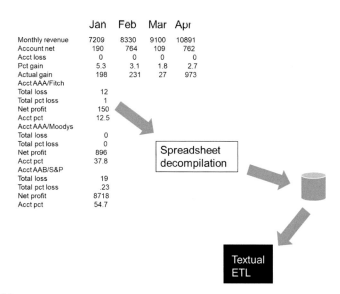

	Jan	Feb	Mar	Apr
Monthly revenue	7209	8330	9100	10891
Account net	190	764	109	762
Acct loss	0	0	0	0
Pct gain	5.3	3.1	1.8	2.7
Actual gain	198	231	27	973
Acct AAA/Fitch				
Total loss	12			
Total pct loss	1			
Net profit	150			
Acct pct	12.5			
Acct AAA/Moodys				
Total loss	0			
Total pct loss	0			
Net profit	896			
Acct pct	37.8			
Acct AAB/S&P				
Total loss	19			
Total pct loss	.23			
Net profit	8718			
Acct pct	54.7			

Spreadsheet decompilation

Textual ETL

FIG. 4.6.14
Report decompilation.

Taxonomies

Taxonomies are classifications of information. Taxonomies play a large and important role in the disambiguation of narrative information. Fig. 4.7.1 shows that taxonomies are to unstructured data what the data model is to structured data.

DATA MODELS/TAXONOMIES

The data model classically has played the role of serving as a map—an intellectual guideline—to the understanding and management of data in the structured environment. The taxonomy plays the same role in the unstructured textual environment. While not perfectly equivalent to each other, the taxonomy serves much the same purpose as the data model.

There is one anomaly in the world of unstructured data that must be explained. The classification of information that has been developed in this book has one very confusing anomaly. Unfortunately, that anomaly is important in understanding the role and function of taxonomies.

Consider the classification of data shown in Fig. 4.7.2.

Fig. 4.7.2 shows that there is unstructured data. Then, a subclassification of unstructured data is repetitive and nonrepetitive unstructured data. Then, beneath nonrepetitive data, there is a lower classification of repetitive and nonrepetitive data. Using this classification scheme, there are repetitive and nonrepetitive data. And this is confusing (apologies!) but is not a mistake.

In order to explain this anomaly and explain why it is important, consider the following real example.

In general, unstructured data can be considered to be repetitive and nonrepetitive. Repetitive unstructured data are unstructured data whose content and structure are highly repetitive. Into this classification of data fall clickstream data, analog data, metering data, and so forth. Into the other classification of data fall all data that are written. There are e-mails, call center data, customer feedback, contracts, and a whole host of other written and spoken narrative data.

111

Data Architecture. https://doi.org/10.1016/B978-0-12-816916-2.00016-4

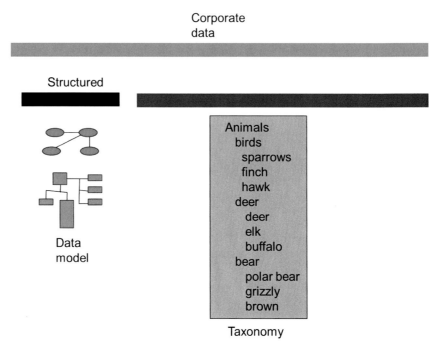

FIG. 4.7.1
Taxonomies—one of the keys to unlocking unstructured data.

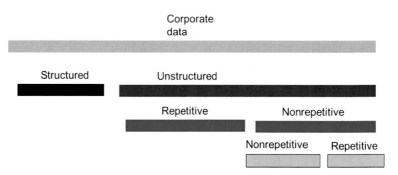

FIG. 4.7.2
Creating confusion—the fact that there is repetitive nonrepetitive data.

Now, consider that in the classification of narrative data, there appears a further subclassification of data. For all written data, there can be nonrepetitive written data and repetitive written data. For example, lawyers who write contracts use what is called "boilerplate." A boilerplate contract is a contract where the primary body of the contract is predetermined. The lawyer only fills in a few details into the contract such as the name, address, and social security number of the recipient of the contract. There may be a few other terms that are negotiated, but at the end of the day, the boilerplate contracts are very, very similar.

This then is an example of a repetitive nonrepetitive occurrence of data. The contract is nonrepetitive because it is in narrative form. But it is repetitive because it is essentially boilerplate.

The reason why making the distinction between nonrepetitive nonrepetitive text and nonrepetitive repetitive text is that taxonomies apply to nonrepetitive nonrepetitive text. Some examples are needed here to explain this anomaly.

APPLICABILITY OF TAXONOMIES

Taxonomies are most applicable to text such as e-mails, call center information, conversations, and other free-form narrative text. In free-form text, it is necessary to classify words using only the context associated by the taxonomy. As an example, the word ice cream is encountered. Ice cream belongs in the taxonomy of "dessert." It is assumed that the e-mail is about food and meals and desserts. Another e-mail mentions cake. Cake too is a dessert. So, the e-mails are related to each other, even though the words—"ice cream" and "cake"—are very different. Using taxonomic classification in free-form text is very useful for understanding the text.

However, suppose you have a boilerplate contract. Suppose the contract is for the purchase of apples. The term "apples" appears in every contract as part of the boilerplate. Certainly, an apple is a fruit. But the fact the apple is classified as a fruit appears in every instance of a contract. And there are many instances of the contract. Therefore, using a taxonomy to classify apple is not terribly useful in boilerplate data because the classification occurs repeatedly and adds very little to the understanding of the text.

For this reason, taxonomies are not very useful or applicable to boilerplate contracts and other places where there is repetitive narrative text.

The previous discussion is very difficult to explain. It is hoped that the examples make it clear what is being said.

WHAT IS A TAXONOMY?

So what is a taxonomy? In its simplest form, a taxonomy is simply a list of words that provides a classification of some larger topic. Fig. 4.7.3 shows some simple taxonomies.

Transportation
automobile
make
Ford
Honda
Porsche
Saturn
type
SUV
sedan
sports
station wagon
airplane
make
Boeing
....

Car
Honda
Toyota   German products
Porsche   sausage
Buick   beer
Chevrolet   Porsche
Yugo   Volkswagen
Subaru   skis
Kia   clothes
                    steel
                    bread

FIG. 4.7.3
Some simple taxonomies.

FIG. 4.7.4
An ontology.

In Fig. 4.7.3, it is seen that a car can be a Honda, Porsche, Volkswagen, and so forth. Or a German product may be sausage, beer, a Porsche, software (such as SAP), and so forth.

Of course, there are many other ways to classify these items. A car may be a sedan, an SUV, a sports car, and so forth. Or American products may be a hamburger, software, movies, corn, wheat, and so forth.

There are indeed almost an infinite number of taxonomies. Taxonomies are applied to nonrepetitive unstructured data on the basis of applicability. For example, an automaker may use taxonomies relating to engineering and manufacturing. Or an accounting firm may choose taxonomies that apply to taxes and to the rules of accounting. Or a retailer may choose taxonomies that relate to products and sales.

Conversely, it would be very unusual to have an engineering firm use a taxonomy relating to religion or lawmaking. Or it would be unusual for a construction firm have an interest in taxonomies about ethnicity.

Related to a taxonomy is an ontology. Fig. 4.7.4 depicts an ontology.

A simple definition of an ontology is that an ontology is a taxonomy where there are interrelationships of the elements within the taxonomy.

As a rule, either taxonomies or ontologies (or both) can be used when creating the foundation for textual disambiguation of nonrepetitive unstructured data.

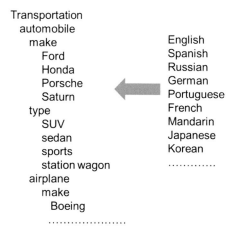

FIG. 4.7.5
Taxonomies—in multiple languages.

TAXONOMIES IN MULTIPLE LANGUAGES

One of the issues relating to taxonomies is that taxonomies can exist in multiple languages. Fig. 4.7.5 shows that taxonomies can exist in multiple languages.

COMMERCIAL OR PRIVATE TAXONOMIES?

A related issue is whether to use commercially created taxonomies or to use individually created taxonomies when doing textual disambiguation. One of the major advantages of a commercially created taxonomy is that the commercially created taxonomy can be easily and automatically translated into different languages. One of the features of commercially created taxonomies is that the taxonomy is normally created and supported in multiple languages. With a commercially created taxonomy, you can read a document in one language and create the associated analytic database in a different language.

But the largest advantage of using a commercially created taxonomy is that the commercially created taxonomy does not require a large investment in the creation of the taxonomy. If an organization decides to manually create their own taxonomies, the organization is inviting a disaster because of the organization's inability to estimate how much effort is required to actually build and maintain the taxonomies that it needs.

DYNAMICS OF TAXONOMIES AND TEXTUAL DISAMBIGUATION

The dynamics of how a taxonomy interacts with textual disambiguation is illustrated in the simple example seen in Fig. 4.7.6.

In Fig. 4.7.6, raw text is shown. The raw text is passed against the taxonomies for a car and another taxonomy for a motor thoroughfare. The output shows that where the word "Porsche" is encountered, it is recognized to be part of the taxonomy for car. The word "Porsche" is changed to the expression "Porsche/car" in the output. The same processing occurs for "Volkswagen" and "Honda."

Using the taxonomy for thoroughfare, the term "highway" is seen to be a form of "road." The output for "highway" is written out as "highway/road."

The example in the figure is very simple. But the example serves to illustrate the dynamics of how the taxonomy is used to interact with raw text inside the textual disambiguation process. In reality, the actual uses of taxonomies are usually much more sophisticated and elaborated than this simple example.

It is the use of taxonomies that has been described that is the key to opening the door to sophisticated analysis of text.

Note that on output of the processed text, the analyst can now create a query on "car" and find all mentions of any type of car. Also note that the term "car" appears nowhere in the raw text. This is just a glimpse at the value added by taxonomies when taxonomies are applied to text.

The ability to classify data externally is extremely useful when disambiguating nonrepetitive unstructured data.

TAXONOMIES AND TEXTUAL DISAMBIGUATION— SEPARATE TECHNOLOGIES

Taxonomies—the gathering, classification, and maintenance of the taxonomy—require their own care and handling. Usually, it makes sense to

Raw text –
"she drove her Porsche past the Volkswagen on the highway.
And soon they both passed a Honda on the right hand side…"

Processed text –
"she drove her Porsche/car past the Volkswagen/car on the highway/road.
And soon they both passed a Honda/car on the right hand side…"

FIG. 4.7.6
The application of a taxonomy to raw text.

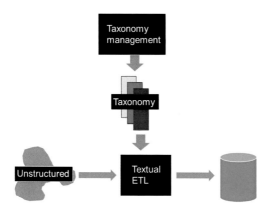

FIG. 4.7.7
Taxonomies serve as input to textual ETL.

build and manage the taxonomy external to the technology for textual disambiguation. Fig. 4.7.7 shows that arrangement.

There are many reasons for the logic behind separating the building and management of the taxonomies from textual disambiguation. But the primary reason is that textual disambiguation is complex enough without adding the further complexity of the building and management of taxonomies to the process.

Another way to explain the differences between the two processes is to look at the representation of taxonomies in the different technologies. In the world of taxonomy management, taxonomies require a robust and complex representation. But in the world of textual disambiguation, taxonomies are represented as a series of word pairs.

Fig. 4.7.8 shows this distinct difference between the two technologies.

DIFFERENT TYPES OF TAXONOMIES

An interesting point about taxonomies is that taxonomies themselves can be classified in many ways. Stated differently, there are many different ways to create the lists and classifications that make up taxonomies. Some taxonomies are made up of words that are synonyms. Other taxonomies are simply a list of words that happen to be gathered together. Other taxonomies are categories of words and so forth.

Fig. 4.7.9 shows that there are many different kinds of taxonomies.

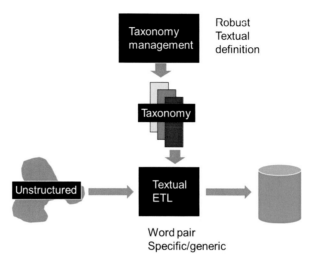

FIG. 4.7.8
The output from processing taxonomies is a word pair specification.

Taxonomies –
synonyms
lists
categories
preferred
many more
. . . .

FIG. 4.7.9
Different kinds of taxonomies.

TAXONOMIES—MAINTENANCE OVER TIME

A final observation about taxonomies is that over time, taxonomies require maintenance. Taxonomies require maintenance because language is constantly changing. For example, in the year 2000, if you referred to a "blog," no one would have known what you are talking about. But 10 years later, the term "blog" is a commonly used term.

Over time, language and terms change. And as language and terms change, the taxonomies that track those changes must be brought up to date.

Fig. 4.7.10 shows that over time, taxonomies require periodic maintenance.

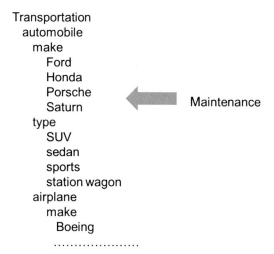

FIG. 4.7.10
Over time taxonomies require periodic maintenance.

The Siloed Application Environment

The road to siloed applications starts simply and innocently enough. One day, the corporation sees a need for a computerized system. They build an application. Soon, another group in the organization also spots a need for computerization in another place. A new application is spawned. Soon, there are lots of applications that have been built.

THE CHALLENGE OF SILOED APPLICATIONS

The challenges presented by siloed systems start innocently enough. The problems with siloed applications begin as a minor irritation or inconvenience. But over time, the problems escalate from inconvenience to calamity. And there is never any easing of the problems. It is eternal escalation.

Fig. 5.1.1 depicts the siloed applications that management wakes up to one day.

So, what are the problems that eternally escalate in the face of siloed applications? There are many.

> *Maintenance.* Once an application is built, it needs constant maintenance. And over time, the need for maintenance never de-escalates. The completion of one maintenance project spawns three other new projects for maintenance. And as there are more applications that arise, the need for maintenance grows exponentially.
>
> *Integrity of data.* It is one thing to have data. It is quite another thing to have data that can be believed. Multiple siloed applications breed disintegrity of data. Marketing says we are losing money. Finance says we are breaking even. Sales says we are making money. Who to believe is like drawing straws. One day, we believe one source. The next day, we believe the next source. And nobody is saying the same thing as anyone else. Who to believe is a constant political battle within the walls of the organization. The problem is not in having data. There is plenty of that. Instead, the issue becomes which data to actually believe. Making good corporate decisions becomes difficult in the face of data that cannot be believed.

121

Data Architecture. https://doi.org/10.1016/B978-0-12-816916-2.00017-6

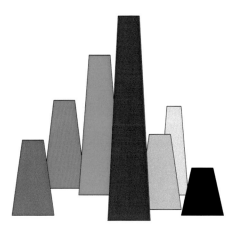

FIG. 5.1.1
Siloed applications.

Fig. 5.1.2 shows that there are multiple versions of the same data within different siloed applications.

Not only do siloed applications have conflicting values of information, but also trying to resolve the issues across the different applications is an intractable problem. There are a multiplicity of reasons why the unbelievability of data across siloed applications presents an intractable problem. But the single greatest reason for the intractability stems from the fact that data cannot be meaningfully shared from one siloed application to the next.

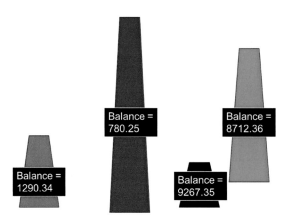

One of the problems with siloed application systems

FIG. 5.1.2
Integrity of data—one of the problems with siloed data.

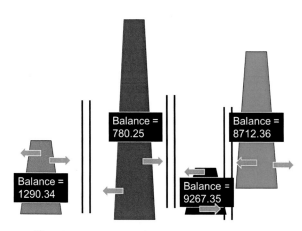

There is no sharability of data across siloed applications

FIG. 5.1.3
No sharability across applications.

Fig. 5.1.3 shows this issue.

Certainly, data can be shared from a mechanical standpoint. But merely passing data from one application to another does no good when the data mean something different in each application. As a simple example of why data are not interchangeable among applications, consider the following example. Suppose that there are three siloed applications—application A, application B, and application C.

Suppose that all three applications have a field of data—amount of sale—and in each amount of sale is a dollar value. It seems like it would be easy enough to exchange the values between the applications. But a closer examination turns up the fact that application A measures American dollars, application B measures Australian dollars, and application C measures Canadian dollars. At first glance, there is consistency among the applications. But a closer examination shows that it would be a very misleading thing to do to merely start exchanging dollar values between the different applications. The data are not the same at all.

Unfortunately, the differences between applications run much more deeply than a conversion of money. There are many other reasons why merely transferring data values from one application to the next is a dangerous thing to do.

Older technology can become an issue. When an application is built, it is built in the technology that is available at the time of development. Unfortunately, the siloed application often times outlives the technology it was built in. Because a siloed application is extremely difficult to change, the siloed application becomes "trapped" inside older technology.

There are then many reasons why siloed applications in corporations become an ever-increasing vexation.

BUILDING SILOED APPLICATIONS

So, exactly how did corporations get into the dilemma that they find themselves in when it comes to their siloed applications?

The sojourn to siloed systems starts innocently enough. Simply stated, developers were building applications in what they thought were the best methods and approaches for development at the time.

One of the fundamentals of application development was the tenet that applications are to be built from end user requirements. That notion sounds simple and straightforward. But time has shown that this simplistic approach has some major shortcomings.

Fig. 5.1.4 depicts this simple notion—that applications are built based on end user requirements.

Indeed, whole books and methodologies are built on this simple notion. And to an extent, these books and methodologies are correct. Applications must be based on end user requirements.

However, there is a major flaw with this line of thinking. The flaw is that only the *direct* user of the systems is used to determine the requirements. The thinking is that if ALL the people—direct users and indirect users of the application—are considered, it will take a very long amount of time to build the application. Therefore, when gathering the requirements of the system, only the direct users of the system are considered. In doing so, the gathering of requirements takes a finite amount of time.

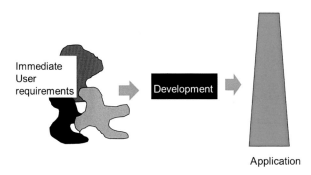

Immediate User requirements → Development → Application

FIG. 5.1.4
How the application was built.

So, who are these indirect users of the application? Typically, the indirect end user of the application includes (but is not limited to) marketing, sales, finance, and accounting.

And when the application was built and just being installed, the direct end user was quite pleased. But shortly thereafter, the dissatisfaction begins to come when the indirect users of the system began to voice their complaint. Some of the things the indirect user of the data complained about were as follows:

Data definitions that were different from those used by the developer
Accessibility to the data found in the application
Difficulty of access to the data found in the application
Accuracy of the data found in the application
Timeliness of access to the data found in the application
Organization of the data found in the application
And so forth

The list of complaints of the indirect end user was long.

Because the data were so hard to get to and so foreign to the thinking of the indirect end user, the indirect end user sets out to build THEIR own application. And in doing so, the indirect end user escalated the issues evolving around siloed systems. Now, there were even MORE siloed applications.

Fig. 5.1.5 shows that—once built—the application did not solve any of the demands for data of the indirect users.

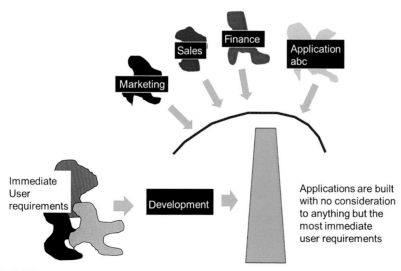

FIG. 5.1.5
Immediate user requirements.

And the hunger for data and information spawned more applications, and each of the new applications exaggerated the dissatisfaction with siloed applications.

WHAT DOES A SILOED APPLICATION LOOK LIKE?

So, what exactly do these applications that turned into silos actually look like? What are some characteristics of these applications?

Most of these siloed applications were the very first applications that were built or were otherwise acquired by the corporation. As a result, these were the very first applications that inhabited the corporation.

In many cases, these applications were the applications that directly connected the corporation to its customers. Typical of these applications were ATM processing, bank teller processing, airline reservation processing, and so forth. These early applications were critical because they were the day-to-day face of the corporation to its customer base.

These early applications had a direct effect on the day-to-day business of the corporation. For example, when the bank teller system went down, the bank had to cease doing business until the system came back up.

CURRENT VALUED DATA

One of the common expectations was that the data found in the application were what can be called "current valued data."

Fig. 5.1.6 shows current valued data.

Current valued data are data that are accurate as of the moment of access. In order to achieve this high degree of accuracy, the application must support online transaction processing.

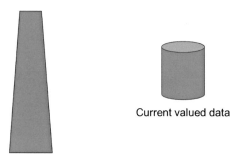

Current valued data

FIG. 5.1.6
Current valued data.

As a simple example of current value data, consider the account balance for a husband and a wife. At 8:00 a.m., their account balance has $5000. At 9:15 a. m., the wife does an ATM withdrawal of $500. At 9:15 a.m. and 5 seconds, the account balance is corrected to $4500.

The husband checks the account balance at 10:00 a.m. and sees that the account balance is $4500. The husband withdraws $175 as of 10:01 a.m. At 10:01 a.m. and 5 seconds, the account now has $4325.

At 4:15 p.m., the wife deposits a check into the account for $2000. As of 4:15 p.m. and 5 seconds, the account balance is now $6325.

At any point in the day, the husband, the wife, and the bank can check the account balance and see what the balance in the account is. The account balance is accurate as of the moment of access to the data.

Current value data are data that are accurate as of the moment of access. Applications that interact directly with the customer are typically populated with current value data.

The converse of current value data is data that are not accurate as of the moment of access. As a simple example of noncurrent value data, consider the stock market where values are captured at the end of the trading day. Suppose there is an application that captures data as of the end of a trading day.

At 9:00 a.m., you look at your favorite stock. You found that its closing value the day before was $76.10. However, the market has been open for several hours now. The stock may well be trading higher or lower than $76.10. But your stock value won't be updated until the end of the trading day.

MINIMAL HISTORICAL DATA

Another characteristic of the data found in siloed applications is that there is relatively little historical data found in the application. If there is any amount of historical information found in the application, it is summarized.

There is a very practical reason why there is little historical data found in an application. The reason for the paucity of historical data is the need for efficient transactional performance. In a customer facing application, it is typical to do transactions. In order to execute transactions quickly, it is necessary to wade through and process the minimum amount of data. When an application stores massive amounts of historical data, the efficiency of transaction performance is impeded. Therefore, online transaction processing applications shed as much

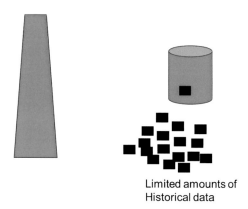

Limited amounts of
Historical data

FIG. 5.1.7
Limited amounts of historical data.

data as possible as soon as possible. In doing so, they optimize the performance of the system.

In order to understand this principle, consider your bank account in the bank. Is it reasonable for you to find the current account balance? Yes, of course it is. Is it reasonable for you to go and look up a transaction that you made last week? The answer is yes, of course. Now, suppose you are going through an IRS audit. Suppose you need to find a check you wrote 5 years ago. Is it reasonable that the 5-year-old check is in the online processing portion of your database? No, it is not reasonable. In order to find your 5-year-old check, the bank will have to look through audit and archive records.

When it comes to detail, applications typically store a month's worth of data or maybe even a quarter's worth of data depending on the nature of the business being accommodated. Beyond that, the data are stored elsewhere.

Fig. 5.1.7 shows that online transaction processing applications focus on very current information.

HIGH AVAILABILITY

Another characteristic of siloed applications is the fact that application data often have the need for a high degree of availability. For systems that are customer facing, anytime the system is down and dysfunctional, the customer grows dissatisfied with the company whose business the application was built for. For example, suppose your ATM machine is down. You cannot transact your activity, and you grow dissatisfied with the bank that owns and manages the ATM machine. As a consequence, applications are up and running as frequently as

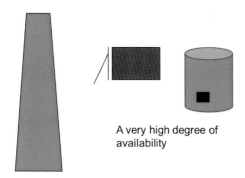

A very high degree of availability

FIG. 5.1.8
A very high degree of availability.

possible. Applications try to achieve 100% uptime. The reality is that no system is up and available 100% of the time. That nevertheless is the goal.

Fig. 5.1.8 shows that applications try to achieve a 100% availability.

OVERLAP BETWEEN SILOED APPLICATIONS

Another consequence of the building of siloed applications is that there is a high degree of overlap—redundancy—among the many siloed applications.

There is a high degree of overlap/redundancy from one application to another

FIG. 5.1.9
A high degree of overlap.

Because the applications are built for individual requirements, it is almost inevitable that there be significant data and process overlap between the different siloed applications.

Fig. 5.1.9 shows the overlap between the different applications.

FROZEN BUSINESS REQUIREMENTS

Another common characteristic of siloed applications is that the siloed applications have their business requirements "frozen in time." The siloed applications are built around requirements of the business that are known as of one moment in time. Once the application is built, the siloed application is very difficult to change. Unfortunately, business conditions change whether the underlying application changes or not. Business change is simply a fact of life.

The result is that one day, the business wakes up and finds that they have a different set of business requirements than those represented by the siloed application. The siloed application represents business requirements of a previous decade. But the siloed application is so difficult to change that new, more modern business requirements are not satisfied by the siloed application.

For this reason, siloed applications are said to be "frozen in time" when it comes to the business that is represented by the siloed application.

Fig. 5.1.10 shows a siloed application that has been frozen in time.

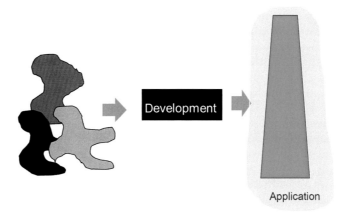

The requirements for the application get to be frozen in time

FIG. 5.1.10
The requirements for the application are frozen in time.

DISMANTLING SILOED APPLICATIONS

Unfortunately for most organizations, dismantling the older siloed application is not an option.

Fig. 5.1.11 shows that dismantling the siloed application is not something that is even considered.

Dismantling the application and rebuilding it was not an option for most organizations

FIG. 5.1.11
Dismantling applications was never an option.

Introduction to Data Vault 2.0

"Data Vault 2.0" is a system of business intelligence that includes modeling, methodology, architecture, and implementation best practices. The components also known as *pillars* of Data Vault 2.0 are identified as follows:

- Data Vault 2.0 modeling—focused on process and data models
- Data Vault 2.0 methodology—following Scrum and agile ways of working
- Data Vault 2.0 architecture—includes NoSQL and big data systems
- Data Vault 2.0 implementation—pattern-based automation and generation

The term "data vault" is merely a marketing term chosen in 2001 to represent the system to the market. The true name for the data vault system of business intelligence (BI) is *common foundational warehouse modeling, methodology, architecture, and implementation.*

The system includes aspects relating to the business of designing, implementing, and managing an enterprise data warehouse. With the Data Vault 2.0 (DV2) system, the organization can build incrementally, distributed or centralized, in the cloud or on-premise with disciplined agile teams.

Each of these components plays a key role in the overall success of an enterprise data warehousing program. These components are combined with industry-accepted practices rooted in Capability Maturity Model Integration (CMMI), Six Sigma, total quality management (TQM), Project Management Professional (PMP), and disciplined agile delivery.

DATA VAULT ORIGINS AND BACKGROUND

Data vault was originally designed for use within Lockheed Martin, the US Department of Defense, National Security Agency, and NASA. The process started in 1990 and was completed in circa 2000. The entire system is composed of 10 years of research and development and over 30,000 test cases. The system is built to overcome the following issues:

Data Architecture. https://doi.org/10.1016/B978-0-12-816916-2.00018-8

- Integrate data from 250+ source systems from ADABAS, to PeopleSoft, to Windchill, to Oracle Financials, to mainframes and midranges, to SAP
- Provide an auditable and accountable data store and process engine
- Ingestion and query parsing of tagged image drawings (unstructured data)
- Rocket data fed in real time from the NASA launch pads
- Multilayered security—including classified data sets
- Subsecond query response times over 15 terabytes of live data
- Four hour turnaround from requirement to "hands-on" data in development for the report writers

These issues may not sound like much, but in 1997, we were dealing with 10BaseT networking as the "fastest" and best network; a 15 TB disk store was $250,000. Joining servers across the globe with subsecond query response times became imperative and challenging work. Flexibility to change and adapt was paramount.

Our team met the goals of the NSA and exceeded the expectations of all corporate management involved. Our team of five people ingested 150 source systems in under 6 months, built over 1500 reports, and delivered over 60,000 data attributes with 100% accountability and auditability. Today, with the better technology, this can be accomplished much easier, especially with the proper automation tooling. This global enterprise data warehouse is still there, still going strong, and of course much larger.

The "Old" Data Vault 1.0

Stepping back in time—in 2001—the Data Vault 1.0 standards were released. As of circa 2018, Data Vault 1.0 is now 17 years old; it is time to innovate. These standards were targeted at traditional relational database solutions on a small scale. In addition, the only standards released to the public were the Data Vault 1.0 model standards.

Data Vault 1.0 modeling utilizes sequence numbering schemes that fails to properly perform under large-volume load cycles. Furthermore, sequence numbering techniques limit the team's ability to distribute the data vault model onto hybrid platforms (on-premise/in-cloud) or onto geographically distributed platforms.

Enter: Data Vault 2.0

The New and Updated Data Vault 2.0

Since 2001, the technology, platforms, capabilities, and hardware have all changed and shifted. Today's focus is on much larger big data systems,

NoSQL platforms, and better processing of unstructured/semistructured data. The methodology has been brought up to date to include disciplined agile delivery (from Mark Lines and Scott Ambler). The architecture includes landing zones, data lakes, and hybrid solution designs.

The data vault has evolved—just like the web, just like automobiles, or just like any system. Data vault is now considered to be at a stable 2.0 release and includes (as mentioned previously) model, methodology, implementation, and architecture. Data Vault 2.0 (DV2) is a foundational system that provides programs and projects with the knowledge and foresight to implement successful enterprise data warehouses.

The issues Data Vault 2.0 is built to solve include the following:

- Global distributed teams
- Global distributed physical data warehouse components
- "Lazy" joining during query time across multicountry servers
- Ingestion and query parsing of images, video, audio, and documents (unstructured data)
- Ingestion of real-time streaming (IOT) data
- Cloud and on-premise seamless integration
- Agile team delivery
- Incorporation of data virtualization and NoSQL platforms
- Extremely large data sets (into the petabyte ranges and beyond)
- Automation and generation of 80% of the work products

From a business perspective, DV2 brings the entire solution to the table—not only the data model but also the workflow, processes, automation, standardization, adaptability, architectural flexibility, agility, and more. From a business perspective, these components can no longer be ignored. Cobbling together multiple different methodologies and hoping for success rarely work.

DV2 brings tried and tested successes, empirical evidence that will not suffer the consequences of reengineering. DV2 also brings confidence from customers, based on solid reliable engineering implementations. Data Vault 2.0 offers all of this, including customer references (some of the largest commercial organizations and government data stores in the world).

This might sound like overkill; however, the team (once properly trained) can deliver sprint work products in a one- and two-day life cycle. The solution is foundational and offers building block components that easily fit together in a standardized fashion. Accelerating the teams' progress by leveraging automation and workflow process tooling (specifically with Data Vault 2.0 authorized tools) becomes a must-do.

Today, there are customers around the world whom have implemented petabyte-level distributed Data Vault 2.0 solutions with some of the latest big data technology. More information from business to technical and from tooling to data platforms can be found in the data vault community: http://DataVaultAlliance.com (free to join).

WHAT IS DATA VAULT 2.0 MODELING?

A Business View

The data vault model is based on a business concept model. Capturing concepts or elements of the business needs to be unified at a logical level and then mapping those concepts to the raw data level and the business process levels. The concept model starts with an individual data item like a customer, product, or service. Then, these concepts are uniquely identified by business keys that travel across the lines of business (from data inception to data "death").

The model separates relationships or associations (links) from identifiers (hubs) from the descriptive data that change over time (satellites). This allows the model to store commonly defined data sets mapped to a concept level and ties that data to multiple business process levels. These business processes are the ones that execute within the source systems.

By capturing the data set in this manner, the model can easily represent multiple logical units of work, along with shifting business hierarchies and shifting processes. Furthermore, the conceptual model can be applied in automation and generation tools, data virtualization tools, and query tools to better meet the needs of the enterprise.

Because this model (at a build process level) is focused on concepts, it can be split or divided into parallel work streams. The model can be built incrementally over time with little to no reengineering efforts when change arrives. The model can be automatically generated (with human input around the concepts and business keys), to expedite and accelerate the process.

A Technical View

The data vault modeling is a hybrid approach based on third normal form and dimensional modeling aimed at the logical enterprise data warehouse. The data vault model is built as a ground-up, incremental, and modular models that can be applied to big data, structured, and unstructured data sets.

DV2 modeling is focused on providing flexible, scalable patterns that work together to integrate *raw* data by business key for the enterprise data warehouse.

DV2 modeling includes minor changes to ensure the modeling paradigms can work within the constructs of big data, unstructured data, multistructured data, and NoSQL.

Data Vault Modeling 2.0 changes the sequence numbers to hash keys. The hash keys provide stability, parallel loading methods, and decoupled computation of parent key values for records. There is an alternative for engines that hash business key values internally—the option of utilizing the true business keys as they are, without sequences or hash surrogates. The pros and cons of each technique will be detailed in the data vault modeling section of this chapter.

HOW IS DATA VAULT 2.0 METHODOLOGY DEFINED?

A Business View

The methodology utilizes best practices from software development best practices such as CMMI, Six Sigma, TQM, Lean Initiatives, and cycle time reduction and applies these notions for repeatability, consistency, automation, and error reduction.

DV2 methodology focuses on rapid sprint cycles (iterations) with adaptations and optimizations for repeatable data warehousing tasks. The idea of DV2 methodology is to enable the team with agile data warehousing and business intelligence best practices. DV2 encompasses methodology as a pillar or key component to achieve the next level of maturity in the data warehousing platform.

Other methodologies are available for use; however, the DV2 methodology is uniquely geared to leverage the benefits of the DV2 model, process designs, and much more.

A Technical View

The methodology (like the modeling components) is based on solid repeatable process designs. These designs require little to no reengineering and can handle scale-out, scale-up, parallelism, and real time with ease. The methodology is also geared around the people. From a technical standpoint, there is nothing better than having an agile team, capable of implementing and rapidly scaling a solution.

Tooling that is offered by both AnalytiX DS and WhereScape assists the team from the process perspective. Automation and generation tooling is beneficial in increasing the delivery speed by a factor of four times (minimum).

WHY DO WE NEED A DATA VAULT 2.0 ARCHITECTURE?

Data Vault 2.0 architecture is designed to include NoSQL (think: big data, unstructured data, multistructured, and structured data sets). Seamless integration points in the model, and well-defined standards for implementation offer guidance to the project teams.

DV2 architecture includes NoSQL, real-time feeds, and big data systems for unstructured data handling and big data integration. The DV2 architecture also provides a basis for defining what components fit where and how they should integrate. In addition, the architecture provides a guideline for incorporating aspects such as managed self-service BI, business write back, natural language processing (NLP) result set integration, and direction for where to handle unstructured and multistructured data sets.

WHERE DOES DATA VAULT 2.0 IMPLEMENTATION FIT?

DV2 implementation focuses on automation and generation patterns for time-savings, error reduction, and rapid productivity of the data warehousing team. The DV2 implementation standards provide rules and working guidelines for high-speed reliable build-out with little to no errors in the process. The DV2 implementation standards dictate where and how specific business rules are to execute in the process chain, indicating how to decouple the business changes or data provisioning from data acquisition.

WHAT ARE THE BUSINESS BENEFITS OF DATA VAULT 2.0?

There are hundreds of benefits, far too many to list—all of which are drawn from the existing best practices of CMMI, Six Sigma, TQM, PMP, Agile/Scrum, automation, and so on. However, the reason for Data Vault 2.0 system of business intelligence can be nicely summed up in one word: *maturity.*

Maturity of the business intelligence and data warehousing systems require the following key elements:

- Repeatable patterns
- Redundant architecture/fault-tolerant systems
- High scalability
- Extreme flexibility
- Managed consistent costs for absorbing changes
- Measurable key process areas (KPAs)
- Gap analysis (for the business of building data warehouses)
- Incorporation of big data and unstructured data

From a business perspective, Data Vault 2.0 addresses the needs of big data, unstructured data, multistructured data, NoSQL, and managed self-service BI. Data Vault 2.0 really is targeted at the evolution of the *enterprise data warehousing (EDW) and business intelligence (BI)*. Data Vault 2.0's goal is to mature the processes of building BI systems for the enterprise in a repeatable, consistent, and scalable fashion while providing seamless integration with new technologies (i.e., NoSQL environments).

The resulting business benefits include (but are not limited to) the following:

- Lowering total cost ownership (TCO) for EDW/BI programs
- Increasing agility of the entire team (including delivery)
- Increasing transparency across the program

The resulting business benefits can be found in the following categories:

Data Vault 2.0 agile methodology benefits:
- Drives agile deliveries (2/3 weeks)
- Includes CMMI, Six Sigma, and TQM
- Manages risk, governance, and versioning
- Defines automation and generation
- Designs repeatable optimized processes
- Combines best practices for BI

Data Vault 2.0 model benefits:
- Follows scale-free architecture
- Based on hub and spoke design
- Backed by set logic and massively parallel processing (MPP) math
- Includes seamless integration of NoSQL data sets
- Enables 100% parallel heterogeneous loading environments
- Limits impacts of changes to localized areas

Data Vault 2.0 architecture benefits:
- Enhances decoupling
- Ensures low impact changes
- Provides managed self-service BI
- Includes seamless NoSQL platforms
- Enables team agility

Data Vault 2.0 methodology benefits:
- Enhances automation
- Ensures scalability
- Provides consistency
- Includes fault tolerance
- Provides proved standards

WHAT IS DATA VAULT 1.0?

Data Vault 1.0 (DV1) is highly focused on the data vault modeling components and relational database technology. A DV1 data model attaches surrogate sequence keys as its primary key selection for each of the entity types. Unfortunately, *surrogate sequences* exhibit the following problems:

- Introduce dependencies on the ETL/ELT loading paradigm
- Contain an upper bound/upper limit, when reached can cause issues

- Are meaningless numbers (mean absolutely nothing to the business)
- Cause performance problems (due to dependencies) on load of big data sets
- Reduce parallelism (again due to dependencies) of loading processes
- Cannot be utilized as MPP partition keys for data placement, to do so would potentially cause hot spots in the MPP platform
- Cannot be reliably rebuilt or reassigned (reattached to old values) during recovery loads
- Are disparate across multiple source applications that are housing the same data sets

DV1 *does not* meet the needs of big data, unstructured data, semistructured data, or very large relational data sets. DV1 is highly focused on just the data modeling section and relational databases.

Are surrogate sequences a *bad* thing to utilize? No, if the data set is small (less than 100M records per table) or if the platform is capable of scaling compute power beyond traditional methods (reducing the cost of a lookup on load). Sequences do work very well for high-performance queries, and most traditional relational engines utilize this to their advantage when data are partitioned by range.

There are platforms where sequences are discouraged and in fact not even available. In those platforms, alternative key structures are needed. The alternative key structure proposed is in fact a hash key, which is discussed in detail, later in this chapter. A third alternative is to utilize the natural business key directly from the source system. This too has its pros and cons and will also be addressed later on in this chapter.

Introduction to Data Vault Modeling

WHAT IS A DATA VAULT MODEL CONCEPT?

From a conceptual level, the data vault model (DVM) is a hub-and-spoke-based model, designed to focus its integration patterns around business keys. These business keys are the keys to the information stored across multiple systems (hopefully the master keys), utilized to locate and uniquely identify records or data. At a conceptual level, these business keys are stand-alone, meaning they don't rely on other information to exist.

The concepts are derived from *business context* (or business ontologies), elements that make sense to the business from a master data perspective like customer, product, and service. These concepts are business drivers at the lowest level of grain. The DVM is built to house data at the level of granularity of the source systems.

The DVM should never be simply designed as a "source system restructuring." If there is no integration by business keys, then there is no point in building a DVM. Business keys need to reflect the concepts as they are defined within the business taxonomy. These taxonomy hierarchies define the context where the business keys live, along with their granularity.

An example of this might be "customer account number" (CAN). In a perfect world, the CAN would be assigned once and never change—it would also be assigned to the same customer, forever. This would be the ultimate in master data management. Regardless of the business process or source application that is processing the CAN, the value would remain the same. Once this occurs, tracing the CAN through the life cycle of the business is an easy undertaking.

DATA VAULT MODEL DEFINED

A DVM is a detail-oriented, historical tracking and uniquely linked set of normalized tables that support one or more functional areas of business.

141

Data Architecture. https://doi.org/10.1016/B978-0-12-816916-2.00019-X

In DV2, the model entities are keyed by hashes, while in DV1, the model enti ties are keyed by sequences.

The modeling style is a *hybrid* of third normal form and dimensional modeling techniques—uniquely combined to meet the needs of the enterprise. The DVM is also based on patterns found in hub-and-spoke-type diagramming, otherwise known as scale-free network design (Fig. 6.2.1).

These design patterns enable the data vault model to inherit scale-free attributes that impose no known inherent limitation on the size of the model or the size of data that the model can represent—other than those limitations introduced by the infrastructure.

COMPONENTS OF A DATA VAULT MODEL

There are three basic entities or structures in a data vault model: hub, link, and satellite. In business terms, the hubs represent the actual business keys or master key sets that exist across the enterprise in a horizontal fashion. The links represent the relationships and associations that exist across the business keys in the enterprise. The real *data warehousing* components are the satellites that store nonvolatile data over time.

The data vault model is based on normalization and separation of classes of data. In this particular case, the business keys (hubs) are considered a different class than the relationships (links). Both of these types are separated by *context* or descriptive information (satellites) that have a tendency to change over time.

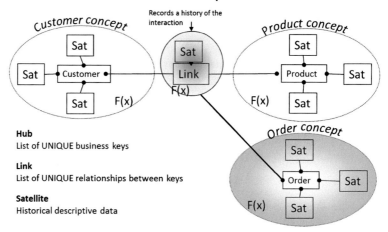

Data vault conceptual model

Hub
List of UNIQUE business keys

Link
List of UNIQUE relationships between keys

Satellite
Historical descriptive data

FIG. 6.2.1
Data vault conceptual model.

WHAT MAKES BUSINESS KEYS SO INTERESTING?

Business keys are the drivers in business. They tie the data set to the business processes and the business processes to the business requirements. Without business keys, the data set has no value. Business keys are the sole source of tracking the data through the business processes and across lines of business.

Fig. 6.2.2 represents several concepts that exist within a full-scale enterprise. The blue boxes represent hundreds of individual business processes that occur within the business. The blue boxes are tied together through a business process life cycle. The objective of organizing the business processes in this manner is to identify the critical path (as these processes are engaged in cycle time reduction and lean initiatives). The critical path of the business processes is depicted by the red dotted line.

Note that the critical path is an important part to overhead cost reduction, time to market delivery, and quality improvements. By identifying the critical path in the organization, the company can achieve "better, faster, and cheaper" throughout the enterprise. Identifying and tracking the data through the business processes is necessary to trace the critical path through the company's business processes.

Within each of the business processes, the business keys are identified. Business keys are how the source systems and the individuals in the organization track and manage the data/contracts underneath. The business keys (in this example, SLS123) originate in the sales systems. As illustrated in this example, when these keys cross the process boundaries from sales to procurement, a manual process takes place. The result of the manual process is a change to the example

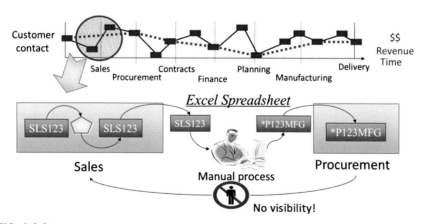

FIG. 6.2.2
Business keys across lines of business.

business key from *SLS123* to *P123MFG*. Unfortunately, the manual change to the business keys in this example is not recorded anywhere except in an external Excel spreadsheet.

WHAT DOES THIS HAVE TO DO WITH DATA VAULT AND DATA WAREHOUSING?

As stated earlier, the objective is to lower total cost of ownership (TCO) in the organization. TCO translates to reducing overhead costs, increasing quality of the deliverable, and decreasing the amount of time to deliver the product or service. A properly designed and implemented data vault data warehouse can help with these tasks, including the discovery and tracing activities needed to identify the critical path.

The ability to track and trace the data set across multiple lines of business is part of creating value or establishing data as an asset on the books. Without traceability back to the business processes, data become nearly valueless.

Introducing critical path analysis in the business and establishing traceability across multiple lines of business mean the organization can engage in cycle time reduction (or lean initiatives); these initiatives aid the organization in identifying their critical path and eliminating business processes that add no value and are apt to slowing down the production and delivery of the product or service. Understanding the path of the data (identified by business keys) across the multiple lines of business can show the critical path and the long-standing business processes that need to be addressed in cycle time reduction efforts.

By linking the business processes to the data through business keys, it is not only easier to assign value but also easier to understand the gaps in the business perception (i.e., requirements they provide the EDW team. The gaps expose the reality of what multiple source systems are capturing and executing on.

One of the end results from this process is to help (hopefully) understand where the business may be hemorrhaging money. When businesses close the gap through TQM best practices, they stop the money loss and potentially increase revenue and quality of the product or service at the same time.

HOW DOES THIS TRANSLATE TO DATA VAULT MODELING?

The data vault model, more specifically the hub table, shows how many different keys there are across the entire business. The hub table tracks when each key

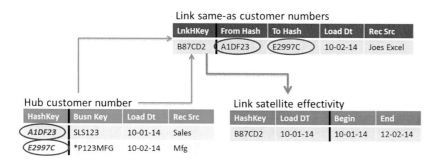

FIG. 6.2.3
Data Vault 2.0 data model.

is inserted to the warehouse and from what source application it arrived. The hub table does not track anything else. To understand the "changing of the business keys" from one line of business to another, the data warehouse needs another table structure and another source feed.

The next table structure that the data vault uses is called a link. The link structure houses the feed from the manual process, FROM SLS123 TO *P123MFG, otherwise known as a same-as link structure.

An example Data Vault 2.0 model for this case is shown in Fig. 6.2.3.

The hub *customer* represents the two keys found in the business process. The link *same-as* shows their connection. The record source (Rec Src) shows "Joes Excel," meaning the data vault load processed an Excel spreadsheet based on the manual process. The link *satellite effectivity* provides the time line for when the relationship between the two keys starts and stops. Satellites are where the descriptive data live and breathe.

Satellites carry more than just effectivity. In the case of customer (not shown here), the satellite may carry additional descriptive details such as the customer name, address, and phone number. Other examples of satellites and satellite data are provided further in this section.

The link in this case carries the key matches (from and to). This type of link structure can be utilized to connect master key selections or to explain the key mapping/changing from one source system to another. It can also be utilized to represent multilevel hierarchies (not shown here).

Note that importing the Excel spreadsheet shows the first step toward managed self-service BI (managed SSBI). Managed SSBI is the next step in the evolution of data warehousing. Allowing the business users to interact with the raw data sets in the warehouse and affect their own information marts by changing the data.

The data vault model not only provides immediate business value but also is capable of tracking all relationships over time. It demonstrates the different hierarchies of data (even though this is highly focused on two particular business keys at the moment) that are possible when loading into the warehouse.

By tracking the changes to business keys that exposes the relationship across and between business keys, the business can then begin to ask and answer the following questions:

- How *long* does my customer account stay in sales before it is passed to procurement?
- Can I compare an AS-SOLD image with an AS-CONTRACTED image and an AS-MANUFACTURED image with an AS-FINANCED image?
- How many customers do I actually have?
- How long does it take for a customer/product/service to make it from *initial sale* to *final delivery* in my business?

Many of these questions cannot be answered without a consistent business key that spans the different lines of business.

WHY RESTRUCTURE THE DATA FROM THE STAGING AREA?

Restructuring allows integration across multiple systems into a single place in the target data warehouse without changing the data set itself (i.e., no conformity). This is called *passive integration.* Data are considered passively integrated by business key because there is no change to the raw data. It is integrated according to the location (i.e., all individual customer account numbers will exist in the same hub, while all corporate customer account numbers exist in a different hub).

In the age of big data, staging areas are also known as landing zones, data dumps, or data junkyards. Staging areas are a logical concept that can manifest themselves physically in multiple environments. A "staging area" may be a file store on Amazon S3 or an Azure Cloud, or it may be a Hadoop distributed file system (HDFS). It may also be a relational database table structure. Staging areas focus the data in a single concept in preparation for moving the data downstream.

WHAT ARE THE BASIC RULES OF THE DATA VAULT MODEL?

There are some fundamental rules in data vault modeling that must be followed, or the model itself no longer qualifies to be a data vault model. These rules are documented in a classroom environment in full. However, some of the rules are listed below:

(1) Business keys are separated by GRAIN and semantic meaning. That means customer corporation and customer individual must exist or be recorded in two separate hub structures.

(2) Relationships, events, and intersections across two or more business keys are placed into link structures.

(3) Link structures have no begin or end dates; they are merely an expression of the relationship at the time the data arrived in the warehouse.

(4) Satellites are separated by the type of data/classification and rate of change. Type of data is typically a single source system.

Raw data vault modeling does not allow nor provide for such concepts or notions as conformity, nor does it deal with super types. Those concepts lie within the business vault models (another form of data vault modeling that is used as an information delivery layer).

WHY DO WE NEED MANY TO MANY LINK STRUCTURES?

Many-to-many link structures allow the data vault model to be future proof/extendable. The relationships expressed in source systems are often a reflection of business rules or business execution *today.* The relationship definition has changed over time and will continue to change. To represent both historical *and* future data (without reengineering the model and the load routines), many-to-many relationship tables are necessary.

This is how the Data Vault 2.0 data warehouse can expose the patterns of relationship changes over time answering questions like where is the gap between "current requirements" and "relationships" in history? The many-to-many table (link) in the raw data vault provides metrics around what percentage of data are "broken" and when that data break the relationship requirement.

For example, let's say that in the past, for a sample customer, it was common to have one portfolio manager. Today, however, the company has changed the business rule so that there might be three or more portfolio managers assigned to a customer. If the data warehouse model enforces the "past" relationship (many customers to one portfolio manager), then to support today's relationship the data model and the ELT/ETL loading routines would have to be reengineered.

There is a reason for having a many-to-many relationship implemented in a link table without the descriptive attributes attached. That reason would be to catch discrepancies across multiple source systems. A link table (for purposes of understanding) may be thought of as a *relationship table*. There are several forms of link structures including nonhistorized links, hierarchical links, and same-as links. These forms are *functionally* defined because they are defined in a manner that indicates the type of function or role the data in these structures play.

Reengineering results in ever-increasing amounts of money because as the data set grows and the model grows, the time, complexity, and cost of modifications also grow. Eventually, this increase in cost and time to maintain the data outgrows the business' ability to pay.

The *only* way to represent both relationships (historical and future) over time is to place the data in a many-to-many link table; then, based on query requirements provided by data marts downstream, the warehouse can tell the business users exactly what they have and when it "breaks" the current rule.

PRIMARY KEY OPTIONS FOR DATA VAULT 2.0

There are three main alternatives for selecting primary key values in a Data Vault 2.0 model:

- Sequence numbers
- Hash keys
- Business keys

Sequence Numbers

Sequence numbers have been around since the beginning of machines. They are system-generated, unique numeric values that are incremental (sequential) in nature. Sequence numbers have the following issues:

- Upper limit (the size of the numeric field for nondecimal values).
- Introduce process issue when utilizing sequences during load because they require any child entity to look up its corresponding parent record to inherit the parent value.
- Hold no business meaning.

The most critical of the issues above is that of negative performance impacts associated with lookup or join processes, particularly in heterogeneous environments or in environments where data are legally not allowed to "live" or be replicated on to other environments (geographically split or on-premise and in-cloud mix). This process issue is exacerbated during high-speed IOT or real-time feeds. Consider what happens in an IOT or real-time feed when data flow quickly to billions of child records, and each record must then wait on a sequence "lookup" (one record at a time); the real-time stream may back up.

Lookups also cause "precaching" problems under volume loads. For example, suppose the parent table is invoice and the child table is order. If the invoice table has 500 million records and the order table has 5 billion records and each order has at least one matching parent row (most likely more), then each record that flows into order must "look up" at least one invoice. This lookup process will happen 5 billion times, once for each child record.

It doesn't matter if the technology is an ETL engine, real-time process engine, or SQL data management-enabled engine. This process must happen to avoid any potential orphan records. If the referential integrity is shut off, the load process can run in parallel to both tables. However, to populate the "parent sequence," it must still be "searched/looked up" on a row-by-row basis. Adding parallelism and partitioning will help with the performance, but eventually, it will hit an upper limit bottleneck.

In an MPP environment (MPP storage), the data will be redistributed to allow the join to occur, and it is not just the sequence that has to be shipped—it's the sequence PLUS the entire business key that it is tied to. In an MPP engine with non-MPP storage (like snowflake DB), the data don't have to be shipped, but the lookup process still must happen.

This act of a single-strung, one record at a time lookup can tremendously (and negatively) impact load performance. In large-scale solutions (think of 1000 "tables" or data sets each with 1 billion records or more), this performance problem is dramatically increased (load times are dramatically increased).

What if there is one child table? What if the data model design has parent-> child->child->child tables? Or relationships that are multiple levels deep? Then, the problem escalates as the length of the load cycles escalates exponentially.

To be fair, let's now address some of the positive notions of utilizing sequence numbers. Sequence numbers have the following positive impacts once established:

- Small byte size (generally less than number(38)) (38 "9's") or $10^{\wedge}125$.
- Process benefit: joins across tables can leverage small byte size comparisons.
- Process benefit: joins can leverage numeric comparisons (faster than character or binary comparisons).
- Always unique for each new record inserted.
- Some engines can further partition (group) in ascending order the numerical sequences and leverage subpartition (micropartition) pruning by leveraging range selection during the join process (in parallel).

Hash Keys

What is a hash key? A hash key is a business key (may be composite fields) run through a computational function called a hash and then assigned as the primary key of the table. Hash functions are called *deterministic.* Being *deterministic* means that based on given input X (every single time the hash function is provided X), it will produce output Y (for the same input, the same output will be generated). Definitions of hash functions, what they are and how they work, can be found on Wikipedia.

Hash key benefits to any data model:

- 100% parallel independent load processes (if referential integrity is shut off) even if these load processes are split on multiple platforms or multiple locations.
- Lazy joins—that is, the ability to join across multiple platforms utilizing technology like drill (or something similar)—even without referential integrity. Note that lazy joins can't be accomplished across heterogeneous platform environments and aren't even supported in some NoSQL engines.
- Single field primary key attribute (same benefit here as the sequence numbering solution).
- Deterministic—it can even be precomputed on the source systems or at the edge for IOT devices/edge computing.
- Can represent unstructured and multistructured data sets—based on specific input hash keys can be calculated again and again (in parallel). In other words, a hash key can be constructed as a business key for audio, images, video, and documents. This is something sequences cannot do in a deterministic fashion.
- If there is a desire to build a smart hash function, then meaning can be assigned to bits of the hash (similar to teradata—and what it computes for the underlying storage and data access).

Hash keys are important to Data Vault 2.0 because of the efforts to connect heterogeneous data environments such as Hadoop and Oracle. Hash keys are also important because they remove dependencies when "loading" the Data Vault 2.0 structures. A hash key can be computed value by value. The "parent" key can also be computed and can be repeated for as many parent keys as there exist values for. There is no lookup dependency, no need to precache, use the temp area, or anything else to calculate each parent value during load processing.

Big data system loads are nearly impossible to scale properly with sequence numbering dependencies in place. Sequences (whether they are in DV1 or dimensional models or any other data model) force the parent to be loaded and then the child structures. These dependencies on "parent first—then lookup parent value" cause a sequential row-by-row operation during the load cycles, thereby inhibiting the scale-out possibilities that parallelism offers.

This type of dependency not only slows the loading process down but also kills any potential for parallelism—even with referential integrity shutoff. Furthermore, it places a dependency into the loading stream in heterogeneous environments. For instance, when loading satellite data into Hadoop (perhaps a JavaScript Object Notation (JSON) document), the loading stream requires a lookup for the sequence number from the hub that may exist in a relational database. This dependency alone defeats the entire purpose of having a system like Hadoop in the first place.

Hash keys do have their issues:

- Length of the resulting computational value when the storage for the hash is greater than sequences.
- Possible collision (probabilities of collision are dependent on the hashing function chosen for utilization).

The first issue leads to slower SQL joins and slower queries. This is because it takes longer to "match" or compare longer length fields than it does to compare numerics. Hashes (in Oracle and SQL Server) are typically stored in fixed binary form (yes, this works as a primary key). Hashes in Hive or other Hadoop-based technologies and some other relational engines must store the hashes as fixed character set lengths. For example, an MD5 hash result is BINARY(16), which results in CHAR(32) fixed length hexadecimal encoded string.

The flip side of using a hash is its unlimited scalability in parallel loading. All data can be loaded in complete parallel all the time across multiple platforms (even those that are geographically split or split on-premise and in-cloud). Hash keys (or business keys) are part of the success of Data Vault 2.0 in a big data and NoSQL world. Hashing is optional in DV2. There are a variety of hashing algorithms available for use that include the following:

- MD5 (deprecated circa 2018)
- SHA 0, 1, 2, and 3—*SHA1* (deprecated circa 2018)
- Perfect hashes

The hash is based on the business keys that arrive in the staging areas. All lookup dependencies are hence removed, and the entire system can load in parallel across heterogeneous environments. The data set in the model now can be spread across MPP environments by selecting the hash value as the distribution key. This allows for better mostly random, mostly even distribution across the MPP nodes *if* the hash key is the MPP bucket distribution key.

"When testing a hash function, the uniformity of the distribution of hash values can be evaluated by the chi-squared test.*"* https://en.wikipedia.org/wiki/Hash_function

Luckily, the hash functions are already designed, and the designers have taken this bit of distribution mathematics into account. The hashing function chosen (if hashing is to be utilized) can be at the discretion of the design team. As of circa 2018, teams have chosen SHA-256.

One of the items discussed is the longer the hashing output (number of bits), the less likely/less probable for a potential collision. This is something to take into consideration, especially if the data sets are large (e.g., big data, 1 billion records on input per load cycle per table).

If a hash key is chosen for implementation, then a hash collision strategy must also be designed. This is the responsibility of the team. There are several options available for addressing hash collisions. One of the recommended strategies is reverse hash.

This is just for the Data Vault 2.0 model that acts as the enterprise warehouse. It is still possible (and even advisable) to utilize or leverage sequence numbers in persisted information marts (data marts) downstream to engage fastest possible joins within a homogeneous environment.

The largest benefit isn't from the modeling side of the house; it's from the loading and querying perspectives. For loading, it releases the dependencies and allows loads to Hadoop and other NoSQL environments in parallel with loads to RDBMS systems. For querying, it allows "late-join" or run-time binding of data across Java database connectivity (JDBC) and open database connectivity (ODBC) between Hadoop, NoSQL, and RDBMS engines on demand. It is not suggested that it will be fast, but rather that it can be easily accomplished.

Deeper analysis of this subject is covered in Data Vault 2.0 boot camp training courses and in Data Vault 2.0 published materials. It is beyond the scope of this book to dive deeper into this subject.

Business Keys

Business keys have been around for a long time, if there have been data in operational applications. Business keys should be *smart* or *intelligent* keys and should be mapped to *business concepts*. That said, most business keys today are source system surrogate IDs, and they exhibit the same problems that sequences mentioned above exhibit.

A *smart* or *intelligent* key is generally defined as a sum of components where digits or pieces of a single field contain meaning to the business. At Lockheed Martin, for example, a part number consisted of several pieces (it was a superkey of sorts). The part key included the make, model, revision, and year of the part, like a vehicle identification number (VIN) found on automobiles today.

The benefits of a smart or intelligent key stretch far beyond the simple surrogate or sequence business key. These business keys usually exhibit the following positive behavior at the business level:

- They hold the same value for the life of the data set.
- They do not change when the data are transferred between and across business OLTP applications.
- They are not editable by business (most of the time) in the source system application.
- They can be considered master data keys.
- They cross business processes and provide ultimate data traceability.
- Largest benefit can allow parallel loading (like hashes) and also work as keys for geographically distributed data sets—without needing recomputation or lookups.

They do have three downfalls: (a) length, generally, smart business keys can be longer than 40 characters; (b) meaning over time, the base definition can change every 5–15 years or so (just look at how VIN number has evolved over the last 100 years); (c) sometimes, source applications CAN change the business keys, which wreaks havoc on any of the analytics that need to be done.

If given the choice between surrogate sequences, hashes, and natural business keys, natural business keys would be the preference. The original definition (even today) states that a hub is defined as a unique list of business keys. The preference is to use natural business keys that have meaning to the business.

One of the functions of a properly built *raw* Data Vault 2.0 model is to provide traceability across the lines of business. To do this, the business keys *must* be stored in the hub structures according to a set of design standards.

Most of the business keys in the source system today are surrogate sequence numbers defined by the source application. The world is full of these "dumb" machine-generated numeric values. Examples include customer number, account number, invoice number, and order number, and the list goes on.

Source System Sequence Business Keys

Source system sequence-driven business keys make up 98% of the source data that any data warehouse or analytic system receives. Even down to transaction ID, e-mail ID, or some of the unstructured data sets, such as document ID, contain surrogates. The theory is that these sequences should never change and should represent the same data once established and assigned.

That said, the largest problem that exists in the operational systems is one the analytic solution is always asked to solve, that is, how to integrate (or master) the data set, to combine it across business processes and make sense of the data that have been assigned multiple sequence business keys throughout the business life cycle.

An example of this may be customer account. Customer account in SAP may mean the same thing as customer account in Oracle Financials or some other customer relationship management (CRM) or enterprise resource planning (ERP) solution. Generally, when the data are passed from SAP to Oracle Financials, typically, the receiving OLTP application assigns a new "business key" or surrogate sequence ID. It's still the same customer account; however, the same representative data set now has a new key.

The issue becomes as follows: how do you put the records back together again? This is a master data management (MDM) question and with an MDM solution in place (including good governance and good people) can be solved and approximated with deep learning and neural networks. Even statistical analysis of "similar attributes" can detect within a margin of error the multiple records that "should" be the same but contain different keys.

This *business problem* perpetuates into the data warehouse and analytic solution typically because no master data management solution has been implemented upstream of the data warehouse. Therefore, to put together what appears to be "one version of the customer record" and not double or triple count, algorithms are applied to bridge the keys together.

In the data vault landscape, we call this a hierarchical or same-as link, hierarchical if it represents a multilevel hierarchy and same-as if it is a single hierarchy (parent to child remap) of terms.

Placing these sequence numbers as business keys in hubs have the following issues:

- They are meaningless—a human cannot determine what the key stands for (contextually) without examining the details for a moment in time.
- They can change—often they do, even with something as "simple" as a source system upgrade—this results in a serious loss of traceability to the historical artifacts. Without an "old-key" to "new-key" map, there is no definitive traceability.
- They can collide. Even though conceptually across the business there is one element called "customer account," the same ID sequence may be assigned in different instances for different customer accounts. In this case, they should never be combined. An example of this would be two different implementations of SAP: one in Japan and one in Canada. Each assigns customer ID #1; however, in Japan's system, #1 represents

"Joe Johnson," whereas in Canada's system, #1 represents "Margarite Smith." The last thing you want in analytics is to "combine" these two records for reporting just because they have the same surrogate ID.

An additional question arises if the choice is made to utilize data vault sequence numbers for hubs and the source system business keys are surrogates. The question is as follows: why "rekey" or "renumber" the original business key? Why not just use the original business key (which by the way is how the original hub is defined)?

To stop the collision (as put forward in the example above)—whether a surrogate sequence, a hash key, or the source business key is chosen for the hub structure—another element must be added. This secondary element ensures uniqueness of this surrogate business key. One of the best practices here is to assign geography codes, for example, JAP for any customer account IDs that originate from Japans' SAP instance and CAN for any customer account IDs that originate from Canadas' SAP instance.

Multipart Source Business Keys

Using a geographic code, as mentioned above, brings up another issue. If the hub is created based solely on source system business key (and not surrogate sequence or hash key), then with the choice above (to add a geography code split), the model must be designed and built with a multipart business key.

The issue with a multipart business key is with performance of a join. There are multiple mathematical tests and quantitative results that show time and time again that multifield join criteria are slower than single field join criteria. It only goes "slower" in large volume or big data solutions. At this point, perhaps, a hash key or surrogate sequence in the data vault may be faster than a multifield join because it reduces the join back to a single field value.

Another alternative is to concatenate the multifield values together, thus forming somewhat of an intelligent key, either with or without delimiters. This would depend on how the business wishes to define a set standard for concatenating the multifield values (i.e., the rules needed—just like the rules needed to define a smart key).

The last thing to watch when choosing a multipart business key is the length of the combined or concatenated field. If the length of the concatenated fields is longer than the length of a hash result or surrogate sequence ID, then the join will execute slower than a join on a shorter field. As a reminder, these differences in performance usually can only be seen in large data sets (500 M or 1 billion records or more). The hardware has advanced and will continue to advance so much so that small data sets exhibit good performance. There is simply not enough of a difference in a small data set to make an informed decision about the choice of the "primary key" for the hubs.

The suggestion ultimately is to rekey the source data solutions and add a smart or intelligent key "up front" that can carry the data across instances, across business processes, across upgrades, through master data, across hybrid environments, and never change. Doing this would centralize and ease the pain and cost of "master data" and would lead to easier use of a virtualization engine. It may not require complex analytics, neural nets, or machine learning algorithms to tie the data sets back together later.

In fact, fixing these rekeying issues, according to one estimate, costs the business seven times the money to "fix" this problem in the warehouse, instead of addressing it in the source applications. Fixing the problem in the data warehouse is one form of technical debt (quote and metrics paraphrased from Nols Ebersohn).

If the source system cannot be rekeyed or the source system cannot add an "intelligent" or "smart key" that is a contextual key, the recommendation is to implement master data management upstream. If MDM cannot be implemented, the next recommendation is leverage the source system business keys (unless there are composite business keys)—in which case, a hash is the base-level default recommendation.

Introduction to Data Vault Architecture

WHAT IS A DATA VAULT 2.0 ARCHITECTURE?

The data vault architecture is based on three tier data warehouse architecture. The tiers are commonly identified as staging or landing zone, data warehouse, and information delivery layer (or data marts).

The multiple tiers allow implementers and designers to decouple the enterprise data warehouse from both sourcing and acquisition functions and information delivery and data provisioning functions. In turn, the team becomes more nimble; the architecture is more resilient to failure and more flexible in responding to changes (Fig. 6.3.1).

The sections are staging, EDW, and information marts or information delivery layer. Regardless of platforms and technology utilized for implementation, these layers will continue to exist. However, as the system nears full real-time enablement, the need and dependency on the staging area will decline. True real-time data will feed directly into the EDW layer.

In addition to the three tiers, the Data Vault 2.0 architecture dictates several different components:

(a) The use of Hadoop or NoSQL to handle big data.
(b) The nature of real-time information flowing both IN and OUT of the business intelligence ecosystem; in turn, this also evolves the EDW into an operational data warehouse over time.
(c) The use of managed self-service BI through write-back and master data capabilities enabling TQM as well.
(d) Split of hard and soft business rules, making the enterprise data warehouse a *system of record* for raw facts that are loaded over time.

Data Architecture. https://doi.org/10.1016/B978-0-12-816916-2.00020-6

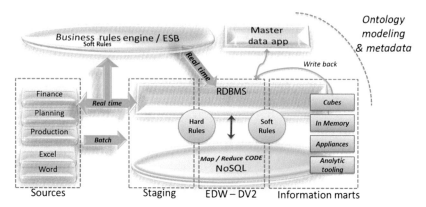

FIG. 6.3.1
Data Vault 2.0 architecture overview.

HOW DOES NOSQL FIT IN TO THE ARCHITECTURE?

NoSQL platform implementations will vary. Some will contain SQL-like interfaces; some will contain relational database technology integrated with nonrelational technology. The line between the two (RDBMS and NoSQL) will continue to be blurred. Eventually, it will be a "data management system" capable of housing both relational and nonrelational simply by design.

The NoSQL platform today, in most cases, is based on Hadoop at its core—which is composed of the Hadoop distributed file system (HDFS) or metadata management for files in the different directories. Various implementations of SQL access layers and in-memory technology will sit on top of the HDFS.

Once atomicity, consistency, isolation, and durability (ACID) compliance is achieved (which is available today with some NoSQL vendors), the differentiation between RDBMS and NoSQL will fade. Note that not all Hadoop or NoSQL platforms offer ACID compliance today and not all NoSQL platforms offer *update* of records in place making it impossible to completely supplant the RDBMS technology.

This is changing quickly. Even as this section is written, the technology continues to advance. Eventually, the technology will be seamless, and what is purchased from the vendors in this space will be hybrid-based.

Current positioning of a platform like Hadoop is to utilize it or leverage it as an ingestion area and a staging area for any and all data that might proceed to the warehouse. This includes structured data sets (delimited files and fixed-width columnar files); multistructured data sets like XML and JSON files; and unstructured data like Word documents, Excel, video, audio, and images.

The reason is to ingest a file into Hadoop is quite simple: copy the file into a directory that is managed by Hadoop. It is from that point that Hadoop splits the file across the multiple nodes or machines that it has registered as part of its cluster.

The second purpose for Hadoop (or best practice today) is to leverage it as a place to perform data mining, utilizing SAS, or R, or textual mining. The results of the mining efforts often are structured data sets that can and should be copied into relational database engines, making them available for ad hoc querying.

WHAT ARE THE OBJECTIVES OF THE DATA VAULT 2.0 ARCHITECTURE?

There are several objectives of the Data Vault 2.0 architecture; they are listed below:

(a) To seamlessly connect existing relational database systems with new NoSQL platforms
(b) To engage business users and provide space for managed self-service BI (write back and direct control over data in the data warehouse)
(c) To provide for real-time arrival direct to the data warehouse environment without forcing a landing in the staging tables
(d) To enable agile development by decoupling the always changing business rules from the static data alignment rules

The architecture plays a key role in separation of responsibilities, isolating data acquisition from data provisioning. By separating responsibilities and pushing ever-changing business rules closer to the business user, agility by the implementation teams is enabled.

WHAT IS THE OBJECTIVE OF THE DATA VAULT 2.0 MODEL?

The objective is to provide seamless platform integration or at least make it available and possible via design. The design that is leveraged includes several basic elements. The first is found in the Data Vault 2.0 model, the use of the hash keys (to replace the surrogates as primary keys). The hash keys allow the implementation of parallel decoupled loading practices across heterogeneous platforms. The hash keys and loading process are introduced and discussed in the implementation and modeling sections of this chapter.

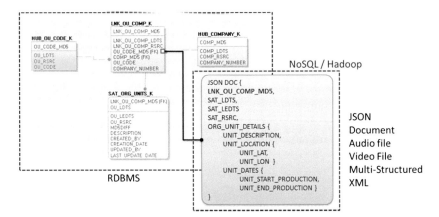

FIG. 6.3.2
Hadoop-based satellite.

That said, the hash keys provide the *connection* between the two environments, allowing cross system joins to occur where possible. Performance of the cross system join will vary depending on the NoSQL platform chosen and the hardware infrastructure underneath. Fig. 6.3.2 shows an example data model that provides a *logical* foreign key between relational DBMS and Hadoop-stored satellite.

In other words, the idea is to allow the business to *augment* their current infrastructure by adding a NoSQL platform to the mix while retaining the value and use of their currently existing RDBMS engines, not to mention all the historical data they already contain.

WHAT ARE HARD AND SOFT BUSINESS RULES?

Business rules are the requirements translated into code. The code manipulates the data and in some cases turns data into information. Part of Data Vault 2.0 system of BI is to enable agility (which will be covered a bit more in the methodology section of this chapter). Agility is enabled by first splitting the business rules into two distinct groups: hard rules and soft rules (Fig. 6.3.3).

The idea is to separate data interpretation from data storage and alignment rules. By decoupling these rules, the team is enabled to be increasingly agile. Also, the business users can be empowered, and the business intelligence solution can be moved toward managed self-service BI.

Beyond that, the Data Vault 2.0-based data warehouse carries *raw* data, in a nonconformed state. That data are aligned with the business constructs known

- **_Hard rules:_**
  - Any rule that does **not** change content of individual fields **or** grain

- For example:
  - Data type alignment
  - Normalization / denormalization
  - Tagging (adding system fields)
  - De-duplication
  - Splitting by record structure

- **_Soft rules:_**
  - Any rule that **changes** or **interprets** data, or changes grain of the data
  - (turning data in to information)

- For example:
  - Concatenating name fields
  - Standardizing addresses
  - Computing monthly sales
  - Coalescing
  - Consolidation

FIG. 6.3.3
Hard and soft business rules.

as business keys (which are defined in the data vault modeling section of this chapter).

The raw data, integrated by business keys, serve as a foundation for passing audits, especially, since the data set is **not** in a conformed format. The idea of the Data Vault 2.0 model is to provide for data-warehousing-based storage of raw data, so that if necessary (due to an audit or other needs), the team can reconstruct or reassemble the source system data.

This, in turn, makes the Data Vault 2.0-based data warehouse a system of record. Mostly because after warehousing the data from the source systems, those systems are either shut down or replaced by newer sources. In other words, the Data Vault 2.0 data warehouse becomes the only place where one can find the raw history integrated by business key.

HOW DOES MANAGED SELF SERVICE BI FIT IN THE ARCHITECTURE?

First, understand that *self-service BI* in and of itself is a misnomer. It emerged in the market in the 1990s as *federated query* engines, also known as enterprise information integration. While it is a grand goal, it never truly was able to overcome technical challenges that vendors touted it would. In the end, a data warehouse and business intelligence ecosystem are still needed in order to make accurate decisions. Hence, the term *managed self-service BI* is feasible and readily applicable to the solution space discussed in this book.

That said, Data Vault 2.0 architecture provides for the managed SSBI capabilities with the injection of write-back data (reabsorbing data on multiple levels) either from direct applications (sitting on top of the data warehouse) or from external applications like SAS, Tableau, QlikView, and Excel, where the data sets are physically "exported" from the tools after having been altered and fed back into the warehouse as another source.

The difference then is that the aggregations and the rest of the soft business rules rely on the new data in order to assemble the proper output for the business. The soft business rules (i.e., code layers) are managed by IT, while the processes are data-driven, and the business manages the data. An example of this can be found in the simple example of allowing businesses direct access to managing their own hierarchies.

Introduction to Data Vault Methodology

DATA VAULT 2.0 METHODOLOGY OVERVIEW

The Data Vault 2.0 standard provides a best practice for project execution, which is called the "Data Vault 2.0 methodology." It is derived from core software engineering standards and adapts them for the use in data warehousing. Fig. 6.4.1 shows the standards that have influenced the Data Vault 2.0 methodology.

The methodology for data vault projects is based on best practices pulled from disciplined agile delivery (DAD), automation and optimization principles (CMMI, KPAs, and KPIs), Six Sigma error tracking and reduction principles, Lean Initiatives, and cycle time reduction principles.

In addition, the data vault methodology takes in to account a notion known as managed self-service BI. The notion of managed self-service BI is introduced in the Data Vault 2.0 architecture section of this chapter.

The idea of the methodology is to provide teams with current working practices and a well-laid out IT process for building data warehouse systems (business intelligence systems) in repeatable fashion, reliably and rapidly.

HOW DOES CMMI CONTRIBUTE TO THE METHODOLOGY?

Carnegie Mellon's Capability Maturity Model Integration (CMMI) contains the foundations of management, measurement, and optimization. These components are applied to the methodology at the levels of key process areas (KPAs) and key performance indicators (KPIs). These pieces are necessary in order to understand and define what the business processes are and should be around the implementation and life cycle of the business intelligence build-out.

The business of building business intelligence solutions needs to mature. In order to accomplish these goals, the implementation team must first accept that a BI system is a software product. As such, software development life cycle

163

Data Architecture. https://doi.org/10.1016/B978-0-12-816916-2.00021-8

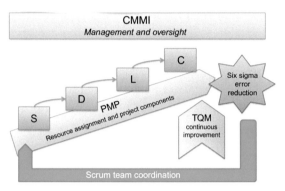

FIG. 6.4.1
Data Vault 2.0 methodology overview.

	Data vault 2.0 methodology
Level 1—initial chaos	N/A
Level 2—Managed	Predefined document templates Implementation standards Pattern based architecture
Level 3—Defined	Defined project process
Level 4—Quantitatively managed	Estimates and actuals captured Measured lead times Measured complexity Measured defects
Level 5—Optimizing	Automation tools Rapid delivery Reduced cost Parallel teams

FIG. 6.4.2
CMMI mapped to Data Vault 2.0.

(SDLC) components, along with best practices of managing, identifying, measuring, and optimizing must be applied—particularly if the team is to become and remain agile going forward. Fig. 6.4.2 demonstrates how CMMI levels map to Data Vault 2.0 methodology. It is not a complete map, just a representative portion of the entire piece.

The end goal of CMMI is optimization. Optimization cannot be achieved without metrics (quantitative measurements) or KPIs. These KPIs cannot be achieved without the KPAs or definitions of key areas to be measured, which of course cannot be achieved without first managing the project.

The road to agility is paved with metrics and well-defined/well-understood business processes. The Data Vault 2.0 methodology relies on the necessary components of CMMI in order to establish a solid foundation on which to build and automate enterprise business intelligence systems.

Taking a step back, here is a simplified definition of what CMMI cares about:

> In CMMI, process management is the central theme. It represents learning and honesty as demonstrated through work according to a process. Process also enables transparency by communicating how work should be done. Such transparency is within the project, among projects, and being clear about expectations. Also, measurement is part of process and product management and provides the information needed to make decisions that guide product development. http://resources.sei.cmu.edu/asset_files/TechnicalNote/2008_004_001_14924.pdf
> Page 17

CMMI brings consistency to the processes; it also brings manageability, documentation, and cost control. CMMI helps the people assigned to the project execute with a specific quality metric in mind. It also assists with the measurements of those metrics by identifying common processes that must happen in every business intelligence system.

CMMI provides the *framework* to operate within. Teams implementing Data Vault 2.0 methodology inherit the best parts of CMMI level 5 specifications and can successfully hit the ground running. Why? Because Data Vault 2.0 methodology provides the transparency, defines many of the KPAs and KPIs, and also enriches the project process by allocating template-based predefined deliverables, utilized during the implementation phases.

Transparency is implemented in the Data Vault 2.0 projects in different manners. The first recommendation for teams is to set up an in-company wiki, one that can reach any and all employees (including executives) in the firm. All meetings, all models, all templates, designs, metadata, and documentation should be recorded in the wiki.

The wiki should be updated at least once a day (if not more) by different members of the team. There will be more updates at the start or kickoff of new projects than at any other time during the life cycle. This should indicate a level of communication (which is stressed in agile/Scrum) with the business users.

The second component is the recording of business requirement meetings. All business requirement meeting "time" can be shortened, and the quality of the requirements increases when the meetings themselves are actually recorded utilizing an MP3 recorder. The audio files should be submitted to the wiki, so that team members (if out of the office) can retroactively attend or review when necessary.

This leads to a more agile business requirement meeting. Noise makers in these meetings tend to be quiet when it is recorded until or unless they have a significant contribution to make that would impact the outcome of the project goals. Please note that the rest of the explanation of how and why this works is beyond the scope of this book and is available in Data Vault 2.0 Boot Camp training classes and online at http://LearnDataVault.com.

IF CMMI IS SO GREAT, WHY SHOULD WE CARE ABOUT AGILITY THEN?

Agility and Scrum or disciplined agile delivery (DAD) is still necessary to manage the individual sprint cycles or miniprojects that need to occur. CMMI manages the overall enterprise goals and provides a baseline consistency to the enterprise-wide efforts—so everyone in IT is on the same page (at least those involved with the BI project).

> An agile implementation should be tailored to match an organization's actual maturity level; however, implementing agile when an organization is at CMMI level three can result in less rework and improve the overall CMMI initiative while providing the significant benefits of agile. Implementing a CMMI compliant software development process that is also agile will bring the repeatability and predictability offered by CMMI. Agile, by design, is highly adaptable and therefore can be molded into a CMMI-compliant software development process without altering the primary objectives set forth by the Agile Manifesto. https://www.scrumalliance.org/community/articles/2008/july/agile-and-cmmi-better-together

Please keep in mind that teams don't wake up one day and just decide to be agile right there on the spot. It's an evolutionary process; the team must undergo training both in agile and in Data Vault 2.0 methodology in order to achieve the desired goals. Most teams that undertake training with Data Vault 2.0 start with 7-week sprint cycles (if they have had zero exposure to CMMI and agile previously).

Usually, the second sprint cycle reduces 7 weeks to 6 weeks. The third (if the team is working in earnest and measuring their productivity and following the agile and Scrum review process) can see sprint cycles drop to about 4 weeks. From there, it simply improves to 2 weeks as the team gets better at it. Currently, there is a team implementing Data Vault 2.0 methodology and attempting to achieve 1-week sprint cycles. There doesn't seem to be a bottleneck to optimizing the processes.

But as a reminder, where does the optimization of these processes come from? CMMI—in direct correlation with the KPAs and KPIs of building a data warehouse. It is tied as well to repeatable designs, pattern-based data integration, pattern-based models, and yes—pattern-based business intelligence build cycles. This is the value of Data Vault 2.0 methodology—it provides the patterns out of the gate, to get the teams kick-start in the right direction.

WHY INCLUDE PMP, SDLC IF CMMI AND AGILE SHOULD BE ALL THAT'S NEEDED?

That said, CMMI doesn't describe *how* to achieve these goals; it just describes *what* should be in place. Agile doesn't describe *what* you need, but rather *how* to manage the people and the life cycle. Projects and SDLC components are necessary for the next step: pattern-based development and delivery. The next pieces of the puzzle come from project management professional (PMP) and software development life cycle (SLDC). PMP lays the project foundation for the common project best practices.

While the team strives to be agile in the end, at some level, waterfall project practices must be adhered to. Otherwise, a project cannot progress through its lifecycle to completion.

According to project management body of knowledge (PMBOK) guide:

The project management framework embodies a project life cycle and five major project management process groups:

- Initiating
- Planning
- Executing
- Monitoring and controlling
- Closing

Reference: http://encyclopedia.thefreedictionary.com/Project+Management +Professional

The difference is that this "lifecycle" is now assigned to a 2-week sprint, with disciplined agile delivery (DAD) overseeing the process.

There are several components to how this fits in with the Data Vault 2.0 methodology. First, there is the master project—the overall enterprise-wide vision. This generally consists of a multiyear, large-scale effort (for large enterprises). These projects are then often broken into subprojects (as they should be), with outlined goals and objectives within 6-month time frames.

Then, the subprojects should be broken into 2-week sprint cycles (to meet agile requirements). The idea is to not have the project levels become top-heavy and full of planning, but rather to act as an overall guide or map from start to finish in terms of what the enterprise business intelligence solution needs to provide.

At the end of the day, project managers should have a firm grasp on what they are managing (CMMI), how they will manage the people (agile/Scrum/DAD), how the sprints have to be lined up in order to accomplish the goals and objectives of the enterprise, and how to measure the success/failure of particular parts of the process. Otherwise, without hindsight or measurement, then there will be no room for improvement or optimization.

SO THEN, WHAT DOES SIX SIGMA CONTRIBUTE TO THE DATA VAULT 2 METHODOLOGY?

Six Sigma is defined to be

> Six Sigma seeks to improve the quality of process outputs by identifying and removing the causes of defects (errors) and minimizing variability in manufacturing and business processes. It uses a set of quality management methods, including statistical methods, and creates a special infrastructure of people within the organization ("Champions," "Black Belts," "Green Belts," "Yellow Belts," etc.) who are experts in these methods.
> http://en.wikipedia.org/wiki/Six_Sigma

To paraphrase for enterprise BI projects, Six Sigma is all about measuring and eliminating *defects* that plague the enterprise warehouse build process. Data Vault 2.0 methodology attaches Six Sigma school of thought to the metrics that are captured in the life cycle of each sprint (i.e., the KPIs and the Scrum review process—what's broken, why, and how do we fix it).

In order to *reach full optimization* (or *full maturity*) for the enterprise BI initiatives, all miniprojects or minisprints must reach their full optimization as well. Otherwise, the organization *cannot* achieve CMMI level 5. The Data Vault 2.0 methodology outlines (in some levels of detail) how to tie these components together.

Once the team understands that all work is measured, monitored, and eventually optimized, then Six Sigma mathematics can provide the business with a confidence rating—showing improvement (or not) of the enterprise BI team and their progress, as a whole. This is only part of the nature of total cost of ownership (TCO) and reducing TCO while improving return on investment (ROI) for the business.

The Data Vault 2.0 methodology provides the patterns, the artifacts, and the repeatable processes for building an enterprise BI solution, effectively and in a measured and applied manner. Six Sigma seeks to assist the optimization of the teams, and the implementation methods in order to streamline the agility and improve quality overall. In other words, without Six Sigma, the words "better faster cheaper" cannot apply to business intelligence projects.

WHERE DOES TQM (TOTAL QUALITY MANAGEMENT) FIT IN TO ALL OF THIS?

Total quality management (TQM) is the cream of the crop. TQM is necessary in order to keep the moving parts of the enterprise BI solution well-oiled and running smoothly. TQM is the icing on the cake (as it were). Turns out, TQM plays several roles in the Data Vault 2.0 methodology; these roles will be briefly introduced and discussed below. In order to better understand TQM, a definition is in order:

> Total quality management (TQM) consists of organization-wide efforts to install and make permanent a climate in which an organization continuously improves its ability to deliver high-quality products and services to customers.
> http://en.wikipedia.org/wiki/Total_quality_management

The Data Vault 2.0 methodology incorporates and aligns the goals and functions of TQM with the purpose of producing *better faster cheaper* business intelligence solutions. It is actually hard to imagine enterprise focused projects being run any other way. TQM offers a view consistent with the business users and the deliverables that the enterprise BI project strives to provide. Some of the fundamental primary elements behind TQM include the following:

- Customer-focused
- Total employee involvement (within the reach of the enterprise BI team and business users)
- Process-centered
- Integrated system
- Strategic and systematic approach
- Continual improvement
- Fact-based decision-making
- Communications

http://asq.org/learn-about-quality/total-quality-management/overview/overview.html

It is clear by now that TQM plays a vital role in the success of the data warehousing and BI projects. TQM is aligned (as previously described) with the desired outcomes of CMMI, Six Sigma, Agile/Scrum, and DAD.

The Data Vault 2.0 methodology is process-centered, provides for an integrated system, is a strategic and systematic approach, requires total employee involvement, is customer-focused, and relies on transparency and communications. The Data Vault 2.0 model brings fact-based decision-making to the table, rather than "truth" or subjective-based decision-making. The other part of the fact-based decision-making is impacted by the collected KPAs and KPIs in the enterprise BI project (don't forget, these are a part of the optimization steps in CMMI level 5).

As it turns out, accountability (both for the system as a whole and the data living in the data warehouse) is a necessary part of TQM as well. How is this possible? TQM is customer-focused; the customer (in this case, the business user) needs to stand up and take ownership of their data (no *not their information* but their *data*).

The only place in the organization that these data exist in raw form integrated by business key is in the Data Vault 2.0 data warehouse. It is precisely this understanding of facts that draws the business users' attention to Six Sigma metrics—demonstrating quantitatively, the gaps between business perception of operation, and business reality of data capture over time.

Addressing these gaps by filing change requests to the source systems or renegotiating the SLAs with the source data provider is part of the TQM process and part of reducing TCO and improving data quality across the enterprise. TQM plays a role in enriching the BI ecosystem, if and only if the business users are forced to be accountable for their own data and decide to engage in gap analysis (the old-fashioned way) by leveraging statistics that show where and what percentage of their current business perception (business requirements) are broken. The DV2 methodology provides pathways in the project that the teams and business users can follow to achieve these results.

Without the business taking action to *close* the gaps, TQM dissolves to simple data quality initiatives and does not contribute as heavily or as well to the TCO reduction strategy. Improving the quality of the data and understanding the gaps that exist are vital to the overall success and future of an enterprise BI solution.

Introduction to Data Vault Implementation

IMPLEMENTATION OVERVIEW

The data vault system of BI provides implementation guidelines, rules, and recommendations as standards. As noted in previous sections of this chapter, well-defined standards and patterns are the *key* to success of agile, CMMI, Six Sigma, and TQM principles. These standards guide the implementation of

- the data model, finding business keys, designing entities, and applying key structures;
- the ETL/ELT load processes;
- the real-time messaging feeds;
- information mart delivery processes;
- virtualization of the information mart;
- automation best practices;
- business rules—hard and soft;
- write-back capabilities of managed self-service BI.

Some of the objectives of managing implementation through working practices include meeting the needs of TQM, embracing master data, and assisting in alignment across business, source systems, and the enterprise data warehouse.

Before going any further, it is necessary to understand that the highest level of optimization can only be reached *if* the process, design, and implementation are pattern-based and data-driven.

WHAT'S SO IMPORTANT ABOUT PATTERNS?

Patterns make life easier. In the enterprise BI world, patterns enable automation and generation while reducing errors and error potential. Patterns are the heartbeat of the Data Vault 2.0 system of business intelligence. Once the team has accepted the principles that building a data warehouse or BI system is the same as building software, it is possible to extend that thought to pattern-driven design.

171

Data Architecture. https://doi.org/10.1016/B978-0-12-816916-2.00022-X

> A pattern is a recurring solution to a problem within a context.
>
> **Christopher Alexander**

Think about it, how often have IT teams said they "need one pattern for loading history, one pattern for loading current, and yet another pattern for loading data in real-time?" Other teams have made the statement that "this part of the data model works for these reasons, and this other part of the data model was constructed differently because of exceptions to the design rules." Much of this contributes to what is commonly called *conditional architecture.*

Conditional architecture is defined as a pattern that only works for a specific case often based on an IF condition. When the case changes (i.e., volume or velocity or variety) the boundaries, the architecture needs to change. Thus, conditional architecture is born.

Conditional architecture is a horrible way to construct/design an enterprise BI solution. The reason is because when volume grows and timelines (velocity changes) shrink, then reengineering takes place in order to rectify or correct the design. This leads to a solution that continues to cost more and more money and take longer and longer to change. In other words, it leads to a brittle architecture over time. This (especially in a big data solution) is a very bad construct.

At some point, the business can't or won't be able to pay for the reengineering costs. This is typically when the solution is torn down and rebuilt (green-field approach). With the patterns of Data Vault 2.0 (both architecture and implementation), rearchitecture and reengineering are avoided for 98% of the cases where volume grows, velocity changes, and variety increases.

Having the right pattern/design based on mathematical principles means that the team no longer suffers reengineering because of changing requirements.

WHY DOES REENGINEERING HAPPEN BECAUSE OF BIG DATA?

Reengineering/redesign/rearchitecture happens because big data pushes three of the four available axes in the following diagram. The more processing that has to happen in smaller and smaller time frames requires a highly optimized design. The more variety needing to be processed in smaller time frames also requires a highly optimized design. Finally, the more volume needing to be processed in smaller time frames (you guessed it) requires a highly optimized design.

Fortunately for the community, there is a finite set of process designs that have been proved to work at scale, and by leveraging MPP, scale-free mathematics, and set logic, these designs work both for small volumes and extremely large volumes without redesign.

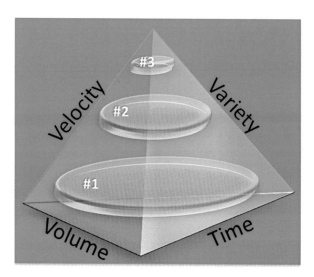

FIG. 6.5.1
Architectural changes and reengineering.

Fig. 6.5.1 contains four axis labels: velocity, volume, time, and variety. In this figure, velocity is the speed of arrival of the data (i.e., latency of arrival); volume is the overall size of the data (on arrival to the warehouse); variety is defined to be the structural, semistructural, multistructural, or nonstructured classification of the data; and time is the allotted time frame in which to accomplish the given task (e.g., loading to the data warehouse). Let's examine a case study for how this impacts reengineering or even conditional architecture.

Scenario #1: Ten rows of data arrive every 24 hours, highly structured (tab delimited and fixed number of columns). The requirement is to load the data to the data warehouse within a 6-hour window. The question is as follows: how many different architectures or process designs can be put together in order to accomplish this task? For sake of argument, let's state that there are 100 possibilities (even typing the data in by hand or typing it in to Excel and then loading it to the database).

The design that is chosen by this team is to type it in by hand to a SQL prompt as "insert into" statements.

Now, the parameters change:

Scenario #2: 1,000,000 rows of data, arriving every 24 hours, highly structured (tab delimited, fixed number of columns). The requirement is to load the data warehouse in a 4-hour window. The question is as follows: can the team use the same "process design" in order to accomplish the task?

Chances are the answer is *no.* The team must redesign, reengineer, and rearchitect the process design in order to accomplish the task in the allotted time frame. So, the redesign is complete. The team now deploys an ETL tool and introduces logic to loading the data set.

> Scenario #3: One billion rows of data, arriving every 45 minutes, highly structured. The requirement is to load the data warehouse in a 40-minute time frame (otherwise the queue of incoming data backs up). The question again is as follows: can the team use the same "process design" they just applied, in order to accomplish this task? Can the team execute without redesign?

Again, most likely the answer is *no.* The team must once again redesign the process because it doesn't meet the service level agreement (requirements). This type of redesign occurs again and again until the team reaches a CMMI level 5 *optimized* state for the pattern.

The problem is that any *significant change* to any of the axis' on the pyramid causes a *redesign to occur.* The only solution is to mathematically find the right solution, the correct design that will scale regardless of time, volume, velocity, or variety. Unfortunately, this leads to unsustainable systems that try to deal (unsuccessfully) with big data problems.

The Data Vault 2.0 implementation standards hand these designs to the BI solution team, regardless of the technology underneath. The implementations or patterns applied to the designs for dealing with the data sets scale. They are based on mathematical principles of scale and simplicity, including some of the foundations of set logic, parallelism, and partitioning.

Teams that engage with the Data Vault 2.0 implementation best practices inherit the designs, as an artifact for big data systems. By leveraging these patterns, the team no longer suffers from rearchitecture or redesigns just because one or more of the axis/parameters change.

WHY DO WE NEED TO VIRTUALIZE OUR DATA MARTS?

They should no longer be called *data marts*—they provide information to the business—therefore, they should be called *information marts.* There is a split between data, information, knowledge, and wisdom that should be recognized by the business intelligence community.

Virtualization means many things to many people. In this context, they are defined to be view-driven—whether or not they are implemented in a relational or nonrelational technology. Views are logical collections of data (mostly structured) on top of physical data storage. Note that it may not be a relational table anymore; it might be a key-value pair store or a nonrelational file sitting in Hadoop.

The more virtualization (or views) that can be applied, the quicker and more responsive the IT team is to change. In other words, less physical storage means less physical management and maintenance costs. It also means faster reaction time for IT to implement, test, and release changes back to the business.

WHAT IS MANAGED SELF-SERVICE BI?

Unfortunately, there is a term called *self-service BI* being thrown about in the marketplace. This was in the 1990s, something applied to federated query engines—otherwise known as enterprise information integration (EII). The purpose and use for this type of engine has morphed in to the cloud and virtualization space.

One of the marketing statements in the 1990s (by these vendors) was as follows: "You don't need a data warehouse…" The industry and the vendors learned that this simply isn't a true statement. It wasn't true then, and it certainly isn't true now. Data warehouses (and business intelligence systems) are as important to the enterprise as the operational systems are, because the enterprise warehouse captures an *integrated* view of historical information, allowing *gap analysis* to occur across multiple systems.

If you give a child a bunch of finger paint (with no training and no instruction), will it make them a master artist, or will they simply make a big mess?

If a child is taught what to do with finger paint and where to paint—then provided some paper and paints—chances are they will paint on the paper instead of themselves. IT wants business to succeed; IT should be an enabler, helping to integrate the proper paints for the right colors and providing the paper along with basic instruction on how to get at the information (Fig. 6.5.2).

Self service BI | *IT helps manage* | *Managed self-service BI*

FIG. 6.5.2

Illustrating managed self-service BI.

What the market realized is that IT is still needed in order to prepare the data, turn them in to information and make them usable by the business. IT is also needed to secure the data and offer access paths and encrypted information where necessary. Finally, IT is needed to assemble the data and integrate the historical data in an enterprise data warehouse. At the end of the day, *managed* self-service BI is necessary, because IT must manage the information and the systems being utilized by the business users.

Data Vault 2.0 provides the groundwork for understanding how to properly implement managed SSBI in enterprise projects. It covers the standards and best practices for achieving optimal goals.

The Operational Environment: A Short History

The computer profession is immature. This is not a pejorative statement about IT and computers but simply a fact. When you compare IT versus other professions, it is no contest. The streets of Rome that we use today were laid out by an engineer 2000 years ago. The majority of the hieroglyphics in the pyramids in Egypt is some accountant documentation of how much grain is owed the pharaoh. In the mountains of Chile are found skulls that are estimated to be 10,000 years old that indicate that at least an early form of medicine was practiced long ago.

So, when you compare the profession of IT to the engineering, accounting, and medical professions, it is no contest. The IT profession is historically very immature compared to other professions. That is a historical fact that is inarguable.

The very earliest uses of the computer were for the purpose of calculating military matters in World War II. The military first used computers to calculate the trajectory and landing zone of projectiles.

COMMERCIAL USES OF THE COMPUTER

The commercial uses of the computer started in approximately the 1960s. And the commercial use of the computer has been growing and advancing ever since.

The very early days of the computer were (rightfully so) centered around the early technology. In the very earliest days were paper tape, wired boards, and then punched cards.

The language of the day was assembler. It was quickly recognized that trying to code and debug assembler was going to be a long and arduous process. Soon, there were more sophisticated languages such as COBOL and Fortran.

Fig. 7.1.1 shows that there were early fascinations with the technology of the day.

Soon, it was discovered that applications could be built. The early applications automated what would otherwise be tedious activities. The first applications centered around human resources, payroll, and accounts payable/receivable.

The first applications used the computer to automate human activities.

177

Data Architecture. https://doi.org/10.1016/B978-0-12-816916-2.00023-1

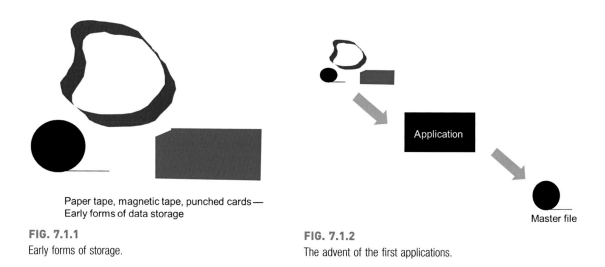

Paper tape, magnetic tape, punched cards—
Early forms of data storage

FIG. 7.1.1
Early forms of storage.

Application

Master file

FIG. 7.1.2
The advent of the first applications.

THE FIRST APPLICATIONS

Fig. 7.1.2 depicts the advent of the first applications.

Once organizations discovered that they could write applications, soon, applications began to spring up everywhere. In the very earliest days of application development, the coding practices were very nonuniform, to say the least. The code that was produced was very difficult to maintain and was often inefficient. In the early days, there were no standard coding practices. Everyone "did his/her own thing." As a result, the code that was produced was very unstable.

Fig. 7.1.3 illustrates the many new applications that were being produced.

ED YOURDON AND THE STRUCTURED REVOLUTION

Into this fray stepped Ed Yourdon and Tom Demarco. Ed Yourdon recognized that discipline in the creation of code was needed. Ed began what was termed

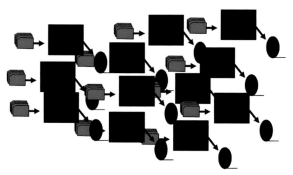

FIG. 7.1.3
Lots of applications.

the "structured" revolution. Ed began with structured programming and then extended his philosophy for the discipline in the creation of systems to general design principles.

Thus, structured programming and design was born. Given the development practices of the day, Ed Yourdon made significant contributions with the notion that computer systems should be developed with order and discipline.

THE SDLC

One of the significant products of the structured revolution was the notion of the system development life cycle (SDLC).

Fig. 7.1.4 shows the SDLC.

The SDLC is sometimes called the "waterfall" approach to the development of systems.

DISK TECHNOLOGY

Into this fray at about the time of structured development of systems came the disk storage device. With disk storage, data could be accessed directly. Prior to the advent of disk storage, data had been stored on magnetic tape files. Even though magnetic tape files could hold a lot of data, all the data on the magnetic tapes had to be accessed sequentially. In order to find a single record, you had to process the entire file.

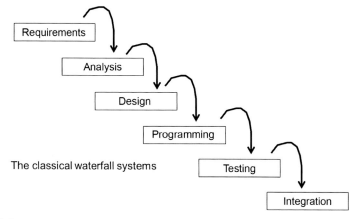

FIG. 7.1.4
The SDLC.

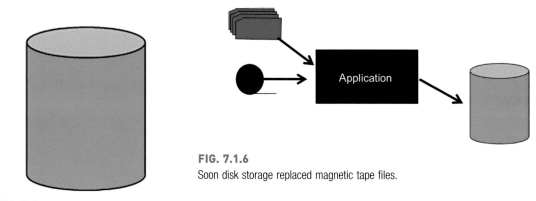

FIG. 7.1.6
Soon disk storage replaced magnetic tape files.

FIG. 7.1.5
Disk storage.

In addition, magnetic tape files were notoriously unreliable for the long-term storage of data. Over time, the oxide was stripped off of the magnetic tape files, thus rendering the file unusable.

With disk storage, data could be accessed directly. This meant that there was no longer a need to access an entire file in order to get to one record.

Fig. 7.1.5 shows the symbol for a disk storage device.

The first iterations of disk storage were expensive and fragile. But over time, the capacity, cost, and stability of the disk files improved.

And soon, applications were using disk storage, not magnetic tape files.

Fig. 7.1.6 shows that applications were built where data could be accessed on disk storage.

ENTER THE DBMS

Applications were built with the aid of software called a database management system—a *DBMS*. The DBMS allowed the application programmer to focus on the logic of processing. The DBMS focused on the placement and accessing of data stored on the disk.

It wasn't long after the DBMS appeared that it was recognized that since data could be accessed directly, rather than sequentially, a new type of application could be built. The new application that could be built was the online transaction processing application.

Fig. 7.1.7 shows the online transaction processing application.

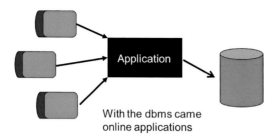

With the dbms came
online applications

FIG. 7.1.7
Online applications.

The advent of the online transaction processing application had a profound and long-lasting effect on business. For the first time, business was able to incorporate the computer into the very fabric of business. Prior to online transaction processing, the computer was useful to business. But with online transaction processing, the computer became a normal aspect of the day-to-day processing that occurred.

Suddenly, with online transaction processing, there were reservation systems; bank teller systems; ATM systems; and many, many more types of business applications.

RESPONSE TIME AND AVAILABILITY

With the integration of the computer into business came a new concern. Suddenly, the business was concerned with response time and availability. Response time was crucial to the business ability to function properly. When the computer did not yield proper response time, the business directly and immediately suffered. When the computer went down and was unavailable, the business suffered.

Prior to online transaction processing systems, response time and availability were theoretical subjects that were only of passing interest to the business. But in the face of online transaction systems, response time and availability became central concerns of the business.

Because of the elevated importance of response time and availability, there were significant advances in technology. Suddenly, the operating system, the database management systems, and other internal components needed to operate with efficiency that was never before needed.

Fig. 7.1.8 shows the increasing sophistication of the technical environment.

There have been many advancements in technology. Some of the more prominent advances in early technology are listed here (Fig. 7.1.9).

Data base Management system
Input/ output
Operating system
Application

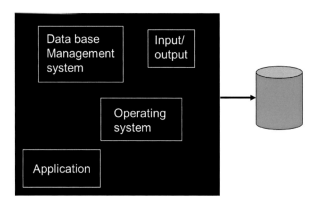

FIG. 7.1.8
The basic components of an application.

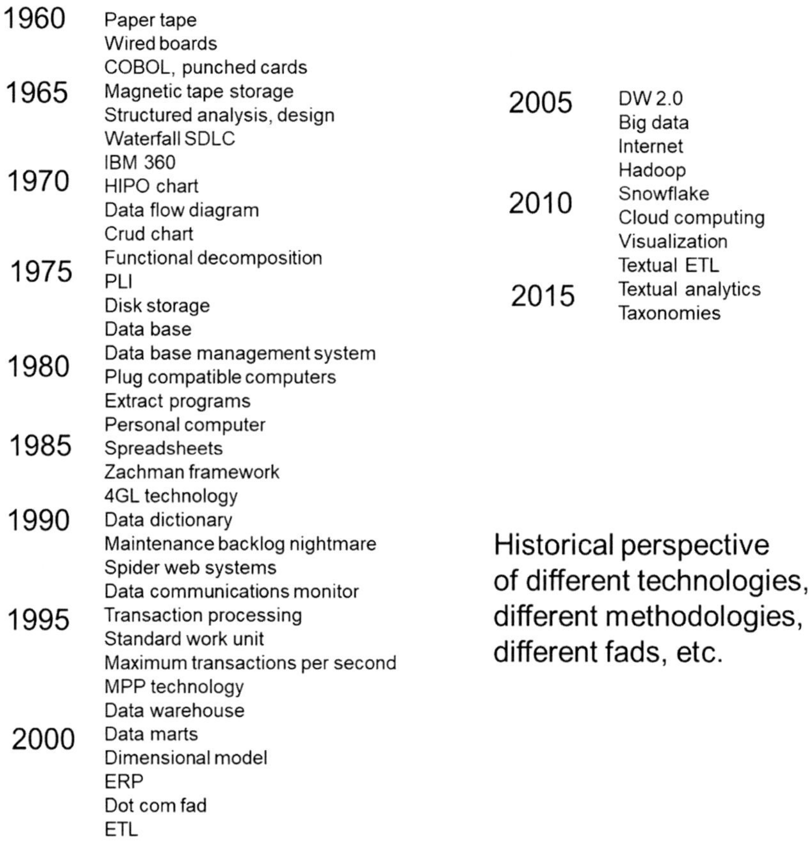

1960
Paper tape
Wired boards
COBOL, punched cards
1965
Magnetic tape storage
Structured analysis, design
Waterfall SDLC
IBM 360
1970
HIPO chart
Data flow diagram
Crud chart
Functional decomposition
1975
PLI
Disk storage
Data base
Data base management system
1980
Plug compatible computers
Extract programs
Personal computer
1985
Spreadsheets
Zachman framework
4GL technology
1990
Data dictionary
Maintenance backlog nightmare
Spider web systems
Data communications monitor
1995
Transaction processing
Standard work unit
Maximum transactions per second
MPP technology
Data warehouse
2000
Data marts
Dimensional model
ERP
Dot com fad
ETL
2005
DW 2.0
Big data
Internet
Hadoop
Snowflake
2010
Cloud computing
Visualization
Textual ETL
2015
Textual analytics
Taxonomies
Historical perspective of different technologies, different methodologies, different fads, etc.

FIG. 7.1.9
A historical perspective.

The corporate computing environment has arrived where it is at today as a result of many advances. In almost every case, the advances are built on top of each other.

CORPORATE COMPUTING TODAY

The world of corporations and technology today is a world in transition. Once, the IT department did everything imaginable that dealt with technology. Today, technology is to be found everywhere—in the hands of end user, in the hands of customers, on management's desk, and elsewhere. Much of computing is migrating to the cloud, where professional technology managers store and process data. The classic IT function has been relegated to a caretaker function, looking after older operational systems. Leadership in new and innovative uses of technology is directly in the hands of the end user.

The Standard Work Unit

At the heart of online transaction processing is good response time. Response time in the online transaction environment is not a "nicety"—it is a "necessity." Organizations depend on their online systems for running day-to-day business. If response time is not good, business suffers. Therefore, in the world of online transaction processing, response time is an absolute necessity.

ELEMENTS OF RESPONSE TIME

There are many facets to achieving good response time. In order to achieve good response time:

- The organization has to be using the right technology.
- There has to be adequate capacity.
- The workload passing through the system must be understood.
- The data being processed must be understood.

But, having all these items in place is not enough. At the heart of success for achieving good response time is something called the "standard work unit."

So what is response time? Fig. 7.2.1 shows the elements of response time.

Response time is the amount of time from the moment of the initiation of the transaction until the moment in time when the results of the transaction are returned to the end user. Fig. 7.2.1 shows that the transaction is initiated, the transaction is sent to the processor, the processor commences execution, the processor goes out and finds data, the data are processed, and the results are sent to the end user.

Typically, all of this activity occurs in a second or less. Given all the activity that takes place, it is a wonder that it occurs as fast as it does.

AN HOURGLASS ANALOGY

In order to understand how good response time is achieved, it makes sense to study an hourglass.

Consider the hourglass shown in Fig. 7.2.2.

185

Data Architecture. https://doi.org/10.1016/B978-0-12-816916-2.00024-3

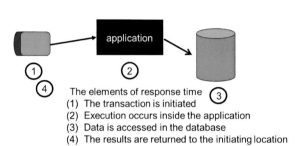

The elements of response time
(1) The transaction is initiated
(2) Execution occurs inside the application
(3) Data is accessed in the database
(4) The results are returned to the initiating location

FIG. 7.2.1
The elements of response time.

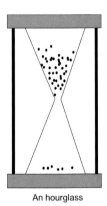

An hourglass

FIG. 7.2.2
The movement of sand through an hourglass.

When you examine the flow of sand through the hourglass, the flow is steady and at an even pace. All things considered, the flow of sand is done efficiently.

So, how is the flow through the hourglass done in such an efficient manner? Consider the grains of sand as they pass through the center of the hourglass. Fig. 7.2.3 shows the flow of sand through the center of the hourglass.

One of the reasons (other than gravity) why the hourglass exhibits an even flow of sand is that the grains of sand are small and uniform in size. Consider what would happen if the hourglass was to have pebbles inserted in among the grains of sand.

Fig. 7.2.4 shows what happens if pebbles are inserted into the hourglass along with the grains of sand.

The neck of
the hourglass

FIG. 7.2.3
The neck of the hourglass is the critical gating factor.

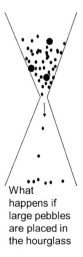

What
happens if
large pebbles
are placed in
the hourglass

FIG. 7.2.4
Placing large pebbles in the hourglass.

The result of placing pebbles in the hourglass is that the flow of sand is interrupted and the flow is erratic and inefficient.

In many ways, the transactions that run through an online system are like the grains of sand. As long as the transactions are small and uniform in size, the efficiency of the system is quite good. But when large transactions are mixed in with small transactions in the workload of an online transaction processing system, the flow is very mixed and inefficient.

And when the flow is inefficient, the result is poor response time.

THE RACETRACK ANALOGY

Another way to express the same thing is seen in Fig. 7.2.5.

In Fig. 7.2.5, a pathway with different workloads is pictured. You can think of it as a roadway where there are cars running. The cars are all fast and uniform in size. The speeds that are attained are quite high. The roadway could be the old Brickyard in Indianapolis or Daytona. The only cars running on the track are Porsches and Ferraris. Everything is running efficiently.

Now, consider another roadway. The next roadway is seen in Fig. 7.2.6.

In this roadway, there are some small fast cars and some semitrucks. This could be Mexico City at rush hour. Everything is slow.

The difference between the speeds that are attained is remarkable. On one track, there are very high rate of speeds. On another track, there are very low rates of speed that are attained. The major difference between the tracks is that large, slow vehicles are allowed onto the road. The large vehicles slow everything down.

A racetrack

FIG. 7.2.5

Cars on a racetrack.

A racetrack with a cement truck

FIG. 7.2.6

A racetrack with a cement truck on the track.

YOUR VEHICLE RUNS AS FAST AS THE VEHICLE IN FRONT OF IT

There is another way of thinking of the speeds that can be attained. That way is the vehicle you are in is as slow as the vehicle in front of you. And if the vehicle in front of you is a large, slow vehicle, then that is your optimal speed.

Stated differently, how fast can a Porsche run on a race track? The Porsche can run as fast as the slowest car in front of the Porsche.

The way then to achieve speed and efficiency in the online transaction environment is to allow only small fast-moving transactions into the system.

The size of an online transaction is measured in terms of how much data the transaction accesses and whether the transaction does update. The update a transaction does affects the amount of records that are locked during the update process. In general, an online DBMS "locks" records that might be updated while a transaction is in execution.

Fig. 7.2.7 shows what constitutes a "large" online transaction and a "small" online transaction.

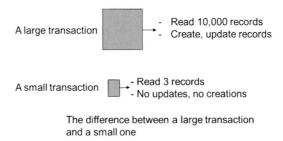

A large transaction
- Read 10,000 records
- Create, update records

A small transaction
- Read 3 records
- No updates, no creations

The difference between a large transaction and a small one

FIG. 7.2.7
A small transaction and a large transaction.

THE STANDARD WORK UNIT

The standard work unit then states "in order to achieve good and consistent online transaction time, each online transaction running in the system needs to be small and uniform in size."

THE SLA

Related to the standard work unit is the notion of a *service-level agreement* or SLA. An SLA is an agreement stating what amounts to an acceptable level of performance and service in the online transaction environment.

A typical SLA might look like the following:

> Mon–Fri, between the hours of 7:30 a.m. and 5:30 p.m.
>> All transactions will execute in no more than 3 seconds.
>> There will be no outages of greater than 5 minutes.

The SLA covers both average response time and system availability. The SLA covers only working hours. Outside working hours, the computer operation staff is free to do whatever is needed to be done to the computer—running large statistical programs, doing maintenance, running database utilities, and so forth.

Data Modeling for the Structured Environment

The structured environment contains a lot of complex data with a lot of possibilities for organizing and arranging that data. In the structured environment, the analyst has the opportunity to shape the data according to his/her needs. And given the many ways that data can be shaped, the organization needs a "road map" to guide the organization in its efforts to shape the data.

THE PURPOSE OF THE ROADMAP

The road map serves several important purposes:

- The road map serves as a direction for the organization to go.
- The road map serves as a guide to different people with different agendas who still must build a collaborative effort.
- The road map allows a large effort to be sustained over time.
- The road map serves as a guide to end users who ultimately must navigate the final product.

There are many reasons then why large, complex organizations need a data model.

The data that are modeled are the data that sit at the heart of the business of the company. The data model is shaped around whatever is at the core of the business of the organization.

GRANULAR DATA ONLY

The data model is shaped around _ONLY_ the granular detailed data of the organization. Bad things happen when the data modeler allows summarized or aggregated data to enter the data model. When summarized or aggregated, data are allowed to enter the data model:

- There is a HUGE amount of data to be modeled.
- The formula for calculating the summarized data changes faster than the modeler can create and change the model.

191

Data Architecture. https://doi.org/10.1016/B978-0-12-816916-2.00025-5

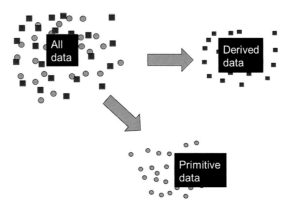

Separating derived, summarized data from primitive, singular data

FIG. 7.3.1
Separating detailed and summarized data.

- Different people have different formulas for the same or similar calculations.

The first step in building the data model is to remove all derived data—summarized or aggregated data—from the data model.

Fig. 7.3.1 shows that detailed granular data are separated from summarized or aggregated data when building the data model.

After the granular data are identified, the next step is to "*abstract*" the data. The data are abstracted to its highest meaningful level. The highest meaningful level is called an *entity*.

As a simple example of abstraction, suppose a corporation has female customers, male customers, foreign customers, corporate customers, and governmental customers. The data model creates the entity known as "customer" and wraps all of the different types of customer together.

Or suppose the company produces sports cars, sedans, SUVs, and trucks. The data model abstracts the data into the entity—vehicle.

THE ERD

The highest level of abstraction for the data model is called the entity relationship diagram (ERD). The ERD reflects data at its highest level of meaningful abstractions and their relationship to each other. The entities of the organization are identified, as well as the relationships between those entities.

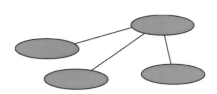

FIG. 7.3.2
The high level data model.

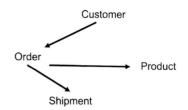

FIG. 7.3.3
Some simple entities and their relationship.

Fig. 7.3.2 shows the symbol that identifies the entities and relationships in an ERD.

As an example of the ERD for a manufacturing company, the ERD might look like that seen in Fig. 7.3.3.

The ERD is important as a high-level statement of what the data model is all about. But—of necessity—there is very little detail found at the ERD level.

THE DIS

The next level of the data model is the place where much detail is found. This level of the data model is called the "data item set" (*dis*).

Each entity identified in the ERD has its own dis. Using the simple example shown in Fig. 7.3.3, there would be one dis for customer, another dis for order, another dis for product, and yet another dis for shipment.

The dis contains keys and attributes, and the dis shows the organization of the data.

The symbol for a simple dis is seen in Fig. 7.3.4.

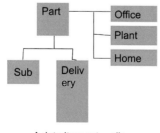

A data item set — dis
The md level data model

FIG. 7.3.4
A data item set—dis.

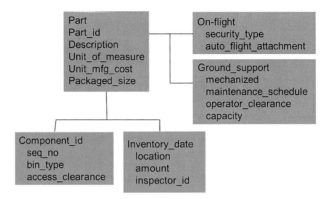

A simple data item set

FIG. 7.3.5
A simple dis.

The basic construct of a dis is a box. In the box are the elements of data that are closely related and that belong together. The different lines between the groupings of data have meaning. A downward-pointing line indicates multiple occurrences of data. A line to the right indicates a different type of data.

As a simple example of a dis, consider the dis shown in Fig. 7.3.5.

The anchor or primary data are indicated by the box of data that is at the top left of the diagram. The anchor box indicates that the data that relate directly to the key of the box are description, unit of measure, unit manufacturing cost, packaged size, and packaged weight. The elements of data exist once and only once for each product.

Data that can occur multiple times are shown beneath the anchor box of data. One such grouping of data is component id. There can exist multiple components for each product. Another grouping of data that is independent of component id is inventory date and location. The product may have been inventoried in multiple places on different dates.

The lines going to the right of the anchor box indicate types of data. In this case, a product may be used in flight or in ground support.

The dis indicates the keys, attributes, and relationships for an entity.

PHYSICAL DATA BASE DESIGN

Once the dis is created, the physical design of the dis is created. Each grouping of data in the dis results in a separate database design.

Part	
Part_id	char nvarchar(56)
Description	char nvarchar(250)
Weight	dec(5,3)
UM	char (10)

FIG. 7.3.6
The physical model.

Fig. 7.3.6 shows the database design that has resulted from the design of the grouping of data found in the dis.

The physical database design takes into account the physical structure of the data, the physical characteristics of the data, the specification of keys, the specification of indexes, and so forth.

The result of the physical specification of the data is a database design, as shown in Fig. 7.3.7.

The elements of the database design include keys, attributes, records, and indexes.

RELATING THE DIFFERENT LEVELS OF THE DATA MODEL

The different levels of the data model are akin to the different levels of mapping that exist in the world. Fig. 7.3.8 shows how the different levels of mapping relate to each other.

In Fig. 7.3.8, it is seen that the ERD is the equivalent to a globe of the world. The dis is the equivalent to the map of Texas. And the physical database design is the equivalent of the city map of Dallas, Texas. The globe—the ERD—is complete but not detailed. The map of Texas—the dis—is

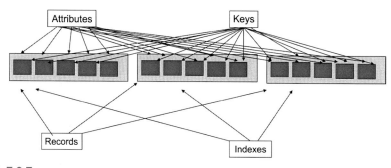

FIG. 7.3.7
The elements of a database.

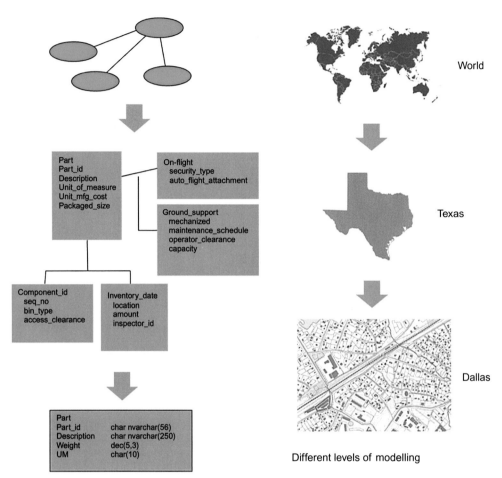

FIG. 7.3.8
Different levels of modelling.

incomplete in that you can't find your way to and from Chicago with a map of Texas. But the map of Texas has a great deal more detail than the globe. The city map of Dallas—the physical data model—is even less complete. You cannot find your way from El Paso to Midland with a city map of Dallas. But you have even more details in the city map of Dallas than you do in the state map of Texas.

AN EXAMPLE OF THE LINKAGE

The complete linkage of the different forms of data modeling to each other is shown in Fig. 7.3.9.

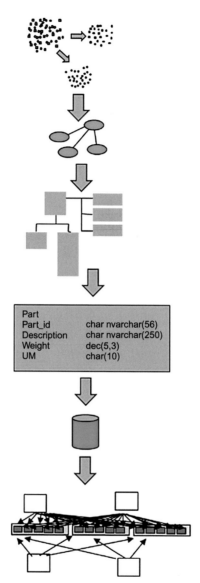

FIG. 7.3.9
The sequence of the steps in doing database design.

GENERIC DATA MODELS

It has been noticed that when a data model is created, it oftentimes applies very nicely to other companies in the same industry. For example, a bank—ABC—creates a data model. Then one day, it is discovered that the data model for bank ABC is very similar to the data model for bank BCD, CDE, and DEF.

Because of the great similarity of data models within the same industry, there are models called *"generic data models."* The idea behind a generic data model is that it is much less expensive and much faster to acquire a generic data model than it is to build a data model from scratch. It is true that any generic data model is going to need customization. But even with customization, using a generic data model is much preferable to having to build the data model by itself.

OPERATIONAL DATA MODELS/DATA WAREHOUSE DATA MODELS

There are different types of data models. There are operational data models and data warehouse data models. An operational data model is one that models the day-to-day operations of the company. The data warehouse data model is one that is based on the informational needs of the organization. The operational data model includes some information that is needed for operational processing only, such as a specific telephone number. The data warehouse data model does not contain data that are specific to operational processing. The data warehouse data model does not contain any summarized data. The data warehouse data model does contain a time stamp for every record in the model.

A Brief History of Data Architecture

Data have been around since the first computer program was written. In many ways, data are the gasoline that fuels the engine of the computer. The way that data are used, the way data are shaped, and the way that data are stored has progressed to the point that there is actually now an area of study that can be called data architecture.

There are many facets to data architecture because—as we shall see—data are complex. The four most interesting aspects of data architecture are the following:

- The physical manifestation of data
- The logical linkage of data
- The internal format of data
- The file structure of data

Each of these aspects of data has evolved interdependently over time. Data architecture can best be explained in terms of the evolution of each of these aspects of data architecture.

The evolution of data architecture is seen in Fig. 8.1.1.

The simplest evolution that has occurred (and has been described in many places) is that of the physical evolution of the media on which data have been stored. Fig. 8.1.2 shows this well-documented evolution.

The beginning of the computer industry harks back to paper tape and punched cards. In the very earliest days, data were stored by means of paper tape and punched cards. The value of paper tape and punched cards was that it was easy to create storage. But there were many problems with paper tape and cards. Hollerith punched cards were fixed format only (everything was stored in 80 columns). Cards were dropped and soiled. Cards could not be repunched. And all things considered cards were expensive.

Only so much data could be stored on cards. Very quickly, an alternative to punched cards was needed.

Fig. 8.1.3 shows that punched cards and paper tape were early storage mechanisms for data.

Data Architecture. https://doi.org/10.1016/B978-0-12-816916-2.00026-7

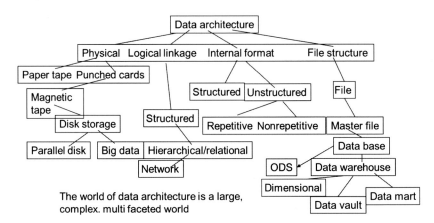

FIG. 8.1.1

The world of data architecture.

Next came magnetic tape. Magnetic tape could store much more data than could ever be stored on punched cards. And magnetic tape was not limited to the single format of a punched card. But there were some major limitations to magnetic tape. In order to find data on a magnetic tape file, you had to scan the entire file. And the oxide on magnetic tape files was notoriously unstable.

Magnetic tape file represented a major step forward from punched cards. But magnetic tape files had their own serious limitations.

Fig. 8.1.4 shows the symbol for magnetic tape files.

After magnetic tape files came disk storage. With disk storage, data could be accessed directly. No longer was it necessary to search the entire file to find a single record.

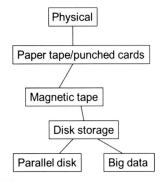

FIG. 8.1.2

The physical dimension of data architecture.

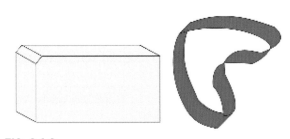

FIG. 8.1.3

Punched cards and paper tape.

FIG. 8.1.4
Magnetic tape file.

FIG. 8.1.5
Disk storage.

The early forms of disk storage were expensive and slow. And there was relatively little capacity for the early forms of disk storage. But quickly, the costs of manufacturing dropped significantly, the capacity increased, and the speed of access decreased. Disk storage was a superior alternative to magnetic tape files.

Fig. 8.1.5 shows the symbol for disk storage.

The demand for volumes of data increased dramatically. In short order, it was necessary to manage disk storage in a parallel manner. By managing disk storage in a parallel manner, the total amount of data that could be controlled increased significantly. Parallel management of storage did not increase the volume of data that could be managed on a single disk. Instead, parallel storage of data decreased the total elapsed time that was required to access and to manage storage.

Fig. 8.1.6 shows the symbol for parallel management of storage.

Yet, another increase in the volume of data that could be managed on disk arrived in the form of big data. Big data was really just another form of parallelism. But with big data, even more data could be managed at an increasingly lower unit cost.

Fig. 8.1.7 shows the symbol for big data.

Over the years then, the total amount of data that could be managed, at an amazing decrease in the unit storage of data, with an ever-increasing speed of access, has evolved.

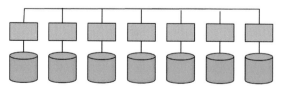

FIG. 8.1.6
Parallel disk storage.

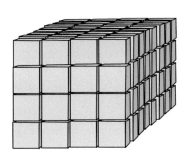

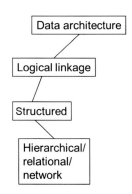

FIG. 8.1.7
Big data.

FIG. 8.1.8
The logical linkage of data.

But the physical storage of data was hardly the only evolution that was occurring. Another concurrent evolution that was occurring was the evolution of the way that data were logically organized. It is one thing to physically store data. It is another thing to logically organize data so that it can be easily and rationally accessed.

Fig. 8.1.8 shows the evolutionary progression of the logical organization of data.

In the very earliest days, data were logically organized in almost a random fashion. Every programmer and every designer "did his/her own thing." To say that the world was in chaos when it came to logical organization of data was an understatement.

Into this world of chaos came Ed Yourdon and Tom DeMarco. Yourdon espoused a concept called the "structured" approach. (NOTE that the term of "structured" as used by Yourdon is quite different; then, the same term is used in describing the internal formatting of data. When Yourdon used the term "structured," he was referring to a logical and organized way of arranging information systems. Yourdon was referring to programming practices, design of systems, and many other aspects of information systems. The term "structured" is also used in describing the internal formatting of data. Even though the terms that are used are the same, they mean something quite different.)

In Yourdon's approach to structured systems, one of the aspects of structured was in reference to how data elements should be logically organized in order to create a disciplined system approach for the building of information systems. Prior to Yourdon, there were many schemes for the logical organization of data.

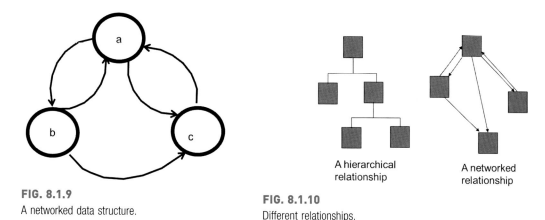

FIG. 8.1.9
A networked data structure.

FIG. 8.1.10
Different relationships.

Fig. 8.1.9 is a symbol depicting the Yourdon approach to structured programming and development.

A while later came the idea of database management systems as a means of logically organizing data. With the DBMS came the idea of organizing data hierarchically and in a network. An early hierarchical organization of data was used by IBM's IMS. An early form of network organization of data was Cullinet's IDMS.

In the hierarchical organization of data was the notion of a parent/child relationship. A parent could have zero or more children. And a child had to have a parent.

Fig. 8.1.10 depicts a diagram that has a parent-child relationship and a networked relationship.

The DBMS were useful for organizing data both for batch processing and for online transaction processing. Many systems were built running transactions under the DBMS.

Soon, there came another notion about the way data should be logically organized. That method was through what was termed a relational database management system.

In the relational database management system, data were "normalized." Normalization meant that there was a primary key for each table and the attributes in the table depended on the key of the table for their existence. The tables were able to be related to each other by means for a key/foreign key relationship. Upon access of the tables, the tables could be "joined" by means of pairing up the appropriate key and foreign key.

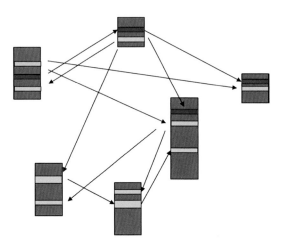

FIG. 8.1.11
Some related relational tables.

Fig. 8.1.11 shows a relational table.

As interesting and as important as the logical organization of data is, it was not the only aspect of data architecture.

Another aspect of data architecture is that of the internal formatting of data. When you look at the logical organization of data, all the DBMS was applied to what is called "structured" data. The structured data imply that there is some way that the computer can comprehend the way the data are organized. The structured way of organizing data applies to many aspects of the corporation. The structured approach is used for organizing customer information, product information, sales information, accounting information, and so forth. The structured approach is used for capturing transaction information.

The unstructured approach is for data that are not organized in a manner that is intelligible to the computer. The unstructured approach applies to images, audio information, downloads from satellites, and so forth. But far and away, the biggest use of the unstructured approach is for textual data.

Fig. 8.1.12 shows the evolution of the internal formatting of data.

The structured approach implies that the data are organized enough to be able to be defined to a database management system. Typically, the DBMS has attributes of data, keys, indexes, and records of data. The "schema" of the data is determined as the data are loaded. Indeed, the content of the data and its place in the schema dictate where and how the data are loaded.

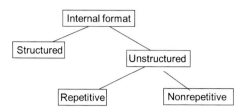

FIG. 8.1.12
Internal formatting of data architecture.

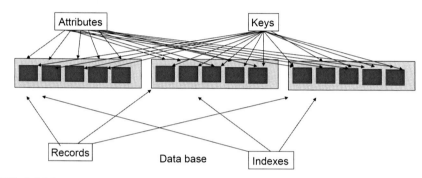

FIG. 8.1.13
A classical index.

Fig. 8.1.13 illustrates data loaded in a structured format.

The unstructured internal organization of data contains all sorts of data. There are a wide variety of data here. The unstructured internal organization of data includes e-mail, documents, spreadsheets, analog data, log tape data, and many varieties of data.

Fig. 8.1.14 shows unstructured internally organized data.

The world of unstructured data is a world where there is a basic division between repetitive and nonrepetitive data.

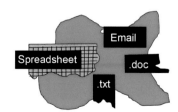

FIG. 8.1.14
Unstructured data.

FIG. 8.1.15
Repetitive unstructured data.

Repetitive unstructured data are data where the data are organized in many records where the structure and content of the records are very similar or even the same.

Fig. 8.1.15 shows repetitive unstructured data.

The other kind of data found in the unstructured environment is that of non-repetitive data. With nonrepetitive data, there is no correlation between one record of data and any other. If there is a similarity of data between any two records of data in the nonrepetitive environment, it is purely a random event.

Fig. 8.1.16 depicts the nonrepetitive unstructured environment.

Yet, another aspect of data is the file organization of the data. Starting with a very simple file organization, the world has progressed to a very elaborate and sophisticated organization of data.

Fig. 8.1.17 shows the evolution of file structures of data.

In the early days was very crude and simple file organization. Soon, the vendors of technology recognized that a more formal approach was needed. Thus, born were simple files, as seen in Fig. 8.1.18.

In Fig. 8.1.18 were found very simple files. These files were simple collections of data organized; however, the designer thought they needed to be organized. In almost every case, the files were designed to be optimized around the needs of an application.

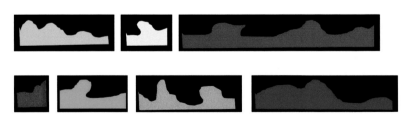

FIG. 8.1.16
Nonrepetitive unstructured data.

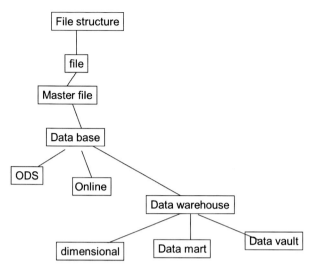

FIG. 8.1.17
Data architecture file structures.

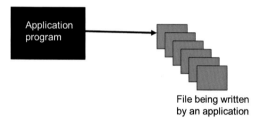

File being written
by an application

FIG. 8.1.18
A file being written by an application.

But soon, it was recognized that the same or very similar information was being collected by more than one application. It was recognized that this overlap of effort was both wasteful and resulted in redundant data being collected and managed. The solution was the creation of a master file.

The master file was a place where data could be gathered in a nonredundant manner.

Fig. 8.1.19 shows a master file.

The master file was a good idea and worked well. The only problem was that a master file existed on a tape file. And tape files were clumsy to use. Soon, the idea of a master file evolved into the idea of a database. Thus, born was the database concept, as seen in Fig. 8.1.20.

FIG. 8.1.19
A magnetic tape file being written by an application.

FIG. 8.1.20
Disk storage being written by an application.

The early notion of a database was as a "place where all data resided for a subject area." In a day and age where lots of data were still lying in files and master files, the idea of a database was an appealing approach. And given that data could be accessed on disk storage in a database, the idea of a database was especially appealing.

Soon, however, the database concept morphed into the online database concept. In the online database concept, not only could data be accessed directly but also could be accessed in a real-time, online mode. In the online, real-time mode, data could be added, deleted, and changed as business needs changed.

Fig. 8.1.21 depicts the online, real-time environment.

The online database environment opened up computing to parts of the business where never before had any interaction been possible. Soon, there were applications everywhere. And in short order, the applications spawned what was known as the spider's web environment.

With the spider's web environment came the need for integrity of data. Soon, the concept of the data warehouse arose.

Fig. 8.1.22 shows the advent of the data warehouse.

The data warehouse provided the organization with the "single version of the truth." Now, there was a basis for reconciliation of data. With the data warehouse—for the first time—came a place where historical data could be

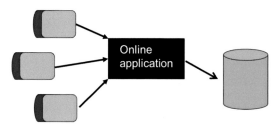

FIG. 8.1.21
Online transaction processing, OLTP.

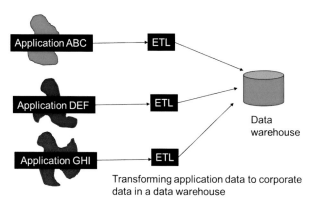

Transforming application data to corporate data in a data warehouse

FIG. 8.1.22
Transforming application data to corporate data.

stored and used. The data warehouse represented a fundamental step forward for the information processing systems of the organization.

As important as the data warehouse was, there were other elements of architecture that were needed. It was soon recognized that something between a data warehouse and a transactional system was needed. Thus, born was the ODS or operational data store.

Fig. 8.1.23 shows the ODS.

The ODS was a place where online high-performance processing could be done on corporate data. Not every organization had need of an ODS, but many did.

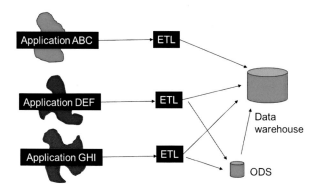

Occasionally there is need for an ODS

FIG. 8.1.23
Sometimes there is a need for an operational data store (ODS).

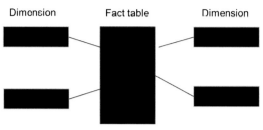

Star joins are built for data marts

FIG. 8.1.24
A star join.

FIG. 8.1.25
The integrated analytical environment.

At about the time that the data warehouse was born, it was recognized that organizations had need of a place where individual departments could go to and find data for their own individual analytic needs. Into this analytic environment came the data mart or the dimensional model.

Fig. 8.1.24 shows the star join, the foundation of the data mart.

It was then recognized that a more formal treatment of data marts was needed than just having dimensional models. The notion of the dependent data mart was then created.

Fig. 8.1.25 shows dependent data marts.

The evolution that has been described did not happen independently. The evolution happened concurrently. Indeed, the evolution to some levels of development depended on evolutionary developments that occurred in other arenas. For example, the evolution to online databases could not have occurred until the technology that supported online processing had been developed.

Or the movement to data warehouses could not have occurred until the cost of storage dropped to an affordable rate.

Big Data/Existing System Interface

One of the challenges of information systems is determining how they all fit together. In particular, how does big data fit with the existing system environment? There is no question that big data brings new opportunities for information and decision-making to the organization. And there is no question that big data has great promise. But big data is not a replacement for the existing system environment. In fact, big data accomplishes one task, and the existing system environment accomplishes another task. They are (or should be!) complementary to each other.

So exactly, how does big data need to interface with and interact with the existing system environment?

THE BIG DATA/EXISTING SYSTEMS INTERFACE

Fig. 8.2.1 shows the recommended way in which big data and existing systems interface with each other.

Fig. 8.2.1 shows the overall system flow between big data and the existing system environment.

Each of the interfaces will be discussed in detail.

Raw big data is divided into two distinct sections (see the "great divide"). There is repetitive raw big data and nonrepetitive raw big data. Repetitive raw big data is handled entirely differently than nonrepetitive raw big data.

THE REPETITIVE RAW BIG DATA/EXISTING SYSTEMS INTERFACE

The interface from repetitive raw big data to existing system environment in some ways is the simplest interface. In many ways, this interface is like a *distillation* process. The mass of data found in raw repetitive big data is winnowed down—distilled—into the few records that are of interest.

211

Data Architecture. https://doi.org/10.1016/B978-0-12-816916-2.00027-9

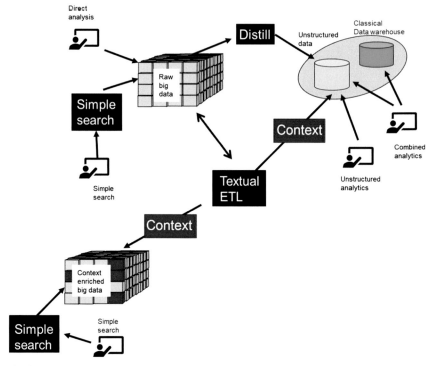

FIG. 8.2.1
The big data/data warehouse interface.

The repetitive raw big data is processed by parsing each record. And when the records that are of interest are located, the records of interest are then edited and passed to the existing system environment. In such a fashion, the data that are of interest are distilled from the mass of records found in the raw repetitive big data environment. One assumption made by this interface is that the vast majority of records found in the repetitive component of raw big data will not be passed to the existing system environment. The assumption is that only a few records of interest are to be found.

In order to explain this assumption, consider a few cases.

Manufacturing—a manufacturer makes a product. The quality of the product is quite high. On the average, only one out of 10,000 products is defective. However, the defective products are still a bother. All the product manufacturing information is stored in big data. But only the information about the defective products is brought to the existing systems environment for further analysis. In this case, based on a percentage basis, very little data are brought to the existing system environment.

Telephone calls (call record details)—on a daily basis, millions of telephone calls are made. But of those millions of telephone calls, only a handful—maybe three or four—are of interest. Only the phone calls that are of interest are brought from the big data environment to the existing system environment

Log tape analysis—a log tape of transactions is created. In a day, tens of thousands of log tape entries are created. But only a few hundred entries on the log tape are of interest. Those few hundred log tape entries that are of interest are the only entries that find their way back into the existing system environment for further analysis.

Metering—an organization collects metering data. The vast majority of the metering activity is normal and not of particular interest. But on a few days of the year, certain metering data react in an unexpected manner. Only those readings that have reacted abnormally are brought to the existing system environment for further analysis.

And there are many more examples of repetitive raw big data being examined for exceptional data.

As a rule when data go from the big data environment to the existing system environment, it is convenient to place the data in a data warehouse. However, if there is a need, data can be sent elsewhere in the existing system environment.

EXCEPTION BASED DATA

Once the data in the raw repetitive big data environment are selected (usually chosen on an "exception basis") and are then moved to the existing system environment, the exception-based data can undergo all sorts of analysis, such as the following:

- Pattern analysis. Why are the records that have been chosen exceptional? Is there a pattern of activity external to the records that match with the behavior of the records?
- Comparative analysis. Is the number of exceptional records increasing? Decreasing? What other events are happening concurrent to the collection of the exceptional records?
- Growth and analysis of exceptional records over time. Over time, what is happening to the exceptional records that have been collected from big data?

And there are _MANY_ more ways to analyze the data that have been collected.

Fig. 8.2.2 shows the interface from big data to the existing system environment.

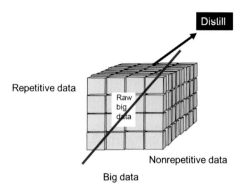

FIG. 8.2.2

Big data contains repetitive data and nonrepetitive data.

THE NONREPETITIVE RAW BIG DATA/EXISTING SYSTEMS INTERFACE

The interface from the nonrepetitive raw big data environment is one that is very different from the repetitive raw big data interface. The first major difference is in the percentage of data that are collected. Whereas in the repetitive raw big data interface, only a small percentage of the data are selected, in the nonrepetitive raw big data interface, the majority of the data are selected. This is because there is business value in the majority of the data found in the nonrepetitive raw big data environment, whereas there is little business value in the majority of the repetitive big data environment.

But there are other major differences as well.

The second major difference in the environments is in terms of context. In the repetitive raw big data environment, context is usually obvious and easy to find. In the nonrepetitive raw big data environment, context is not obvious at all and is not easy to find. It is noted that context is in fact there in the nonrepetitive big data environment; it just is not easy to find and is anything but obvious.

In order to find context, the technology of textual disambiguation is needed. Textual disambiguation reads the nonrepetitive data in big data and derives context from the data. (See the chapter on textual disambiguation and taxonomies for a more complete discussion of deriving context from nonrepetitive raw big data.)

While *most* of the nonrepetitive raw big data is useful, some percentage of data are not useful and are edited out by the process of textual disambiguation.

Once the context is derived, the output can then be sent to either the existing system environment.

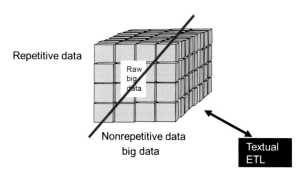

Repetitive data

Raw big data

Nonrepetitive data big data

Textual ETL

FIG. 8.2.3
Textual ETL is used for nonrepetitive data.

Fig. 8.2.3 shows the interface from nonrepetitive raw big data to textual disambiguation.

INTO THE EXISTING SYSTEMS ENVIRONMENT

Once data have come from nonrepetitive raw big data and have passed through textual disambiguation, the data can be passed to the existing system environment.

As the data are passed through textual disambiguation, they are greatly simplified. Context is derived, and each unit of text that passes the filtering process is turned into a flat file record. The flat file record is very reminiscent of a standard relational record. There are key and dependent data, as is found in a relational format.

The output can be sent to a load utility so that the output data can be placed in whatever DBMS is desired. Typical output DBMS include Oracle, Teradata, UDB/DB2, and SQL Server.

Fig. 8.2.4 shows the movement of data into the existing system environment in the form of a standard DBMS.

THE "CONTEXT ENRICHED" BIG DATA ENVIRONMENT

The other route that data can take after they pass through textual disambiguation is that the output of data can be placed back into big data. There may be several reasons for wanting to send output back into big data. Some of the reasons include the following:

- The volume of data. There may be a lot of output from textual disambiguation. The sheer volume of data may dictate that the output data be placed back into the big data environment.

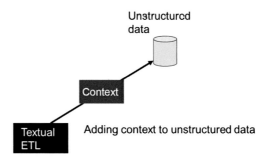

FIG. 8.2.4
Among other things, textual ETL adds context to nonrepetitive data.

- The nature of the data. In some cases, the output data may have a natural fit with the other data placed in the big data environment. Future analytic processing may be greatly enhanced by placing output data back into big data.

In any case, after data pass through textual disambiguation and are placed back into big data, they enter big data in a very different state. When data have passed through textual disambiguation and are placed back into the big data environment, they are placed into the environment with the context of the data clearly identified and prominently a data part of the data in big data.

By placing the output of textual disambiguation back into big data, there now is a section of big data that can be called the *context-enriched* section of big data. From a structural standpoint, the context-enriched component of big data looks to be very similar to repetitive raw big data. The only difference is that the content-enriched component of big data has context open and obvious and attached to the data in this component of big data.

Fig. 8.2.5 shows that output data from textual disambiguation can be placed back into big data.

Another perspective of the big data environment is shown in Fig. 8.2.6.

In Fig. 8.2.6, it is seen that there is the division of big data into the repetitive and nonrepetitive sections. However, in the repetitive section, it is seen that when content-enriched big data is added to the big data environment, those content-enriched data simply become another type of repetitive data. Stated differently, there are two types of repetitive data in big data—simple repetitive data and content-enriched repetitive data.

This division becomes important when doing analytic processing. Repetitive data are analyzed in a completely different fashion than content-enriched repetitive data.

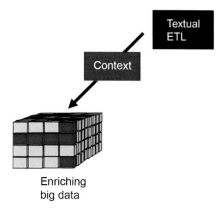

FIG. 8.2.5
Textual ETL can place its results back into big data.

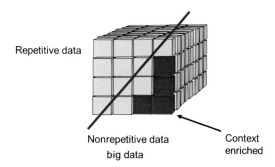

FIG. 8.2.6
Nonrepetitive data can contain raw data and context enriched data.

ANALYZING STRUCTURED DATA/UNSTRUCTURED DATA TOGETHER

The final interface of interest in the big data environment is those data that have come from big data either through the distillation process or textual disambiguation. The data that arrive here can be placed into a standard DBMS.

Fig. 8.2.7 shows the database that has been created from unstructured data being placed in the same environment as the classical data warehouse. Of course, the data in the classical data warehouse have been created from structured data entirely.

Fig. 8.2.7 shows that data whose origin is quite different can be placed in the same analytic environment. The DBMS may be oracle or Teradata. The operating system may be Windows or Linux. In any case, doing analytic processing against the two databases is as easy as doing a relational join.

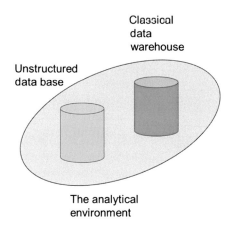

FIG. 8.2.7
The analytical environment can encompass both classical structured data and data whose origins are unstructured.

In such a manner, it is easy and natural to do analytic processing against data from the two different environments. This means that structured data and unstructured data can be used together analytically.

By combining these two types of data together, entirely new vistas of analytic processing open up.

The Data Warehouse/Operational Environment Interface

As interesting as the big data/existing system interface is, it is not the only interface the data architect needs to know about. The other major interface in the corporate systems environment that is of interest is the interface between the operational environment and the data warehouse.

THE OPERATIONAL/DATA WAREHOUSE INTERFACE

Fig. 8.3.1 shows the interface between the operational environment and the data warehouse environment.

The operational environment is the place where day-to-day corporate decisions are made at the detailed level. The data warehouse environment is the place where the data that serve as the basis for corporate decision-making are stored.

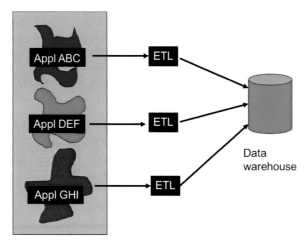

FIG. 8.3.1
Transforming application data to corporate data.

219

THE CLASSICAL ETL INTERFACE

The interface between the two environments is called the "ETL" layer. ETL stands for *extract/transform/load*. It is in the ETL interface that application data are transformed to corporate data. The transformation is one of the most important transformations of data the corporation has.

Fig. 8.3.2 shows the classical ETL interface.

The transformation of data in this interface is from application data to corporate data. The operational data are defined by each application. As a consequence, there are inconsistent definitions of data, inconsistent formulas, inconsistent structures of data, and so forth. But when the data pass through the ETL layer, the inconsistencies are resolved.

THE ODS AND THE ETL INTERFACE

There are however several variations to the classical ETL interface between the operational environment and the data warehouse environment. One of those variations is the inclusion of the ODS into the interface.

Fig. 8.3.3 shows that the ODS can participate in the interface.

Data that flow to the ODS can flow directly into the ODS from the operational environment, or data that pass to the ODS can pass through the ETL transformation layer. Whether or not the data pass through, the ETL layer depends entirely on the class of the ODS. In the case of a class I ODS, data pass directly from the operational system to the ODS. In the case of a class II or class III ODS, data pass through the ETL interface.

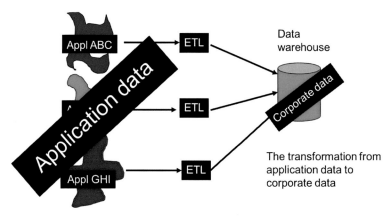

FIG. 8.3.2
ETL performs the transformation.

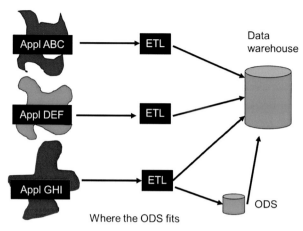

FIG. 8.3.3
The operational data store (ODS).

Not every corporation has or needs an ODS. Usually, it is those corporations where there is a high degree of online transaction processing where the ODS is found.

THE STAGING AREA

Another variation of the classical ETL interface between the operational environment and the data warehouse environment is the case where there is a staging area.

Fig. 8.3.4 shows a staging area.

There are some very specific cases where a staging area is called for. One of those instances is the case where data from two or more files must be merged and

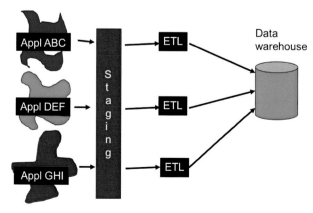

FIG. 8.3.4
Staging area.

there is a timing issue. The data from file ABC are ready for merger at 9.00 am, and the data from file BCD are not ready for a merger until 5:00 pm in the afternoon. In this case, the data from file ABC must be "staged" until the merge is ready to occur.

A second case for the staging area is where there is a large volume of data and the data must be separated into different workloads in order to accommodate the parallelization of the ETL process. In this case, a staging area is needed to separate the volume of data.

A third case for the staging area is the case where the data coming from the operational environment must pass through a *preprocessing* step. In the preprocessing step, data pass through edit and correction process.

One of the issues with the staging area is whether or not analytic processing can be done against data found in the staging area. As a rule, data in the staging area are not used for analytic processing. This is because the data found in the staging area have not yet been passed through the transformation process. Therefore, it does not make sense to do any analytic processing against data found in the staging area.

Note that a staging area is optional and most organizations do not need one.

CHANGED DATA CAPTURE

Yet, another variation on the classical interface between operational systems and data warehouse systems is that of what is termed the *CDC* option. "CDC" stands for *"changed data capture."* For high-performance online transaction environments, it is difficult or inefficient to scan the entire database every time data need to be refreshed into the data warehouse environment. In these environments, it makes sense to determine what data need to be updated into the data warehouse by examining the log tape or journal tape. The log tape is created for the purposes of online backup and recovery in the eventuality of a failure during online transaction processing. But the log tape contains all the data that need to be updated

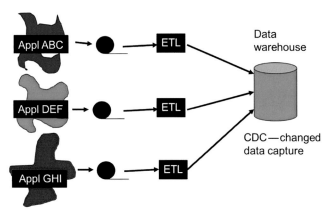

FIG. 8.3.5
Transaction processing systems, changed data capture option.

into the data warehouse. The log tape is read offline and is used to gather the data that need to be updated into the data warehouse.

Fig. 8.3.5 depicts the CDC option.

INLINE TRANSFORMATION

Another alternative to the classical operational to data warehouse interface is that of the inline transformation. In the inline transformation, the data that need to flow to the data warehouse are captured and processed as part of online transaction processing.

Inline transformation is not used very often because the coding needs to be part of the original coding specifications and because of the resource consumption that is required during high-performance online transaction processing. In truth, most code for online transaction processing is created before any one realizes that the results of online transaction processing need to be reflected in the data warehouse environment.

However, on occasion, this option is seen.

Fig. 8.3.6 shows the inline transformation option.

ELT PROCESSING

A final variation on the classical ETL interface is one that can be called the ELT interface. The ELT interface is one where the data are loaded directly from the

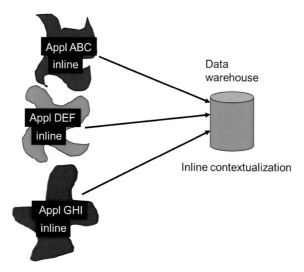

FIG. 8.3.6
Textual data, inline contextualization option.

operational environment to the data warehouse. Once in the data warehouse, the data are then transformed.

The problem with the ELT option is that there is the temptation to simply not execute the "T" step (i.e., the transformation step). In this case, the data warehouse turns into a "garbage dump." And once the data warehouse is loaded with garbage, it becomes worthless as a foundation for decision-making.

If an organization has the will power to not neglect to do the "T" step, then there is nothing wrong with the ELT approach. But few organizations have the willpower and discipline to use the ELT approach properly.

Fig. 8.3.7 illustrates the ELT approach to interfacing operational systems and data warehouses.

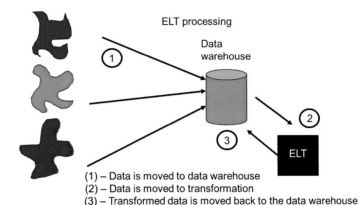

(1) – Data is moved to data warehouse
(2) – Data is moved to transformation
(3) – Transformed data is moved back to the data warehouse

FIG. 8.3.7
An alternative to ETL is ELT.

Data Architecture: A High-Level Perspective

One of the aspects of architecture is to provide a high-level perspective. For a high-level perspective, data architecture looks like the diagram seen in Fig. 8.4.1.

A HIGH LEVEL PERSPECTIVE

Fig. 8.4.1 shows representative components. For example, on the left-hand side where there are cathode ray tubes (CRTs) emanating from an application, the diagram is representative of online transaction processing systems. In reality, there are MANY applications and MANY databases represented by the application, database, and CRTs.

The diagram shows that there are two major types of big data—repetitive data and nonrepetitive data. And of the repetitive data, there is simple repetitive data and context-enriched repetitive data.

The typical sources of the different types of big data are shown as well.

The diagram shows that repetitive data are distilled into data that can be placed into the analytic data warehouse environment. In addition, nonrepetitive data can be disambiguated and placed either in the data warehouse or back into big data as context-enriched repetitive big data.

REDUNDANCY

There are many issues raised by the diagram. One of the issues is that of redundant data. One looks at the diagram, and it appears that there is redundant data everywhere.

In fact, there is data that have been transformed. And if a value of data remains the same after transformation, then you may want to consider the data to be redundant. Then again, you may not.

Consider redundancy in the real world. Take the time of day. You can find the time of day on the Internet, on the telephone, on the radio, on television, and

Data Architecture. https://doi.org/10.1016/B978-0-12-816916-2.00029-2

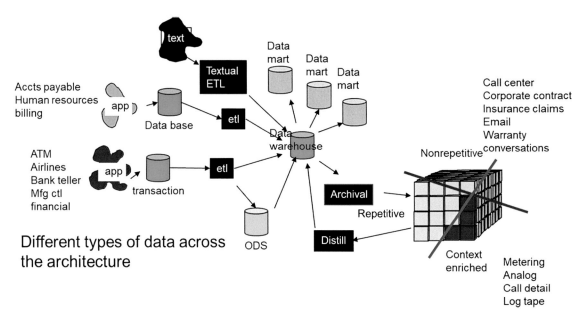

Different types of data across the architecture

FIG. 8.4.1
A high level architecture.

many other places, for that matter. Does the fact that time of day appears redundantly in many places becomes a bother? The only time it becomes a bother is if there is no way to determine what the accurate time is. If there were no definitive source of time, then having time appear redundantly would be a problem. But as long as there is some definitive source somewhere and as long as most redundant sources adhere to that definitive source, then there is no problem. In fact, having redundant sources of time is actually quite helpful, as long as there is no problem with the integrity of that time.

Therefore, having redundant data across the enterprise as seen in Fig. 8.4.1 is not an issue as long as the integrity of the data is not an issue.

THE SYSTEM OF RECORD

The integrity of the data in data architecture is established by what can be called the "system of record." The system of record is the one place where the value of data is definitively established. Note that the system of record applies only to detailed granular data. The system of record does not apply to summarized or derived data.

In order to understand the system of record, think of a bank and your bank account balance. For every account in every bank, there is a single system of record for account balance. There is one and only one place where the account balance is

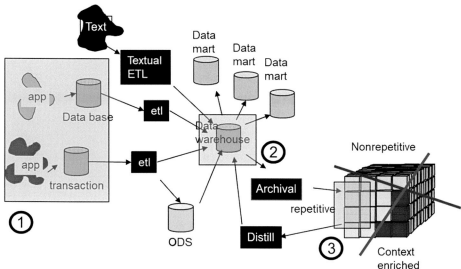

The system of record throughout the architecture

(1) – current data — applications
(2) – 1-5 year old data — data warehouse
(3) – archival data — Big Data

FIG. 8.4.2
The system of record.

established and managed. Your bank account balance may appear in many places throughout the bank. But there is only one place where the system of record is kept.

The system of record moves throughout the data architecture that has been described.

Fig. 8.4.2 depicts the movement of the system of record.

Fig. 8.4.2 shows that as data are captured, especially in the online environment, the data have its first occurrence of the system of record. Location 1 shows that the system of record for current valued data is found in the online environment. You can think of calling the bank and asking for your account balance that exists right now, and the bank looks into its online transaction processing environment to find your account balance right now.

Then one day, you have an issue with a bank transaction that occurred 2 years ago. Your lawyer requires you to go back and prove that you made a payment 2 years ago. You can't go to your online transaction processing environment. Instead, you go to your record in the data warehouse. As data age, the system of record moves for older data to the data warehouse. That is location 2 in the diagram.

Time passes and you get audited by the IRS. This time, you have to go back 10 years time to prove what financial activity you have had a decade ago. Now, you go to the archival store in big data. That is location 3 in the diagram.

So, as time passes, the system of record for data changes in data architecture.

DIFFERENT TYPES OF QUESTIONS

Another way to look at the data found in data architecture is in terms of what types of questions are answered in different parts of the architecture.

Fig. 8.4.3 shows that different types of questions are answered in different parts of the architecture.

Fig. 8.4.3 shows that in location 1, details up to the second questions are answered. Here is where you ask up to the second accurate account balance information. Location 2 indicates that in the data warehouse, you look at your historical activity that has been passed through your bank account.

Location 3 is the ODS. In the ODS, you find up to the second accurate integrated information. In the ODS, you look across information such as ALL your account information—your loans, your savings accounts, your checking account, your IRA, and so forth.

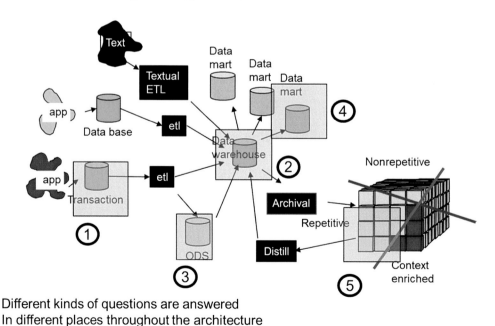

Different kinds of questions are answered
In different places throughout the architecture

FIG. 8.4.3
Answering different questions throughout the architecture.

In location 4, there are the data marts. In the data marts is where bank management combines your account information with thousands of other accounts and looks at the information from the perspective of a department. One department looks at the data in the data marts from an accounting perspective. Another department looks at the data from the perspective of marketing and so forth.

There is yet another perspective of data afforded by the data found in location 5. In location 5, big data is found. There is deep history there and a variety of other data. The kinds of analysis that can be done in location 5 are miscellaneous and diverse.

Of course, the differences in data and the types of analysis that can be done are different for different industries. The example that has been used is of a bank for the purposes of making the example clear. But for other industries, there are other types of usage information.

DIFFERENT COMMUNITIES

Different communities use the information found in data architecture. In general, the clerical community uses information found in locations 1 and 2. Everyone uses the data found in location 3. The data warehouse serves as a cross roads for information throughout the organization. Different functional departments use the information found in location 4. And location 5 serves as an omnibus for the entire organization.

Repetitive Analytics: Some Basics

There are some basic concepts and practices regarding analytics that are pretty much universal. These practices and concepts apply to repetitive analytics and are essential for the data scientist.

DIFFERENT KINDS OF ANALYSIS

There are two distinct types of analysis—open-ended continuous analysis and project-based analysis. Open-ended continuous analysis is analysis that is typically found in the structured corporate world but is occasionally found in the repetitive data world. In open-ended continuous analysis, the analysis starts with the gathering of data. Once the data are gathered, the next step is to refine the data and analyze the data. After the data are analyzed, someone's decision or a set of decisions are made, and the results of those decisions affect the world. Then, more raw data are gathered, and the process starts over again.

The process of gathering data, refining it, analyzing it, and then making decisions based on the analysis on an ongoing basis is actually very common. An example of such a continuous feedback loop might be a bank's decision to raise or lower the loan rate. The bank gathers information about loan applications and loan payments. Then, the bank digests that information and decides to raise or lower loan rates. The bank raises the rate and then tests to see what the results have been. Such is an example of an open-ended continuous analytic loop.

The other type of analytic system is a project-based analysis. In a project-based analysis, the intent is to do the analysis just once. For example, the government may do an analysis on how many illegals have been integrated successfully into society. The intent is to make such a study exactly once. There may be safety studies conducted by an automobile manufacturer. Or there may be chemical analysis of a product. Or there may be a study about the content of ethanol in gasoline and so forth. There can be any sort of and any number of onetime studies.

Fig. 9.1.1 shows that there are two types of analytic studies.

231

Data Architecture. https://doi.org/10.1016/B978-0-12-816916-2.00030-9

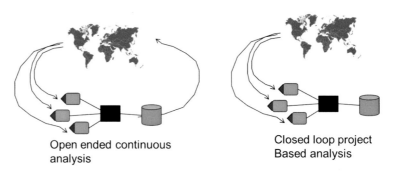

Open ended continuous
analysis

Closed loop project
Based analysis

FIG. 9.1.1
Two types of analytics.

Whether a study is one time or ongoing greatly affects the infrastructure sur-rounding the study. In a continuous study, there needs to be an ongoing infra-structure that is created. In a onetime study, there is a very different infrastructure that is created.

LOOKING FOR PATTERNS

However, the analytic study is done; the study typically looks for patterns. Stated differently, the organization identifies patterns that lead to conclusions. The patterns are tip-offs that important previously unknown events are occur-ring. By knowing these patterns, the organization can then have insights that allow the organization to manage itself more efficiently or more safely or more economically or whatever the end goal of the study is.

The patterns can come in different forms. Sometimes, the patterns are in the form of measurements of occurrences. In other cases, a variable is measured continuously. Fig. 9.1.2 shows two common forms in which patterns are measured.

Where there are discrete occurrences, the occurrences are pasted onto a "scatter chart." The scatter chart is merely a collection of the points placed onto a chart. There are many issues that relate to the creation of a scatter chart. One of the

Looking for patterns in the data

FIG. 9.1.2
Different ways to find patterns in data.

more important issues is that of determining if a pattern is relevant. On occasion, there may be points that have been collected that should not have been collected. On other occasions, there may be points on the chart that have been created that form more than one pattern. A professional statistician is needed to be able to determine the accuracy and the integrity of the points found on a scatter diagram.

Another form of finding patterns is to look at a continuously measured variable. In this case, there typically are levels of thresholds that are of interest. As long as the continuous variable is within the limits of the threshold, there is no problem. But the moment the variable exceeds one or more level of the threshold, then, the analyst takes interest. Usually, the analysis centers around questions of what else has occurred when the variable has exceeded the threshold value.

Once the points of events have been captured and fit to a graph, the next issue is that of identifying false positives. A false positive is an event that has occurred but for reasons unrelated to the study. If enough variables are studied, there will be occurrences of false positives merely by the fact that enough variables have been correlated to each other.

There once was a famous false-positive correlation that occurred that was widely known and discussed. That false-positive correlation was one that stated that if the AFC won the Super Bowl, then the stock market would go down for the next year. But if the NFC won the Super Bowl, then the stock market would rise. Based on this false positive, one could make money in the stock market knowing what was going to happen in the stock market.

Of course, there is no real correlation between the rise or fall of the stock market and who wins the Super Bowl.

Fig. 9.1.3 shows this infamous false-positive correlation.

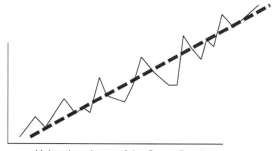

Using the winner of the Super Bowl
to predict the stock market

FIG. 9.1.3
A famous false positive result.

In reality, there is no real correlation between the winner of the Super Bowl and the performance of the stock market. Winning a football game is no indicator of economic performance of the nation. The fact that for many years there actually was a correlation proves that if enough trends are compared, somebody will find a correlation somewhere even if the correlation occurs by simple coincidence.

There may be many reasons why false-positive readings occur. Consider an analysis of Internet sales. One looks at the results of a sale and starts to draw conclusions. In many cases, the conclusion is correct and valid. But one internet sale occurred because someone's cat walked across the keyboard at just the wrong time. There is no legitimate conclusion that can be drawn from an occurrence such as that (Fig. 9.1.4).

False-positive readings can occur for a huge number of unknown and random reasons.

HEURISTIC PROCESSING

Analytic processing is fundamentally different than other types of process. In general, analytic processing is known as "heuristic" processing. In heuristic processing, the requirements for analysis are discovered by the results of the current iteration of processing. In order to understand the dynamics of heuristic processing, consider classical system development life cycle (SDLC) processing.

Fig. 9.1.5 shows a classical SDLC development effort.

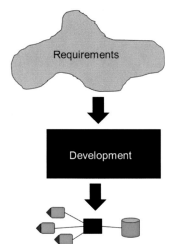

Internet sales

....
10:01 am customer finds product
10:03 am customer likes product
10:15 am customer wants to purchase product
10:23 am child plays with Internet
10:26 am product color is chosen
10:32 am product is placed in checkout basket
....

A "false" positive

Classical systems development

FIG. 9.1.4
A false positive.

FIG. 9.1.5
Classical systems development.

In classical SDLC processing, the first step is to gather requirements. In classical SDLC, the intent is to gather *all* requirements before the next step of development occurs. This approach is sometimes called the "waterfall" approach because of the need to gather all requirements before engaging in the next step of development.

But heuristic processing is fundamentally different than the class SDLC. In heuristic processing, you start with some requirements. You build a system to analyze those requirements. Then, after you have results, you sit back and rethink your requirements after you have had time to reflect on the results that have been achieved. You then restate the requirements and redevelop and reanalyze again. Each time you go through the redevelopment exercise is called an "iteration." You continue the process of building different iterations of processing until such time as you achieve the results that satisfy the organization that is sponsoring the exercise.

Fig. 9.1.6 depicts the heuristic approach to analysis.

One of the characteristics of the heuristic process is that at the beginning, it is impossible to know how many iterations of redevelopment will be done. It just simply is impossible to know how long the heuristic analytic process will take. Another characteristic of the heuristic process is that the requirements may change very little or the requirements may completely change during the life of the heuristic process. Again, it is impossible to know what the requirements will look like at the end of the heuristic process.

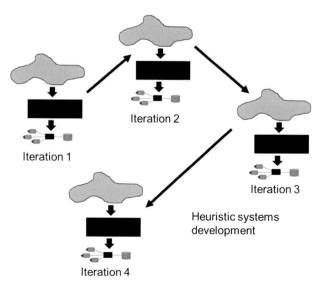

FIG. 9.1.6
The iterative approach.

Because of the iterative nature of the heuristic process, the development process is much less formal and a lot more relaxed than the development process found in the classical SDLC environment. The essence of the heuristic process is on speed of development and the quick production and analysis of results.

FREEZING DATA

Another characteristic of the heuristic process is for the need for data to be "frozen" from time to time. In the heuristic process, the algorithms that process data are constantly changing. If the data that are being operated on are also being changed at the same time, the analyst can never tell whether the new results are a result of the change in algorithms or a change in the data. Therefore, as long as the algorithms going against the data are changing, it is sometimes useful to "freeze" the data that are being operated on.

The notion that data need to be frozen is antithetical to other forms of processing. In other forms of processing, there is a need to operate on the most current data possible. In other forms of processing, data are being updated and changed as soon as possible. Such is not the case at all in heuristic processing.

Fig. 9.1.7 shows the need to freeze data as long as the algorithms processing the data are changing.

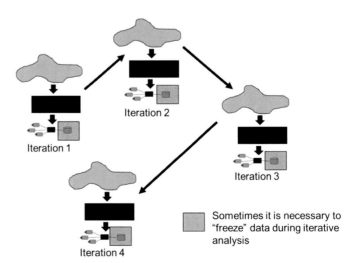

Iteration 2

Iteration 1

Iteration 3

Iteration 4

Sometimes it is necessary to "freeze" data during iterative analysis

FIG. 9.1.7
Freezing data to ensure consistent results.

THE SANDBOX

Heuristic processing is often done in what is called the "sandbox." The sandbox is an environment where the analyst has the opportunity to go and "play" with data. The analyst can look at data one way one day and another way another day. The analyst is not restricted in what kind of processing or in terms of how much processing can be done.

The reason why there is a need for a sandbox is that in standard corporate processing, there is a need for tight control of processing. One reason for the need for tight control of processing in the standard environment is because of resource limitations. In the standard corporate operating environment, there is a need to control the resources that are used for processing by all analysts. That is because there is a need for high performance in the standard operating environment. But in the sandbox environment, there is no such restriction on the analyst. In the sandbox environment, there is no need for high performance. Therefore, the analyst is free to do whatever analytic investigation that he/she wishes to do.

But there is another reason for the sandbox environment. That reason is that in the standard operating environment, there is a need for tight control of data access and calculation. That is because that in the standard operating environment, there are security concerns and data governance concerns. But in the sandbox, there are no such concerns.

The converse of processing in the sandbox is that because there are no controls in the sandbox environment, the results of processing in the sandbox environment should not be used in a formal manner. The results of processing in the sandbox can lead to great new and important insight. But after the insight has been captured, the insight is translated into a more formal system and is incorporated into the standard operating environment.

The sandbox environment then is a great boon to the analytics community.

Fig. 9.1.8 shows the sandbox environment.

FIG. 9.1.8
An analytical sandbox.

THE "NORMAL" PROFILE

One of the most important things that analyst can develop is something that can be called the "normal" profile. The normal profile is the composite of the audience that is being analyzed.

In the case of people, the normal profile may contain such things as gender, age, education, location, number of children, and marriage status.

Fig. 9.1.9 shows a "normal" profile.

A "normal" profile

- Female
- 36 years old
- College educated
- Married
- 2.7 children
- Drives a Honda
- Mortgage of $550,000
- Plays tennis
- Likes Italian food

FIG. 9.1.9
A normal profile.

The normal profile for a corporation may include such attributes as the size of corporation, locations, type of product/service created, and revenue of the corporation. There are different definitions of what is normal for different environments.

There are many reasons why a "normal" profile is useful. One reason is that the profile is just plain interesting. The normal profile tells management at a glance what is going on inside a system. But there is another very important reason why a normal profile is useful. When looking at a large body of data, it is often-times useful to look at a single record and measure just how far from the norm the record is. And you can't determine how far from the norm a record is unless you first understand the norm.

In many cases, the further from the norm a record is, the more interesting it becomes. But you can't spot a record that is far from the norm unless you first understand what the norm is.

DISTILLATION, FILTERING

When doing analytic processing against the repetitive big data environment, the types of processing can be classified in one of two ways. There is what can be termed "distillation" processing, and there is what can be termed "filtering" processing.

Both of these processes can be done depending on the needs of the analyst.

In distillation processing, the results of the processing are a single set of results, such as the creation of a profile. In retail operations, the desire might be to create a normal profile. In banking, the result of distillation might be to create the new lending rate. In manufacturing, the result might be to determine the best materials for manufacture.

In any case, the results of the distillation process are a single occurrence of a set of values.

In filtering, the results are quite different. In filtering, the result of processing is the selection of and the refinement of multiple records. In filtering, the objective is to find all records that satisfy some criteria. Once those records have been found, the records can then be edited, manipulated, or otherwise altered to suit the needs of the analyst. Then, the records are output for further processing or analysis.

In a retail environment, the results of filtering might be the selection of all high-value customers. In manufacturing, the results of filtering might be the selection of all end products that failed quality tests. In health care, the results of filtering might be all patients afflicted with a certain condition and so forth.

The processing that occurs in distillation and in filtering is quite different. The emphasis in distillation is on analytic and algorithmic processing, and the emphasis in filtering is on the selection of records and the editing of those records.

Fig. 9.1.10 illustrates the types of processing that can be done against repetitive data.

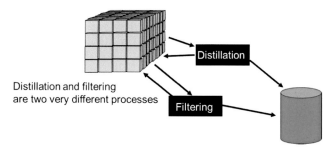

FIG. 9.1.10
Distillation and filtering.

SUBSETTING DATA

One of the results of filtering is the creation of subsets of data. As repetitive data are read and filtered, the result is the creation of data into different subsets. There are lots of practical reasons of subsetting data. Some of those reasons are the following:

- The reduction in volume of data that have to be analyzed. It is much easier to analyze and manipulate a small subset of data than it is to analyze that same data mixed in with many other nonrelevant occurrences of data.
- Purity of processing. By subsetting data, the analyst can filter out unwanted data, so that the analysis can focus on the data that are of interest. Creating a subset of data means that the analytic algorithmic processing that occurs can be very focused on the objective of the analysis.
- Security. Once data are selected into a subset, it can be protected with even higher levels of security than when the data existed in an unfiltered state.

Subsetting data for analysis is a technique that is used commonly and has been used as long as there were data and a computer.

One of the uses of subsetting of data is to set the stage for sampling.

In data sampling, processing goes against a sample of data rather than against the full set of data. In doing so, the resources used for creating the analysis are considerably less, and the time that it takes to create the analysis is significantly reduced. And in heuristic processing, the "turnaround time" to do an analysis can be very important.

Sampling is especially important when doing heuristic analysis against big data because of the sheer volume of data that has to be processed.

Fig. 9.1.11 shows the creation of an analytic sample.

There are some downsides to sampling. One downside is that the analytic results obtained when processing the sample may be different than the processing results achieved when processing against the entire database. For example,

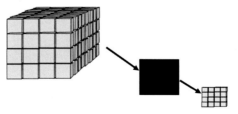

FIG. 9.1.11
Creating the analytical sample.

the sampling may produce the results that the average age of a customer is 35.78 years. When the full database is processed, it may be found that the average age of the customer is really 36.21 years old. In some cases, this small differential between results is inconsequential. In other cases, the difference in results is truly significant. Whether there is significance or not depends on how much difference there is and the importance of accuracy.

If there is not much of a problem with slight inaccuracies of data, then sampling works well.

If in fact, there is a desire to get the results as accurate as possible, then the algorithmic development can be done against sampling data. When the analyst is satisfied that the sampling results are being done properly, then the final run can be made against the entire database, thereby satisfying the needs to do analysis quickly and the need to achieve accurate results.

BIAS OF THE SAMPLE

One issue that arises with sampling is the bias of the sample. When data are selected for inclusion in the sampling database, there is *ALWAYS* a bias of the data. What the bias is and how badly the bias colors the final analytic results are a function of the selection process. In some cases, there is a bias, but the bias of the data really doesn't matter. In other cases, there is a real impact made on the final results because of the bias of the data selected for the sampling database.

The analyst must constantly be aware of the existence of and the influence of the bias of the sampling data.

Fig. 9.1.12 shows that there is an expensive marginal value of accuracy when processing sampling data.

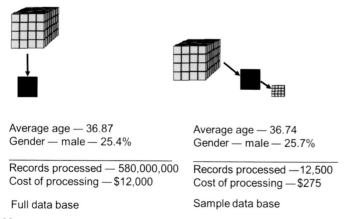

Average age — 36.87
Gender — male — 25.4%
_____
Records processed — 580,000,000
Cost of processing — $12,000

Full data base

Average age — 36.74
Gender — male — 25.7%
_____
Records processed — 12,500
Cost of processing — $275

Sample data base

FIG. 9.1.12
The differences between results obtained from a sample data base and a fully populated data base.

FILTERING DATA

There are many reasons why filtering data—especially big data—is a common practice. The actual practice of filtering data can be done on almost an attribute or any attribute value found in the database.

Fig. 9.1.13 shows that filtering data can be done many ways.

While data can be filtered, at the same time, the data can be edited and manipulated. It is common practice for the output of the filtering process to create records that have some means of ordering the records. Usually, the ordering is done by the inclusion of uniquely valued attributes. For example, the output relating to a person may have the data relating to the person's social security number as part of the output. Or the filtered output for manufacturing goods may have attributes of the part number along with lot number and date of manufacture. Or if the filtered data were from real estate, there may be property address that is an attribute that is included as a key.

Fig. 9.1.14 shows that the data that are produced as part of the filtering process usually contain uniquely valued attributes.

One result of filtering is the production of subsets of data. In fact, when data are filtered, the result is the creation of a subset of data. However, the analyst creating the filtering mechanism may want to use the creation of a subset of data as an opportunity to prepare for future analysis.

Stated differently, when a subset is created, it may be useful to put a little planning into the process to create the subset so that it will be useful to future analytic processing.

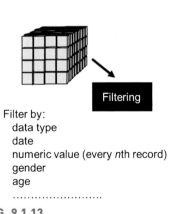

Filter by:
    data type
    date
    numeric value (every nth record)
    gender
    age
    ....

FIG. 9.1.13
Filtering data.

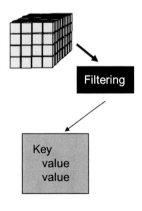

As data is filtered,
keys and values are determined

FIG. 9.1.14
Filtering raw data.

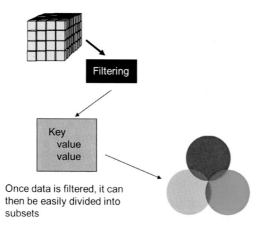

FIG. 9.1.15
Subsetting filtered data.

Fig. 9.1.15 shows that subsets of data are created when data are filtered.

REPETITIVE DATA AND CONTEXT

In general, repetitive data yield its context easily and readily. In general, because repetitive data have so many occurrences of data and because repetitive data are all similarly structured, finding context is easy to do.

When data are in the world of big data, the data are unstructured in the sense that the data are not being managed by a standard database management system. Because the data are unstructured, in order to be used, the repetitive data have to pass through the parsing process (as does all unstructured data). But because the data are structurally repetitive, once the analyst has parsed the first record, all subsequent records will be parsed in exactly the same manner. Because of this parsing, repetitive data in big data still must be done. But doing parsing for repetitive data is an almost trivial thing to do.

Fig. 9.1.16 shows that context for repetitive data is usually easy to find and determine.

When looking at repetitive data, most data are fairly unexceptional. About the only interesting data that occur are in terms of values that occur inside repetitive

■ Context for repetitive data is usually very easy to find

FIG. 9.1.16
Finding the context of repetitive data.

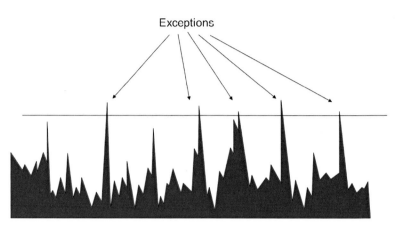

When looking at repetitive data, the vast majority of the data is unexceptional

FIG. 9.1.17
Most nonrepetitive data is non exceptional.

data. As an example of interesting values occurring, consider retail sales. Most retail sales for a retailer are from $1.00 to $100.00. But occasionally, an order is for greater than $100.00. These exceptions are of great interest to the retailer (Fig. 9.1.17).

The retailer is interested in such issues as the following:

- How often do they occur
- How large are they
- What else occurs in conjunction with them
- Are they predictable

LINKING REPETITIVE RECORDS

Repetitive records by themselves have value. But occasionally, repetitive records that have been linked together tell an even larger picture. When records are linked together where there is a logical reason for the linkage, a more complex story can be derived from the data.

Repetitive records can be linked together in many ways. But the most common way to link them together is through common occurrence of data values. For example, there may be a common customer number that links the records. Or there may be a common part number. Or there may be a common retail location number and so forth.

There are in fact many different ways to link together repetitive records, depending on the business problem being studied.

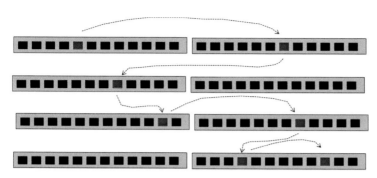

As part of analytical processing, it sometimes makes
sense to link certain records together

FIG. 9.1.18
Linking records.

Fig. 9.1.18 shows it sometimes makes sense to link repetitive records together
based on a business relationship of the records.

LOG TAPE RECORDS

It is common in examining big data to encounter log tapes. Many organizations
create log tapes only to wake up one day and discover that there is a wealth of
information on those tapes that have not ever been used.

As a rule, log tapes contain information that is stored in a cryptic manner. Most
log tapes are written for purposes other than analytic processing. Most log tapes
are written for purposes of backup and recovery or for the purpose of creating a
record of historical events. As a consequence, log tapes require a utility to read
and decipher the log tape. The utility reads the log tape, infers the meaning of
the data found on the log tape, and then reformats the data into an intelligible
form. Once the data are read and reformatted, the analyst can then start to use
the data found on the log tape.

Most log tape processing requires the elimination of irrelevant data. Much data
appear on the log tape that is of no use to the analyst.

Fig. 9.1.19 shows a schematic of what a typical log tape might look like.

Fig. 9.1.19 shows that on the log tape, many different kinds of records are
found. Typically, these records are written onto the log tape in a chronological
manner. As a business event occurs, a record is written to reflect the occurrence
of the event.

At first glance, these data might look like nonrepetitive data. Indeed, from a
physical occurrence of data standpoint, that is a valid perspective. But there

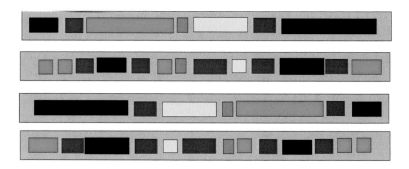

Log tape records are very erose

FIG. 9.1.19
Log tape records are very irregular.

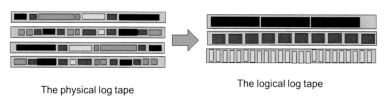

The physical log tape

The logical log tape

FIG. 9.1.20
Two different perspectives of the same thing.

is another way to look at the data found on a log tape. That perspective is that the log tape is merely a chronological accumulation of a bunch of repetitive records. A "logical" perspective of a log tape is seen in Fig. 9.1.20.

In Fig. 9.1.20, it is seen that logically, a log tape is merely a sequential collection of different types of records. The perspective shown in Fig. 9.1.20 shows that the data logically appear to be repetitive records of data.

ANALYZING POINTS OF DATA

One of the ways in which data are analyzed is through the graphing of collection of points of reference data. This technique is called the creation of a scatter diagram and is seen in Fig. 9.1.21.

While gathering and plotting these points can lead to simple observations, there is a mathematical means to expressing the scatter diagram. A line can be drawn through the points. The line represents a mathematically calculated formula using what is called the least squares method. In the least squares approach, the line represents the mathematical function where the square of the distance from each point to the line is the least value.

FIG. 9.1.21
A scatter diagram.

OUTLIERS

On occasion, there is a point of reference that does not seem to fit with all the other points. If this is the case, the point of reference can be discarded. Such a point of reference is referred to as being an "outlier."

In the case of an outlier, the theory is that some other factors were relevant to the calculation of the point of reference. Removing the outlier will not hurt the implications created by the calculation of the least squares regression analysis. Of course, if there are too many outliers, then the analyst must indulge in a deeper analysis of why the outliers occurred. But as long as there are only a few outliers and there are reasons why the outliers should be removed, then removal of outliers is a perfectly legitimate thing to do.

Fig. 9.1.22 depicts a scatter diagram with linear regression analysis and a scatter diagram with outliers.

DATA OVER TIME

It is normal to look at data over time. Looking at data over time is a good way to get insight that would otherwise not be possible.

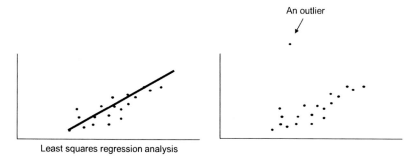

Least squares regression analysis

FIG. 9.1.22
Least squares regression analysis.

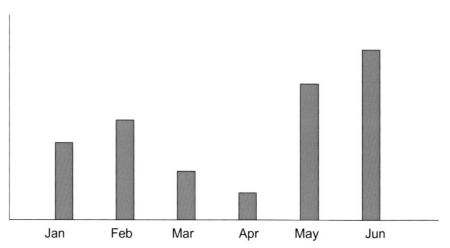

FIG. 9.1.23
A pareto chart.

One of the standard ways to look at data over time is through a Pareto chart. Fig. 9.1.23 depicts data found in a Pareto chart.

While looking at data over time is a standard and a good practice, there is an insidious aspect to looking at data over time. That aspect is this—if the data being examined over time are being examined for a short period of time, then there is no problem. But if the data being examined are being examined over a lengthy enough period of time, then the parameters over which the examination is made change and affect the data.

This effect—of looking at data over limited moments of time—is illustrated by a simple example. Suppose there is an examination of the GNP of the United States over decades. One way to measure GNP is by looking at GNP measured against dollars. So, you plot the national GNP every 10 years or so. The problem is that over time, the dollar means different things in terms of value. The worth of the dollar in 2015 is not the same thing at all as the dollar in 1900. If you do not adjust your parameters of measurement for inflation, your measurement of GNP means nothing.

Fig. 9.1.24 shows that over time, the meaning of the basic measurement of the dollar is not the same over decades.

The fact is that the dollar and inflation are well-understood phenomena. What is not so well understood is that there are other factors over time that cannot be as easily tracked as inflation.

As an example, suppose one were tracking the revenue of IBM over decades. The revenue of IBM over decades is easy enough to find and track because of the fact that IBM is a publicly traded company. But what is not so easy to track are all the

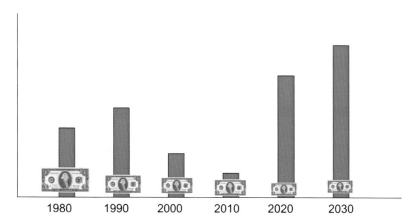
Metadata parameters are constantly changing over time

FIG. 9.1.24
Metadata parameters are changing all the time.

acquisitions of other companies that IBM has made over the years. Looking at IBM in 1960 and then looking at IBM in 2000 are a little misleading because the company that IBM was in 1960 is a very different company than the company that IBM is in 2000.

There is constant change in the parameters of measurement of ANY variable over time. The analyst of repetitive data does well to keep in mind that—given enough time—the very patterns of measurement of data over time gradually change.

Analyzing Repetitive Data

Much of the data found in big data are repetitive. Analyzing repetitive data in the big data environment is quite different than analyzing data in the nonrepetitive environment. As a point of departure, we need to look at what the repetitive big data environment looks like.

Fig. 9.2.1 shows that data in the repetitive big data environment look like lots of units of data laid end to end.

Repetitive data can be thought of as being organized into blocks, records, and attributes. Fig. 9.2.2 shows this organization.

A block of data is a large allocation of space. The system knows how to find a block of data. The block of data is loaded with units of data. These units of data can be thought of as records. Within the record of data are attributes of data.

As an example of the organization of data, consider the record of telephone calls. In the block of data is found the information about many phone calls. In the record for each phone call is found some basic information:

    Date and time of the phone call
    Who was making the phone call
    To whom the call was made
    How long the telephone call was made

There may be other incidental information such as was the phone call operator assisted or was the phone call an international phone call. But at the end of the day, the same attribution of information is found over and over again, for every phone call.

When the system goes to look for data, the system knows how to find a block of data. But once the system finds a block of data, it is up to the analyst to make sense of the data found in the block. The analyst does this by "parsing" the data. The analyst reads the data in the block. Then, the analyst determines where a record is. Upon finding a record, the analyst then determines what attribute is where.

251

Data Architecture. https://doi.org/10.1016/B978-0-12-816916-2.00031-0

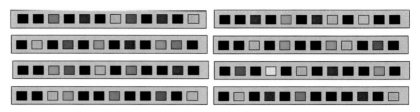

What repetitive data looks like

FIG. 9.2.1
Repetitive data.

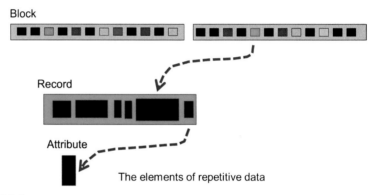

Block

Record

Attribute

The elements of repetitive data

FIG. 9.2.2
The elements of repetitive data.

The process of parsing would be onerous if there were not a high degree of similarity of the records tucked into the block.

Fig. 9.2.3 shows that upon encountering a block of data in big data, there is a need to parse the block.

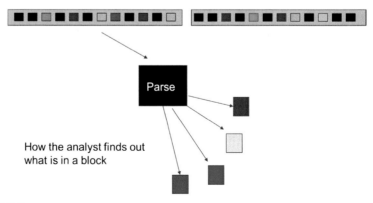

Parse

How the analyst finds out
what is in a block

FIG. 9.2.3
Parsing is done to find out what is in a block.

LOG DATA

One of the most common forms of big data is log data. Indeed, much important corporate information is tucked into the form of logs.

When one looks at log data, log data do not appear to look much like other repetitive data. Consider the comparison seen in Fig. 9.2.4.

In Fig. 9.2.4, repetitive data do not look like log data at all. It appears that in log data, many different kinds of records appear. And indeed, they do. But this apparent contradiction can be resolved by understanding that LOGICALLY, the log tape is nothing more than an amalgamation of repetitive records. This phenomenon is shown by Fig. 9.2.5.

Even though a log tape record is made up of multiple records and must be parsed, the good news is that there typically are a finite number of record types that have to be parsed (unlike other nonrepetitive records where there are anything but a finite number of record types that need to be parsed).

Fig. 9.2.6 shows that there are a finite number of records that need to be examined when parsing a log tape.

The analysis of repetitive data starts with access to the means by which big data is stored. In many instances, big data is stored in Hadoop. However, there are

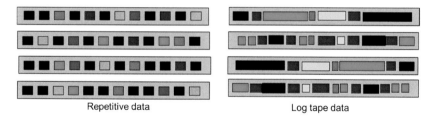

Repetitive data   Log tape data

There is a fundamental structural difference
between repetitive data and log tape data

FIG. 9.2.4
The difference between log tape data and repetitive data.

The physical log tape   The logical log tape

The different perspectives of the
same thing

FIG. 9.2.5
Different perspectives.

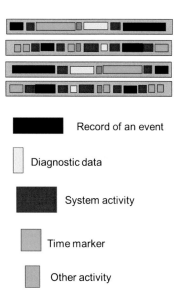

FIG. 9.2.6
Typical contents of a log tape.

other technologies (such as Huge Data) that can manage store and manage large amounts of data.

In an earlier day and age where there were only structured database management systems, the DBMS itself did much of the basic data management. But in the world of big data, much of the management of the data is up to the user.

Fig. 9.2.7 shows some of the different ways in which basic data management needs to be done in big data.

Fig. 9.2.7 shows that with Hadoop, you can access and analyze data through an interface, that you can access and parse data, that you can directly access the data and do basic functions yourself, that there are load utilities, and that there

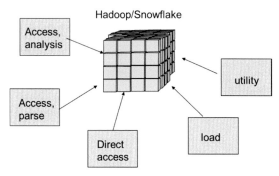

FIG. 9.2.7
Different means of accessing big data.

are other data management utilities. Most of the focus on the technology that directly accesses data in big data is concerned with two things:

The reading and interpretation of the data
The management of large amounts of data

The management of large amounts of data is a consuming issue because there are indeed large amounts of data that need to be handled. There is a science to the handling of large amounts of data unto itself.

Notwithstanding the need to manage large amounts of data, there is still a need for creating an architecture of data.

ACTIVE/PASSIVE INDEXING OF DATA

One of the most useful design techniques the architect can use is that of creating different kinds of indexes of data. In any case, an index is useful in helping find data. It is always faster to locate data through an index than it is to search the data directly. So, indexes have their place in analytic processing.

The way that most indexes are built is through starting with a user requirement to access data and then building an index to satisfy that requirement. When an index is built in this manner, it can be called an active index because there is an expectation that the index will be actively used.

But there is another type of index that can be built, and that index is a passive index. In a passive index, there is no user requirement to start with. Instead, the index is built "just in case" somebody in the future wants to access the data according to how the data are organized. Because there is no active requirement for the building of the index, it is called a "passive" index.

Fig. 9.2.8 shows both active and passive indexes that can be built.

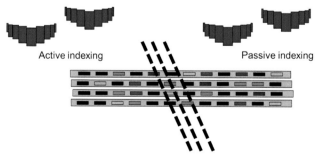

Active indexing   Passive indexing

There are two approaches to
indexing repetitive data

FIG. 9.2.8
Two approaches to accessing repetitive data.

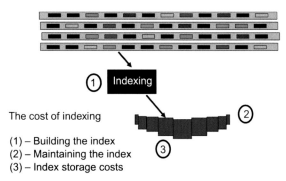

The cost of indexing

(1) – Building the index
(2) – Maintaining the index
(3) – Index storage costs

FIG. 9.2.9
The costs of building and maintaining an index.

With any index, there is a cost. There is the cost of initially building the index. Then, there is the cost of keeping the index current. Then, there is the cost of storage for the index. In the world of big data, indexes are typically built by technology called "crawlers." The crawler technology is constantly searching the big data creating new index records. As long as the data remain stable and unchanged, the data have to only be indexed once. But if data are added or if data are deleted, then there need to be constant updates to the index in order to keep the index current. And in any case, there is the cost of storage for the index itself.

Fig. 9.2.9 shows the costs of building and maintaining an index.

SUMMARY/DETAILED DATA

Another issue that arises is whether detailed and summary data should be kept in big data, and if both summary and detailed data are kept in big data, should there be a connection between the detailed and summary data?

First off, there is no reason why summary and detailed data should not be stored in big data. Big data is perfectly capable of holding both kinds of data. But if big data can hold both detailed and summary data, should there be a logical connection between the detailed data and the summary data? In other words, should the detailed data add up to the summary data?

The answer is that even though detailed and summary data can both be stored in big data, there is no necessary connection between the data once stored in big data. The reason for this is that when the data are calculated and the summary data are created, it is necessary to have an algorithm. The algorithm most likely is NOT stored in big data. So, as long as an algorithm is not stored in big data, there is no necessary logical connection between detailed data and summary data. For this reason, detailed data may or may not add up to the related summary data that can be stored in big data.

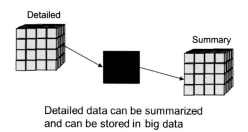

Detailed

Summary

Detailed data can be summarized
and can be stored in big data

FIG. 9.2.10
Detailed data can be summarized and stored in big data.

Fig. 9.2.10 shows this relationship of data inside big data.

But if detailed data and summary data should both be kept in big data and if detailed data should not necessarily add up to the summary data found there, at the very least, there should be documentation of the algorithm that was used to create the summary data.

Fig. 9.2.11 shows that documentation of algorithms and selection of detailed data should be documented alongside the summary data stored in big data.

METADATA IN BIG DATA

While data are the essence of what is stored in big data, it is important not to neglect another type of data. That data are metadata.

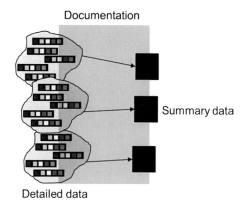

Documentation

Summary data

Detailed data

Whenever summarization is done,
documentation of how the summarization
is needed as well

FIG. 9.2.11
Documenting summarization.

There are MANY forms of metadata, and each of them is important. Two of the more important forms of metadata are native metadata and derived metadata. Native metadata are metadata that addresses the immediate descriptive needs of the data. Typical native metadata include such information as follows:

Field name
Field length
Field type
Field identifying characteristics

Native metadata are used to identify and describe data that are stored in big data.

Derived metadata take many forms. Some of the forms of derived metadata include the following:

Description of how data were selected
Description of when data were selected
Description of the source of data
Description of how data were calculated

Fig. 9.2.12 depicts the different types of metadata.

With metadata stored in big data, there arises the issue—where should metadata be stored? Traditionally, metadata have been stored in a repository. The repository is stored physically separately from the data itself. But in the world of big data, there are some very good reasons for managing metadata differently. In big data, it often makes sense to store the descriptive metadata physically in the same location and same data set as the data being described.

There are several very good reasons for the physical storage of metadata in the same physical location as the data itself. Some of those reasons are the following:

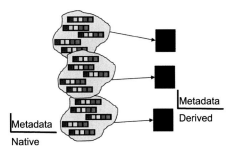

There are many differences between native metadata and derived metadata

FIG. 9.2.12
Differences between native metadata and derived metadata.

Storage is cheap. There is no reason why the cost of storage needed to store the metadata should ever be an issue.

The world of big data is undisciplined. Having the metadata stored directly with the data being described means that the metadata will never be lost or misplaced.

Metadata change over time. When the metadata are stored directly with the data being described, there is ALWAYS a direct relationship between the metadata and the data being described. In other words, the metadata NEVER go out of sync with the data being described.

Simplicity of processing. When the analyst starts to process data in big data, there is never a search for the metadata. It is always easy to locate because it is always with the data being described.

Fig. 9.2.13 shows that embedding metadata along with the data stored in big data is a good idea.

Note that storing metadata directly with the data stored in big data does not preclude the possibility of having a repository of metadata for big data. There is nothing to say that metadata cannot be stored in the data with big data AND reside in a repository as well.

LINKING DATA

One of the fundamental issues of data is that of how data are linked to each other. This issue is an issue in big data just as it has been an issue in other forms of information processing.

In classical information systems, linkage of data was accomplished by matching data values. As an example, one record contained social security number, and another record contained social security number as well. The two units of data could then be linked because of the existence of the same value residing in the record. The analyst could be 99.99999% assured that there was a basis for linkage. (Curiously, since the government reissues social security numbers upon

Embedding metadata along with the actual data is usually a good idea

FIG. 9.2.13

Embedded metadata is a good idea.

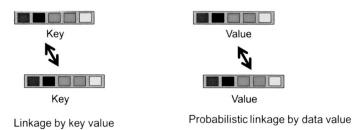

There are two basic kinds of links

FIG. 9.2.14
Different kinds of linkages.

the death of an individual, the analyst cannot be 100% assured that the linkage is real.)

But with the unstructured data (i.e., textual data) that come with big data, it is necessary to accommodate another type of relationship involving the linkage of data. In this case, it is necessary to accommodate what can be called a probable linkage of data.

A probable linkage of data is linkage that is based on probability rather than an actual value.

Probabilistic linkages arise wherever there is text.

As an example of a probabilistic linkage, consider the linkages of data based on name. Suppose there are two names in different records—Bill Inmon and William Inmon. Should these values be linked? There is a high probability that these names should be linked. But it is only a probability, not a certainty. Suppose there are two records where the name William Inmon is found. Should these records be linked?

One record refers to a serial killer in Arizona, and another record refers to a data warehouse writer in Colorado. (This is a true example—look it up on the Internet to verify.) Both individuals have the same name. But they are very different people.

When text is involved, linkage is accomplished on the basis of probability of a match, not the certainty of a match.

Fig. 9.2.14 depicts the different kinds of linkages that are found in big data.

Repetitive Analysis

INTERNAL, EXTERNAL DATA

Because the cost of storage is so inexpensive with big data, it is possible to consider storing data that come from other than internal sources.

In an earlier day, the cost of storage was such that the only data that corporations considered to store were internally generated data. But with the cost of storage diminished by the advent of big data, it is now possible to consider storing external data and internal data.

One of the issues with storing external data is that of finding and using identifiers. But textual disambiguation can be used on external data just as it can against internal data, so it is entirely possible to establish discrete identifiers for external data.

Fig. 9.3.1 shows that storing external data in big data is a real possibility.

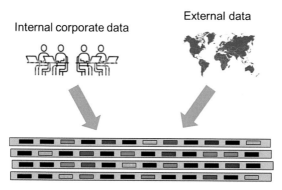

FIG. 9.3.1
Repetitive data can come from almost anywhere.

261

Data Architecture. https://doi.org/10.1016/B978-0-12-816916-2.00032-2

UNIVERSAL IDENTIFIERS

As data are stored in big data and as textual disambiguation is used to bring the data into a standard database format, the subject of universal identifiers or universal measurement arises. Because data come from such diverse sources, because there is little or no discipline or uniformity of data across disparate sources, and because there is a need to relate data to common measurements, there is a need for uniform measurement characteristics across the universe from which data come.

Some universal measurements are fairly obvious; other universal measurements are not.

Three standard or universal measurements of data might include the following:

Time—Greenwich mean time
Date—Julian date
Money—US dollar

Undoubtedly, there are other universal measurements. And each of these measurements has its own quirks.

Greenwich mean time (GMT) is the time that occurs at the meridian that runs through Greenwich, England. The good news about GMT is that there is universal understanding as to what that time is. The bad news is that it is not in agreement with 23 other time zones in the world. But at least, there is an agreed-upon understanding of time in at least one other place in the world.

Julian date is the sequential count of dates starting from day 0, which occurred at Jan 1, 4713 BC. The value of Julian date is that it is universal and that it reduces the number of days to an ordinal number. In a standard calendar, calculating how many days there are between 16 May 2014 and 3 Jan 2015 is a complex thing to do. But with Julian date, such a calculation is very simple to do.

The US dollar is as good a measurement of currency as any other measure. But even with the US dollar, there are challenges. For example, the conversion rate between the dollar and other currencies is constantly changing. If you calculate a value on Feb 15 converting the dollar against another currency, chances are excellent that you will get a different value if you make the same currency conversion on Aug 7. But all other factors being equal, the US dollar serves as a good economic measurement of wealth.

Fig. 9.3.2 shows some of the universal measurements.

Time - GMT

Date - Julian

Money - dollar

FIG. 9.3.2
Some standard measurements of data.

SECURITY

Another significant and serious concern of data (anywhere, not just in big data) is that of security. There are literally hundreds of reasons why data need to be secure:

- Health-care data need to be secure because of privacy reasons.
- Personal financial data need to be secure because of theft and personal loss.
- Corporate financial data need to be secure because of insider trading laws.
- Corporate activity needs to be secure because of the need to keep trade secrets actually secret.
- And so forth.

There are a multitude of reasons why certain data need to be treated with the utmost of care when it comes to security.

Fig. 9.3.3 shows the need for security.

There are many facets to security. Only a few of them will be mentioned here. The simplest (and one of the most effective) form of security is that of encryption. Encryption is the process of taking data and substituting encrypted values for actual values. For example, you might take the text "Bill Inmon" and substitute "Cjmm Jmopm" in its place. In this case, we have merely substituted the next letter in the alphabet for the actual value. It would have taken a good cryptographer about a nanosecond to decrypt the data. But a good encryption analyst could figure out many more ways to encrypt the data that would stump even the most sophisticated of analysts.

In any case, the process of encrypting data is commonly used. Typically, fields of data are encrypted inside a database. In health care, for example, only the identifying information is encrypted. The remaining data are left untouched. This allows the data to be used in research without endangering the privacy of the data.

Fig. 9.3.4 shows encryption being done on a field of data.

FIG. 9.3.3
Security is always an issue.

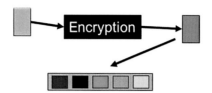

FIG. 9.3.4
Encrypting a field of data.

There are many issues that relate to encryption. Some of the issues are as follows:

- How secure is the encrypting algorithm
- Who can decrypt the data
- Should fields that need to be indexed be encrypted
- How should decryption keys be protected
- And so forth

One of the more interesting issues is consistency of encryption. Suppose you encrypt the name "Bill Inmon." Suppose that at later place, you need to once again encrypt the name—Bill Inmon. You need to ensure that the name—Bill Inmon—is encrypted the same everywhere there is a need for encryption. You need to ensure consistency of encryption everywhere encryption is needed. This is necessary because if you need to link records based on an encrypted value, you cannot do so if there is no consistency of encryption.

Fig. 9.3.5 shows the need for consistency of encryption.

Another interesting aspect of security is looking at who is trying to look at encrypted data. The access and analysis of encryption may be purely innocent. Then, again, it may not be innocent at all. By examining log tapes and seeing who is trying to access what data, the analyst can determine if someone is trying to access data they shouldn't be looking at.

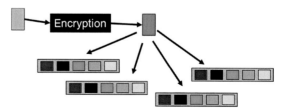

FIG. 9.3.5
Consistency of encryption is an issue.

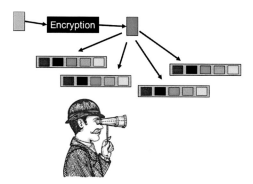

FIG. 9.3.6
Who is looking at our encrypted data?

Fig. 9.3.6 shows that examining log tapes is a good practice in determining if there are breaches of security.

FILTERING, DISTILLATION

There are two basic kinds of processing that occur in the analysis of repetitive data—distillation and filtering.

In distillation of data, repetitive records are selected and read. Then, the data are analyzed, looking for average values, total values, exceptional values, and the like. After the analysis has concluded, a single result is achieved and becomes the out-of-distillation process.

As a rule, distillation is done on a project basis or on an irregular unscheduled basis.

Fig. 9.3.7 shows the process of distillation of repetitive data.

The other type of processing done against repetitive data is that of filtering repetitive and reformatting the repetitive data.

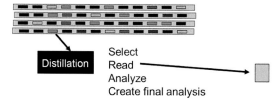

FIG. 9.3.7
The process of distillation.

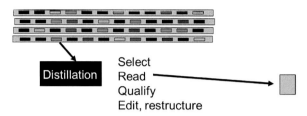

FIG. 9.3.8
The process of filtering.

Filtering of data is similar to distillation in that data are selected and analyzed. But the output of filtering of data is different. In filtering, there are many records that are the output of processing. And filtering is done on a regular, scheduled basis.

Fig. 9.3.8 depicts the filtering of repetitive records of data.

ARCHIVING RESULTS

Much of the analytic processing that is done against repetitive data is of the project variety. And there is a problem with analytic processing done on a project basis. The problem is that once the project is finished, the results are either discarded or put into "mothballs." There is no problem until such time as it comes to do another project. When starting a new project, it is very convenient to see what analysis has preceded this analysis. There may be overlap. There may be complementary processing. If nothing else, a description of how the previous analyses have been developed can be useful.

Therefore, at the end of a project, it is useful to create an archive of the project.

Typical information that might go into the archive might include the following:

    What data went into the project
    How data were selected
    What algorithms were used
    How many iterations were there in the project
    What results were attained
    Where are the results stored
    Who conducted the project
    How long did it take to conduct the project
    Who sponsored the project

Fig. 9.3.9 shows that an archive of projects is a worthwhile thing to do.

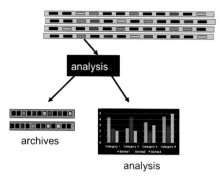

FIG. 9.3.9
Archiving the results of analysis.

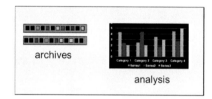

FIG. 9.3.10
Documenting the output.

At the very least, the results created by the project should be gathered and stored, as seen in Fig. 9.3.10.

METRICS

At the outset of the repetitive analysis, it is worthwhile to establish the metrics that will establish whether a project has met its objectives. The optimal time to outline such metrics is at the very outset of the project.

There is a problem with delineating the metrics at the beginning. That problem is that in a heuristically run project that many of the metrics cannot be definitively established.

Nevertheless, outlining the metrics at the very least gives the project a sense of focus.

FIG. 9.3.11
Crossing the finish line.

The metrics can be described in very broad terms. There is no need to have the metrics defined to a very low level of definition.

Fig. 9.3.11 shows that metrics define when a project has been successful or less than successful.

Nonrepetitive Data

There are two types of data that reside in the big data environment—repetitive data and nonrepetitive data. Repetitive data are relatively easy to handle because of the repetitive nature of the structure of the data. But nonrepetitive data are anything but easy to handle because every unit of data in the nonrepetitive environment must be individually interpreted before it can be used for analytic processing.

Fig. 10.1.1 shows a representation of nonrepetitive data as they reside in a raw state in the big data environment.

The nonrepetitive data found in big data are called "nonrepetitive" because each unit of data is unique. Fig. 10.1.2 shows that each unit of data in the nonrepetitive environment is different from the preceding unit of data.

There are many examples of nonrepetitive data in the big data environment. Some of the examples include the following:

    E-mail data
    Call center data
    Corporate contracts
    Warranty claims
    Insurance claims

It is possible for two units of repetitive data to actually be the same. Fig. 10.1.3 shows this possibility.

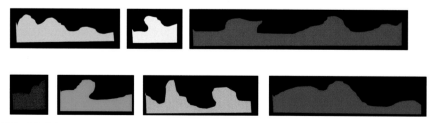

FIG. 10.1.1
Nonrepetitive data.

269

Data Architecture. https://doi.org/10.1016/B978-0-12-816916-2.00033-4

Each unit of data and each structure of data is different and unique

FIG. 10.1.2
Great differences.

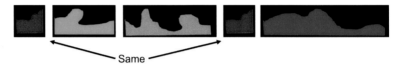

Same

If any two occurrences of data are similar or even the same,
It is an accident

FIG. 10.1.3
The only similarities are accidental.

As an example of two units of nonrepetitive data being the same, suppose there are two e-mails that contain one word—the word "yes." In this case, the e-mails are identical. But the fact that they are identical is merely an act of randomness.

In general, when text finds its way into the big data environment, the units of data stored in big data are nonrepetitive.

One approach to processing nonrepetitive data is to use a search technology. While search technology accomplishes the task of scanning the data, search technology leaves a lot to be desired. The two primary shortcomings of search technology are that searching data do not leave a database that can be subsequently used for analytic purposes and the fact that search technology does not look at or provide context for the text being analyzed. And there are other limitations of search technology as well.

In order to do extensive analytic processing against nonrepetitive data, it is necessary to read the nonrepetitive data and to turn the nonrepetitive data into a standard database format. Sometimes, this process is said to take unstructured data and turn them into structured data. That indeed is a good description of what occurs.

The process of reading nonrepetitive data and turning them into a database is called "textual disambiguation" or "textual ETL." Textual disambiguation is—of necessity—a complex process because the language it processes is complex. There is no getting around the fact that processing text is a complex process.

The result of processing nonrepetitive data in big data with textual disambiguation is the creation of a standard database. Once data are put into the form of a standard database, it can then be analyzed using standard analytic technology.

The mechanics of textual disambiguation are shown in Fig. 10.1.4.

The general flow of processing in textual ETL is this. The first step is to find and read the data. Normally, this step is straightforward. But occasionally, the data have to be "untangled" in order for further processing to continue. In some cases, the data reside in a unit by unit basis. This is the "normal" (or easy) case. But in other cases, the units of data are combined into a single document, and the units of data must be isolated in the document in order to be processed.

The second step is to examine the unit of data and determine what data need to be processed. In some cases, all the data need to be processed. In other cases, only certain data need to be processed. In general, this step is very straightforward.

The third step is to "parse" the nonrepetitive data. The word "parse" is a little misleading because it is in this step that the system applies great amounts of logic. The word "parsing" implies a straightforward process, and the logic that occurs here is anything but straightforward. The remainder of this chapter discusses the logic that occurs here.

After the nonrepetitive data have been "parsed," the attributes of data, the keys of data, and the records of data are identified.

Once the keys, attributes, and records are identified, it is a straightforward process to turn the data into a standard database record.

That then is what takes place in textual disambiguation.

The heart of textual disambiguation is the logic of processing that occurs when nonrepetitive data are analyzed and turned into keys, attributes, and records.

The activities of logic that occur here can be roughly classified into several categories. Fig. 10.1.5 shows those categories.

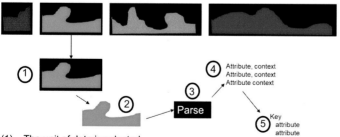

(1) – The unit of data is selected
(2) – The data within the unit of data that is of interest is selected
(3) – The data of interest is "parsed"
(4) – The basic attributes and context are selected
(5) – The basic data base record is selected

FIG. 10.1.4
The mechanics of textual disambiguation.

Textual disambiguation
- Contextualization
- Standardization
- Basic editing

FIG. 10.1.5
The different types of textual disambiguation.

The basic activities of logic applied by textual disambiguation include the activities of the following:

Contextualization, where the context of data is identified and captured
Standardization, where certain types of text are standardized
Basic editing, where basic editing of text occurs

Indeed, there are other functions of textual disambiguation, but these three classifications of activities encompass most of the important processing that occurs.

The remainder of this chapter will be an explanation of logic that is found in textual disambiguation.

INLINE CONTEXTUALIZATION

One form of contextualization is a form that is called "inline contextualization" (or sometimes called "named value" processing). Inline contextualization only applies when there is a repetition and predictability of text. It is noted that in many cases, there is no predictability of text, so inline contextualization cannot be used in these cases.

Inline contextualization is the process of inferring the context of a word or phrase by looking at the text immediately preceding and immediately following the word or phrase. As a simple example of inline contextualization, consider the raw text "2. This is a PAID-UP LEASE."

The context name would be contract type. The beginning delimiter would be "2. This is a" and the ending delimiter would be "." The system would produce an entry into the analytic database that would look like the following:

Document name, byte, context—contract type, value—PAID-UP LEASE

Fig. 10.1.6 shows the activity the system does in processing raw text to determine inline contextualization.

Note that beginning delimiter must be unique. If you were to specify "is a" as a beginning delimiter, then every occurrence where the term "is a" is found would be qualified. And there may be many places where the term "is a" is found that does not specify inline contextualization.

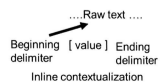

FIG. 10.1.6
Finding beginning and ending delimiters.

Also, note that the ending delimiter must be specified exactly. In this case, if the term does not end in a "." the system will not consider the entry to be a hit.

Because the ending delimiter must be specified accurately, the analyst also specifies a maximum character count. The maximum character count tells the system how far to search to determine whether the ending delimiter has been found.

On occasion, the analyst wants the inline contextualization search to end on a special character. In this case, the analyst specifies the special character that is needed.

TAXONOMY/ONTOLOGY PROCESSING

Another powerful way to specify context is through the usage of taxonomies and ontologies.

There are many important things that taxonomies do for contextualization. The first is applicability. Whereas inline contextualization requires repetitive and predictable occurrences of text to be applicable, taxonomies do not have such a requirement. Taxonomies are applicable just about everywhere. A second valuable feature of taxonomies is that can be applied externally. This means that in choosing the taxonomy to be applied, the analyst can greatly influence the interpretation of the raw text.

For example, suppose the analyst was going to apply a taxonomy to the phrase "President Ford drove a Ford." If the interpretation that analyst wished to infer were about cars, then the analyst would choose one or more taxonomy that would allow "Ford" to be interpreted as an automobile. But if the analyst were to choose a taxonomy relating to the history of the presidents of the United States, then the term "Ford" would be interpreted to be a former president of the United States.

The analyst then has great power in applying the correct taxonomy to the raw text that is to be processed.

The mechanics of how a taxonomy processes against raw text is seen in Fig. 10.1.7.

As a simple example of the application of a taxonomy to raw text, consider the following example.

Raw text—"…she drove her Honda into the garage…." The simple taxonomy used looks like the following:

Car
Porsche
Honda
Toyota

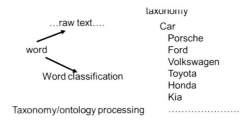

FIG. 10.1.7
Processing a taxonomy against raw text.

    Ford
    Kia
    Volkswagen

When the taxonomy is passed against the raw text, the results look like the following:

    Document name, byte, context—car, value—Honda

In order to accommodate other processing, on some occasions, it is useful to create a second entry:

    Document name, byte, context—car, value—car

The reason why it is sometimes useful to produce a second entry into the analytic database is that on occasion, you want to process all the values and you want the context to be processed as a value. That is why that on occasion, the system produces two entries into the analytic database.

Note that textual ETL operates on taxonomies/ontologies as if the taxonomies were a simple word pair. In fact, taxonomies and ontologies are much more complex that simple word pairs. But even the most sophisticated taxonomy can be decomposed into a series of simple word pairs.

In general, the usage of taxonomies as a form of contextualization is the most powerful tool the analyst has in determining the context of raw text.

CUSTOM VARIABLES

Another very useful form of contextualization is that of the identification of and creation of what can be termed "custom variables." Almost every organization has custom variables. A custom variable is a word or phrase that is recognizable entirely from the format of the word or phrase. As a simple example, a manufacturer may have its part numbers in the form of "AK-876-uy." Looking at a part number, generically, the generic form of the part number would be "CC-999-cc." In this case, "C" indicates a capital character, "-" indicates the literal "-", "9" indicates any numeric digit, and "c" indicates a lower case character.

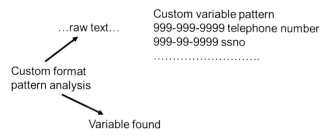

FIG. 10.1.8
Custom variable format processing.

By looking at the format of a word or phrase, the analyst can tell immediately the context of the variable.

Fig. 10.1.8 shows how raw text is processed using custom variables.

As an example of the use of custom variables, consider the following raw text:

...I want to order two more cases of TR-0987-BY to be delivered on...

Upon processing the raw text, the following entry would be created inside the analytic database:

Doc name, byte, context—part number, value—TR-0987-BY

Note that there are a few common custom variables in common use. One (in the United States) is 999-999-9999, which is the common pattern for telephone number. Or there is 999-99-9999 that is the generic pattern for social security number.

The analyst can create whatever pattern he/she wishes for processing against the raw text. The only "gotcha" that sometimes occurs is the case where on occasion more than one type of variable will have the same format as another variable. In this case, there will be confusion in trying to use custom variables.

HOMOGRAPHIC RESOLUTION

A powerful form of contextualization is that known as "homographic resolution." In order to understand homographic resolution, consider the following (very real) example. Some doctors are trying to interpret doctor's notes. The term "ha" gives the doctors a problem. When a cardiologist writes "ha," the cardiologist refers to "heart attack." When an endocrinologist writes "ha," the endocrinologist refers to "hepatitis A." When a general practitioner writes "ha," the general practitioner refers to "headache."

In order to create a proper analytic database, the term "ha" must be interpreted properly. If the term "ha" is not interpreted properly, then people that have had heart attacks, hepatitis A, and headaches will all be mixed together, and that surely will produce a faulty analysis.

There are several elements to homographic resolution. The first element is the homograph itself. In this case, the homograph is "ha." The second element is the homograph class. The homograph class in this case includes cardiologist, endocrinologist, and general practitioner. The homographic resolution is that for cardiologists "ha" means "heart attack"; for endocrinologists, "ha" means "hepatitis A"; and that for general practitioners, "ha" means "head ache."

The fourth element of homographic resolution is that each of the homographic classes must have typical words assigned to the class. For example, a cardiologist may be associated with words like "aorta," "stent," "bypass," and "valve."

There are then four elements to homographic resolution:

> The homograph
> The homograph class
> The homograph resolution
> Words associated with the homograph class

Fig. 10.1.9 shows how homographic processing is done against raw text.

Suppose the raw text looks as follows—"…120/68, 168 lbs, ha, 72 bpm, f, 38,…"

Upon processing the raw text, the entry into the database might look like the following:

> Document name, byte, context—head ache, value—ha

Care must be taken with the specification of homographs. The underlying work done by the system to resolve the homograph is considerable. So, system overhead is a concern.

In addition, the analyst can specify a default homographic class should none of the homographic classes be qualified. In this case, the system will default to the homograph class specified by the analyst.

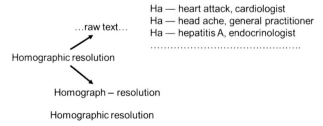

FIG. 10.1.9
Homographic processing.

ACRONYM RESOLUTION

A related form of resolution is that of acronym resolution. Acronyms are found everywhere in raw text. Acronyms are a standard part of communication. Furthermore, acronyms tend to be clustered around some subject area. There are IBM acronyms. There are military acronyms. There are IMS acronyms. There are chemical acronyms. There are Microsoft acronyms and so forth.

In order to clearly understand a communication, it is advisable to resolve acronyms.

Textual ETL is equipped to resolve acronyms. When textual ETL reads raw text and spots an acronym, textual ETL replaces the acronym with the literal value.

Fig. 10.1.10 shows the dynamics of how textual ETL reads raw text and resolves an acronym when it is found.

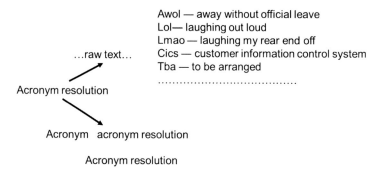

FIG. 10.1.10
Processing an acronym.

As an example of how acronym resolution works, suppose there was the following text:

    Sgt Mullaney was AWOL as of 10:30 p.m. on Dec 25…

The following entry would be placed in the analytic database:

    Document name, byte, context—absent without official leave, value—
    AWOL

Textual ETL has organized the terms of resolution by category class. Of course, the terms of resolution can be customized upon loading into the system.

NEGATION ANALYSIS

On occasion, text will state that something did not happen, as opposed to saying that something happened. If standard contextualization is used, there will be a reference to something that did not happen. In order to make sure that

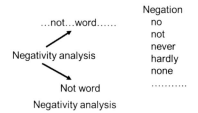

FIG. 10.1.11
Negation analysis.

when a negation is stated in text, the negation needs to be recognized by textual ETL.

For example, if a report says "…John Jones did not have a heart attack…," there does not need to be a reference to John Jones having a heart attack. Instead, there needs to be a reference to the fact that John did NOT have a heart attack.

There are actually many different ways that negation analysis can be done by textual ETL. The simplest way is to create a taxonomy of negative terms— "none, not, hardly, no,…"—and keep track of the negations that have occurred. Then, if a negative term has occurred in conjunction with another term in the same sentence, the inference is made that something did not happen.

Fig. 10.1.11 shows how raw text can be treated to create one form of negation analysis.

As an example of negation analysis, consider the raw text "…John Jones did not have a heart attack…."

The data that would be generated would look like the following:

Document name, byte, context—negation, value—no
Document name, byte, context—condition, value—heart attack

Care must be taken with negation analysis because not all forms of negation are easily handled. The good news is that most forms of negation in language are straightforward and are easily handled. The bad news is that some forms of negation require elaborate techniques for textual ETL management.

NUMERIC TAGGING

Another useful form of contextualization is that of numeric tagging. It is normal for a document to have multiple numeric values on the document. It is also normal for one numeric value to mean one thing and another numeric value to mean something else.

For example, a document may have the following:

Payment amount
Late fee charge
Interest amount
Payoff amount
And so forth

It is most helpful to the analyst who will be analyzing the document to "tag" the different numeric values. In doing so, the analyst can simply refer to the numeric value by its meaning. This makes the analysis of documents that contain multiple numeric values quite convenient. (Stated differently, if the tagging is not done at the time of textual ETL processing, the analyst accessing and using the document will have to do the analysis at the time the document is being analyzed, which is a time-consuming and tedious process. It is much simpler to tag a numeric value at the moment of textual ETL processing.)

Fig. 10.1.12 shows how raw text is read and how tags are created for numeric values.

As an example of how textual ETL might read a document and tag a numeric value, consider the following raw text:

Raw text—"…Invoice amount"—"$813.97,…"

The data placed onto the analytic database would look like the following:

Document name, byte, context—invoice amount, value—813.97

DATE TAGGING

Date tagging operates on the same basis as numeric tagging. The only difference is that date tagging operates on dates rather than numeric values.

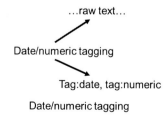

FIG. 10.1.12
Tagging numerical values.

DATE STANDARDIZATION

Date standardization comes in useful when there are multiple documents that have to be managed or when a single document requires analysis based on date. The problem with date is that it can be formatted in so many ways. Some common ways that date can be formatted include the following:

May 13, 2104
23rd of June, 2015
2001/05/28
14/14/09

While a human being can read these forms of data and understand what is meant, a computer cannot.

Data standardization by textual ETL reads data, recognizes them as a date, recognizes what date value is being represented in text, and converts the date value into a standard value. The standard value is then stored in the analytic database.

Fig. 10.1.13 shows how textual ETL reads raw text and converts date values into standardized values.

...Jan 5, 2019.....

Date standardization

Standardized date

Date standardization

FIG. 10.1.13
Converting dates into a standardized format.

As an example of the processing done by textual ETL against raw text, consider the following raw text:

...she married on July 15, 2015 at a small church in Southern Colorado....

The database reference generated for the analytic database would look like the following:

Document name, byte, context—date value, value—20150715

LIST PROCESSING

Occasionally, text contains a list. And occasionally, the list needs to be processed as a list, rather than as a sequential string of text.

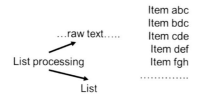

FIG. 10.1.14
List processing.

Textual ETL can recognize and process a list if asked to do so.

Fig. 10.1.14 shows how raw text is read and processed into a recognizable list in textual ETL.

Consider the raw text:

"Recipe ingredients:
   1—Rice
   2—Salt
   3—Paprika
   4—Onions
   ....

Textual could read the list and process it thusly:

Document name, byte, context—list recipe element 1, value—rice
Document name, byte, context—list recipe element 2, value—salt
Document name, byte, context—list recipe element 3, value—paprika

ASSOCIATIVE WORD PROCESSING

Occasionally, there are documents that are repetitive in structure but not in terms of words or content. In cases like these, it may be necessary to use a feature of textual ETL called associative word processing.

In associative word processing, an elaborate definitional structure of data is created; then, the words inside the structure are defined according to a common meaning of words.

Fig. 10.1.15 depicts associative word processing.

As an example of associative word processing, consider the following raw text:

Contract ABC, requirement section, required conferences—every two weeks,...

FIG. 10.1.15
Associative word processing.

The output to the analytic database might look like the following:

Document name, byte, context—scheduled meeting, value—required conference

STOP WORD PROCESSING

Perhaps, the most straightforward processing done in textual ETL is that of stop word processing. Stop words are words that are necessary for proper grammar but are not useful or necessary for the understanding of the meaning of what is being said. Typical English stop words are "a," "and," "the," "is," "that," "what," "for," "to," "by," and so forth. Typical stop words in Spanish include "el," "la," "es," "de," "que," and "y." All Latin-based languages have stop words.

In doing textual ETL processing, stop words are removed.

The analyst has the opportunity to customize the stop word list that is shipped with the product.

Removing unnecessary stop words has the effect of reducing the overhead of processing raw text with textual ETL.

Fig. 10.1.16 shows raw text that is being processed for stop words by textual ETL.

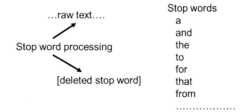

FIG. 10.1.16
Stop word processing.

In order to envision how stop word processing works, consider the following raw text:

> …he walked up the steps, looking to make sure he carried the bag properly…

After stops words are removed, the resulting raw text would look like the following:

> …walked steps looking carried bag…

WORD STEMMING

Another sometimes useful editing feature of textual ETL is that of stemming. Latin-based words have word stems. There are usually many forms of the same word. Consider the stem "mov." The different forms of the word stem mov include move, mover, moves, moving, and moved. Note that the stem itself may or may not be an actual word.

Oftentimes, it is useful to make associations of text that uses the same word stems. It is easy to reduce a word down to its word stem in textual ETL, as seen in Fig. 10.1.17.

In order to see how textual processes word stems, consider the following raw text:

> …she walked her dog to the park….

The resulting database entry would look like the following:

Document name, byte, stem—walk, value—walked

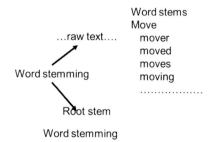

FIG. 10.1.17
Word stemming.

DOCUMENT METADATA

On occasion, it is useful to create an index of the documents that are being managed by the organization. The index can be created where there is only the index or the index can be created in conjunction with all the other features available in textual ETL. There are business justifications for both types of design.

Typical contents for a document index include such data as follows:

> Date document created
> Date document last accessed
> Date document last updated
> Document created by
> Document length
> Document title or name

Fig. 10.1.18 shows that document metadata can be created by textual ETL.

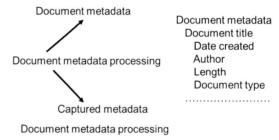

FIG. 10.1.18
Processing document metadata.

Suppose an organization has a contract document. Running textual ETL against the contract document can produce the following entry into the analytic database:

> Document name, byte, document title—Jones Contract, July 30, 1995, 32651 bytes, by Ted Van Duyn,…

DOCUMENT CLASSIFICATION

In addition to document metadata being able to be gathered, it is also possible to classify documents into an index. As an example of classifying documents, suppose the company is an oil company. One way of classifying document in an oil company is according to how the documents belong to a part of the organization. Some documents are about exploration. Some documents are about oil production. Some documents are about refining, oil distribution, and oil sales.

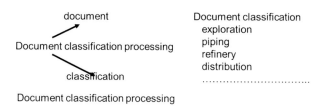

document

Document classification processing

classification

Document classification processing

Document classification
  exploration
  piping
  refinery
  distribution
  ....

FIG. 10.1.19
Classification of documents.

Textual ETL can read the document and determine which classification the document belongs in.

Fig. 10.1.19 shows the reading of raw text and the classification of documents.

As an example of document classification, suppose the corporation has a document on deepwater drilling. The database entry that would be produced looks like the following:

Document, byte, document type—exploration, document name

PROXIMITY ANALYSIS

Occasionally, the analyst needs to look at words or taxonomies that are in proximity to each other. For example, when a person sees the words "New York Yankees," the thought is about a baseball team. But when the words "New York" and "Yankees" are separated by two or three pages of text, the thought is something entirely different.

Therefore, it is useful to be able to do what is referred to as "proximity analysis" in textual ETL.

Proximity analysis operates on actual words or taxonomies (or any combination of these elements).

The analyst specifies the words/taxonomies that are to be analyzed, gives a proximity value for how close the words need to be in the text, and gives the proximity variable a name.

Fig. 10.1.20 shows proximity analysis operating against raw text.

As an example of proximity analysis against raw text, suppose there were raw text that looked like

...away in a manger no crib for a child....

Suppose the analyst had specified that the words manger, child, and crib were the words that made up the proximity variable—baby Jesus.

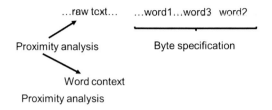

FIG. 10.1.20
Proximity analysis.

The results of the processing would look like the following:

Document name, byte, context—manger, crib, child, value—baby Jesus.

Care must be taken with proximity analysis as a great amount of system resources can be expended if there are many proximity variables to be sought.

FUNCTIONAL SEQUENCING WITHIN TEXTUAL ETL

There are many different functions that occur within textual ETL. Given on the document and the processing that needs to occur, the sequence the functions are done in has a great impact on the validity of the results. In fact, the sequence of the functions may determine whether the results that are achieved are accurate or not.

Therefore, one of the more important features of textual ETL is the ability to sequence the order in which functions are executed.

Fig. 10.1.21 shows that the different functions can be sequences at the discretion of the analyst.

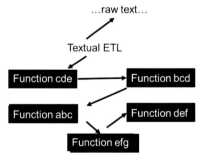

Sequencing the functions internal to
Textual ETL

FIG. 10.1.21
Sequencing the many functions of textual ETL.

INTERNAL REFERENTIAL INTEGRITY

In order to keep track of the many different variables and the many different relationships, textual ETL has an elaborate internal structure. In order for any given iteration of textual ETL to execute properly, the internal relationships MUST be defined properly. Stated differently, if the internal relationships inside textual ETL are not properly defined, textual ETL will not execute properly, and the results obtained will not be valid and accurate.

As an example of internal relationships inside textual ETL, there is a need to define a document. Once a document is defined, the different indexes that can be created for the document can be defined. Once the different indexes are defined, the delimiters that define the index must be defined. This entire infrastructure must be in place before textual ETL can operate accurately.

In order to ensure that ALL internal relationships are accurately defined, textual ETL has to have verification processing executed before textual ETL can be run.

Fig. 10.1.22 shows the need for verification processing.

If any one or more internal relationship is found to be out of place or not defined, the verification process sends a message identifying the relationship that is out of order and declares that the verification process has not been properly passed.

PREPROCESSING, POSTPROCESSING

There is a lot of complexity to the processing inside textual ETL. In most cases, a document can be processed entirely within the confines of textual ETL. However, on occasions, it is possible to either preprocess a document or postprocess the document (or do both) if necessary.

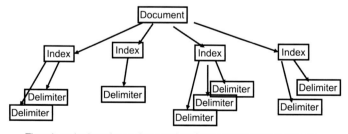

There is an intricate internal structuring of data definitions that requires
That the referential integrity of the relationship be checked and
verified before processing

FIG. 10.1.22
Verification processing.

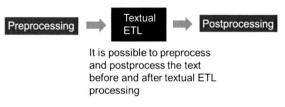

It is possible to preprocess
and postprocess the text
before and after textual ETL
processing

FIG. 10.1.23
Preprocessing and postprocessing.

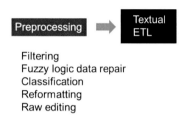

Filtering
Fuzzy logic data repair
Classification
Reformatting
Raw editing

FIG. 10.1.24
Preprocessor.

Fig. 10.1.23 shows that textual ETL can have either or both preprocessing or postprocessing.

Textual ETL is designed to do as much processing as possible within the scope of the program. The reason why neither preprocessing nor postprocessing is a normal part of the workflow is because of overhead. When you do either preprocessing or postprocessing, the overhead of processing is elevated.

There are several activities that occur in preprocessing, if in fact it is necessary to run preprocessing. Some of those activities include the following:

Filtering unwanted and unneeded data
Fuzzy logic repair of data
Classification of data
Raw editing of data

Fig. 10.1.24 shows the processing that occurs inside the preprocessor.

Occasionally, there is a document that simply cannot be processed by textual ETL without being first processed by a preprocessor. In cases like this, a preprocessor comes in handy.

After ETL processing, it is possible to postprocess a document. The functions accomplished in postprocessing are seen in Fig. 10.1.25.

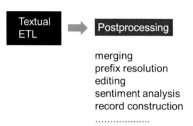

FIG. 10.1.25
Postprocessing.

On occasion, an index entry needs to be edited before it is clean. Or data need to be merged before they are in the form the end user expects.

These are all typical activities that can occur in postprocessing.

Mapping

Mapping is the process of defining the specifications of how a document is to be processed to textual ETL. There is a separate mapping for each type of document to be processed. One of the nice features of textual ETL is that the analyst can build on the specification of previous mappings when it comes time to build a new mapping. On many occasions, one mapping will be very similar to another mapping. It is not necessary for the analyst to create a new mapping if a previous mapping has been created that is similar.

At first glance, creating mappings is a bewildering process. It is like the airline pilot at the control of the airplane. There are many control panels and many switches and buttons. To the uninitiated, flying an airplane seems to be an almost monumental task.

However, once an organized approach is taken, learning to do mapping is a straightforward process.

Fig. 10.2.1 shows the questions the analyst needs to be asking as he/she does the mapping process.

Most of the questions are straightforward, but a few deserve an explanation.

The first observation is that there is a difference between repetitive and nonrepetitive records of text and structural text repetition. It is true that the words repetition and nonrepetition appear in this book. But they do not mean the same thing at all.

Repetitive records of data refer to records of data that repeatedly appear and are very similar in structure and even in context. Nonrepetitive records are records that appear where there is little or no repetition of records from one record to the next.

But repetitive text is something entirely different. Repetitive text refers to text appearing the same way or in a very similar way across more than one document. A simple example of repetitive text is boilerplate contracts. In boilerplate contracts, a lawyer has taken a basic contract and added a few words to it. The same contract appears over and over again in a repetitive manner. Another example of repetitive text is blood pressure. In blood pressure readings, blood

291

Data Architecture. https://doi.org/10.1016/B978-0-12-816916-2.00034-6

Contextualization
Is text repetitive? ──────────────→ Inline contextualization
Is text nonrepetitive? ─────────────→ Taxonomy resolution
Are there custom variables? ─────────→ Custom variable specification
Are there homographs? ──────────────→ Homographic resolution
Are there multiple dates? ───────────→ Date tagging
Are there multiple numerics? ────────→ Numeric tagging
Are there proximity variables? ──────→ Proximity variable specification
Basic editing
Remove stop words? ─────────────────→ Stop word processing
Alternate spelling? ─────────────────→ Alternate spelling processing
Numeric to text conversion? ─────────→ Numeric to text conversion
Negative inference? ─────────────────→ Negation scope of inference
Connectors? ────────────────────────→ Connector analysis
Associations? ──────────────────────→ Associative analysis
Miscellaneous
Document metadata? ─────────────────→ Document metadata stripping
Date standardization ───────────────→ Date standardization
Sub doc processing? ────────────────→ Sub doc specification

FIG. 10.2.1
The process of mapping.

pressure is written as "bp 124/68." The first number is the diastolic reading, and the second number is the systolic reading. When one encounters "bp 176/98," one knows exactly what is meant by the text. The text is repetitive.

Of course, you can use as many techniques and specifications are as applicable. You can use taxonomies, inline contextualization, and custom formatting, all at once. Or you can use only taxonomy processing or only inline contextualization. The data and what you want to do with the data dictate how you will choose to do what is needed.

One of the issues is choosing name for variables. For example, when you create a custom format, you choose a name for the variable. Suppose you wanted to pick up telephone number. You could use a specification of "999-999-9999." You need to name the variable that is created in a meaningful manner. The variable name becomes the context.

For example, for a telephone number, the name "variable001" would be a terrible name. No one would know what you meant when they encountered "variable001." Instead, a name like "telephone_number001" is much more appropriate. When a person reads "telephone_number001," it is immediately obvious what is meant.

The definition of a mapping is meant to be done in an iterative manner. It is HIGHLY unlikely that you will create a mapping and that the first mapping you create becomes the final mapping. It is MUCH MORE likely that you will create a mapping, run the mapping against the document, then go back, and make adjustments to the mapping. Documents are complex, and language is complex. There are plenty of nuances in language that people take for granted. Therefore, it is unrealistic to think that you will create the perfect mapping the first time you create one. It just doesn't happen with even the most experienced people.

Textual ETL often has multiple ways to handle the same interpretation. In many cases, the mapper will be able to accomplish the same results in more than one way. There is no right way or wrong way to do something in textual ETL. You can choose whatever way makes the most sense to you.

Textual ETL is sensitive to resource consumption. In general, textual ETL operates in an efficient manner. The only things to be avoided are the following:

Looking for more than four or five proximity variables. It is possible to swamp textual ETL by looking for many proximity variables.
Looking for many homographs. It is possible to swamp textual ETL by looking for more than four or five homograph resolutions.
Taxonomy processing. Loading more than 10000 words in a taxonomy can slow the system down.
Date standardization. Date standardization causes the system to use many resources. Do not use date standardization unless you really need to use it.

Analytics From Nonrepetitive Data

There is a wealth of information hidden in nonrepetitive data that is unable to be analyzed by traditional means. Only after the nonrepetitive data have been unlocked by textual disambiguation can analysis be done.

There are many examples of rich environments where there is a wealth of information in nonrepetitive data, such as the following:

E-mail
Call center
Corporate contracts
Warranty claims
Insurance claims
Medical records

But talking about the value of analysis of nonrepetitive data and actually showing the value are two different things. The world is not convinced until it sees concrete examples.

CALL CENTER INFORMATION

Most corporations have call centers. A call center is a corporate function where the corporation staffs phone operators to have conversations with customers. With a call center, the consumer has a voice of the corporation with whom a conversation can be made. In many ways, the call center becomes the direct interface the consumer has to the corporation.

The conversations that occur in the call center are many and diverse:

- Some people want to complain.
- Some people want to buy something.
- Some people want product information.
- Some people just want to talk.

There is then a wealth of information that transpires in the conversations that corporations with their customer or prospect base.

295

Data Architecture. https://doi.org/10.1016/B978-0-12-816916-2.00035-8

So, what does management of the corporation know about what takes place in their call center? The answer is that management knows very little about what transpires in the call center. At best, management knows how many calls occur daily and how long those calls are. But other than that, management knows very little about what is being discussed in their call center.

And why does management know so little about what takes place in the call center? The answer is that management needs to look at conversations and conversation is nonrepetitive data. And—prior to textual disambiguation—the computer cannot handle nonrepetitive data for the purposes of analytic processing.

However, with textual disambiguation, organizations can now start to understand the content of what is being discussed in call center conversations.

Fig. 10.3.1 shows the first step in doing analytics against telephone conversations.

The first step in analyzing conversations is to capture the conversations. Recording conversations is an easy thing to do. You just get a tape recorder and record (and make sure you are not breaking a law in doing so!)

After the conversation is recorded, the next step is to use voice recognition technology to convert the conversation to an electronic form. Voice transcription technology is not perfect. There are accents that need to be accounted for. There is slurred speech. There are people that talk really softly. There are angry people. In the best of circumstances, voice to text transcription is not a perfect science.

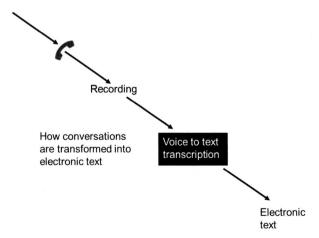

FIG. 10.3.1
Converting conversations into electronic text.

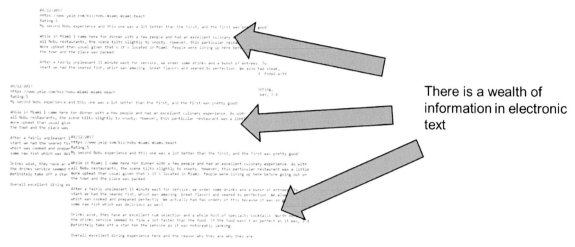

There is a wealth of information in electronic text

FIG. 10.3.2
Wealth of information in electronic text.

But if enough people speak where their words can be understood, then voice transcription works adequately.

Once the voice recordings have been recorded and transcribed, a wealth of information opens up to the analyst.

Fig. 10.3.2 depicts the world that has opened up.

The first step in unlocking the information found in the call center conversations is mapping the transcriptions. Mapping is the process of defining to textual disambiguation how to interpret the conversations. Typical mapping activities include the following:

Editing of stop words
Identification of homographs
Identification of taxonomies
Acronym resolution

While mapping must be done, the mapping that is created on day 1 can be used until day n. In other words, mapping is a onetime only activity. The mapping done the first day can be used thereafter. The analyst only has to do mapping once.

Fig. 10.3.3 shows that mapping is done from the transcriptions.

Once mapping is done, textual disambiguation is ready to process the transcriptions. The input to textual disambiguation is the raw text, the mapping, and

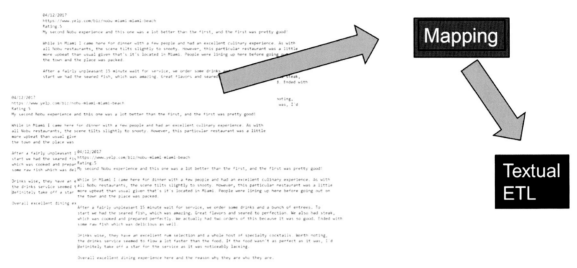

FIG. 10.3.3
Before text can be processed it must be mapped.

taxonomies. The output from textual disambiguation is an analytic database. The analytic database is in the form of any standard database that is used for analytic processing. By the time the analyst gets his/her hands on the database, it appears to be just like any other database the analyst has ever processed. The only difference is that the source of data for this database is nonrepetitive text.

Fig. 10.3.4 shows the processing that occurs inside textual disambiguation.

The output of textual disambiguation is a standard database, often thought of as being in the form of relational data. In many ways, the database that has been produced has text that has been "normalized." There are business relationships

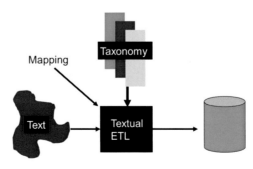

FIG. 10.3.4
Transforming text into a data base.

ndxwktextid	ndxoffset	ndxword	ndxsource	ndxsourcetype	ndxgroup	ndxandcode	ndxworddass
3b45939a-435c-...	223	brother	C:\proof of conc...	taxonomy parent	null	store	family
3b45939a-435c-...	206	card company	C:\proof of conc...	taxonomy parent	null	store	credit card comp...
3b45939a-435c-...	6	consumer	C:\proof of conc...	taxonomy parent	null	store	consumer
3b45939a-435c-...	6	consumer affairs	C:\proof of conc...	taxonomy parent	null	store	public forum
3b45939a-435c-...	186	credit report	C:\proof of conc...	taxonomy parent	null	store	credit report
3b45939a-435c-...	326	credit report	C:\proof of conc...	taxonomy parent	null	store	credit report
3b45939a-435c-...	448	credit report	C:\proof of conc...	taxonomy parent	null	store	credit report
3b45939a-435c-...	237	disability	C:\proof of conc...	taxonomy parent	null	store	me...
3b45939a-435c-...	32	equifax	C:\proof of conc...	taxonomy parent	null	store	
3b45939a-435c-...	310	[and]	C:\proof of conc...	taxonomy parent	null	store	con ... tor
3b45939a-435c-...	145	equifax	C:\proof of conc...	taxonomy parent	null	store	credit bureau
3b45939a-435c-...	32	equifax	C:\proof of conc...	taxonomy parent	null	store	public_agency
3b45939a-435c-...	145	equifax	C:\proof of conc...	taxonomy parent	null	store	public_agency
3b45939a-435c-...	475	investigat	C:\proof of conc...	taxonomy parent	null	store	analysis
3b45939a-435c-...	41	location	C:\proof of conc...	taxonomy parent	null	store	location
3b45939a-435c-...	110	my credit	C:\proof of conc...	taxonomy parent	null	store	consumer
3b45939a-435c-...	323	my credit	C:\proof of conc...	taxonomy parent	null	store	consumer
3b45939a-435c-...	445	my credit	C:\proof of conc...	taxonomy parent	null	store	consumer
3b45939a-435c-...	526	name	C:\proof of conc...	taxonomy parent	null	store	person
3b45939a-435c-...	526	name	C:\proof of conc...	taxonomy parent	null	store	personal_inform...
3b45939a-435c-...	374	[and]	C:\proof of conc...	taxonomy parent	null	store	connector

Text has been transformed into a standard data base

FIG. 10.3.5
Text has been transformed into a standard database.

that are buried in the database. These business relationships are a result of the mapping and the text that has been interpreted by the mapping.

Fig. 10.3.5 shows the database that has been produced.

After the database has been created by textual disambiguation, the next step is the selection of an analytic tool (or tools). Depending on the analysis to be done, it may be necessary to choose more than one analytic tool for analysis.

The analytic tool that is chosen only has to be able to process relational data. That is the only requirement for the analytic tool.

Fig. 10.3.6 shows that an analytic tool needs to be selected.

After the analytic tool has been selected, then analysis can commence. The analyst takes the data derived from the database that was derived from the transcriptions and does the analysis.

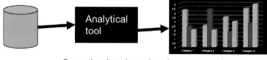

Analytical tool

Once the data base has been created, the data is analyzed and turned into a visualization

FIG. 10.3.6
An analytical tool needs to be selected.

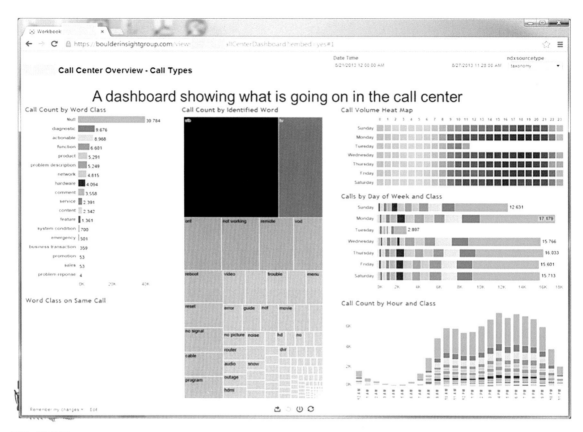

FIG. 10.3.7

A dashboard showing what is going on in the call center.

(NOTE: the following analysis was done by Chris Cox, of Boulder Insights, Boulder, Colorado, in Tableau.)

Each analytic tool has its favored method of presenting data. In this case, Tableau was used, and a dashboard was created.

Fig. 10.3.7 shows a dashboard created for analyzing the call center information.

The dashboard reflects the content of the activity that has transpired within the call center. With the dashboard, the analyst can see the following:

- When activities were processed
- What kind of activities were processed
- The actual content of calls
- The demographics of what was discussed
- And so forth

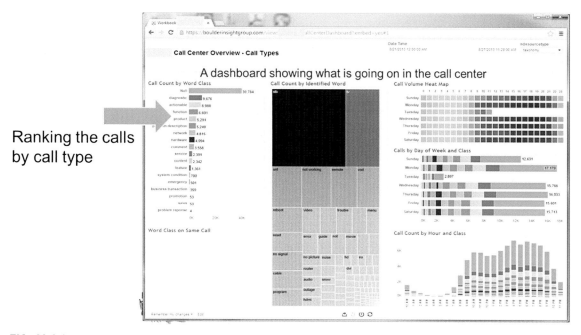

Ranking the calls by call type

FIG. 10.3.8
Ranking the calls by call type.

The dashboard gives a wealth of information that is organized and is graphical. In a glance, management can see what is transpiring in the call center.

As an example of the information contained in the dashboard, consider Fig. 10.3.8.

In Fig. 10.3.8, the diagram is a synopsis of the type of call that has passed through the call center. Each call is categorized as to what the major purpose of the call was. Then, the calls are ranked as to how many of which type occurred during the reporting period. If there were no other information on the dashboard, this information is extremely useful by itself.

Another type of information found on the dashboard is the information relating to what time of day the calls came in at. Fig. 10.3.9 shows this information.

Not only is the hour of day identified, but also the classification by the type of call is identified. It is worth noting that using the dashboard approach, drill down processing is a possibility. For each hour for each category of call, the analyst can invoke drill down processing to investigate more thoroughly each class of call that came in during any given hour.

A related type of information that is available is the type of phone call by day of the week. This type of information is seen in Fig. 10.3.10.

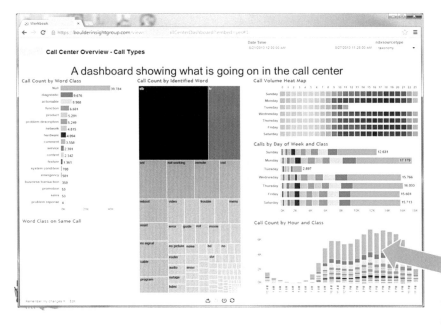

Call center activity on an hour by hour basis

FIG. 10.3.9
Call center activity on an hour by hour basis.

Call center activity on a day by day basis

FIG. 10.3.10
Call center activity on a day by day basis.

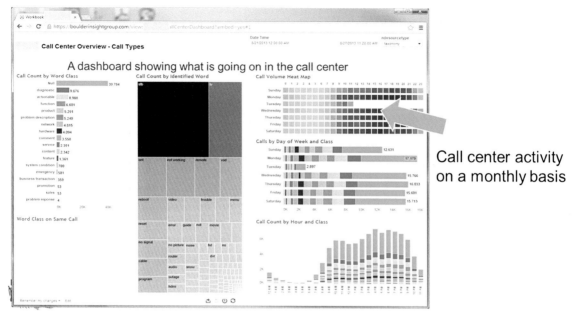

FIG. 10.3.11
Call center activity on a monthly basis.

And yet, another type of information that is available on the dashboard is information about the day of the month when calls occurred. Fig. 10.3.11 shows a "heat map" depicting the pattern of calls throughout the month.

But perhaps, the most useful information on the dashboard is the information shown by Fig. 10.3.12. In Fig. 10.3.12, it is seen in the form of a histogram that the actual subjects were discussed during call center activity. The most discussed subject has the black box that is largest. The next most discussed subject is the next largest box.

By looking at the histogram, the management has a very good idea what subjects are on the mind of their customer base.

Looking at the dashboard tells management in a glance what management needs to know about what is going on in the call center.

As impressive as the dashboard is, the dashboard would not be possible without the data being placed in a standard database.

There is a progression of processing and data that makes possible the creation of the dashboard. That progression looks like the following:

Repetitive data → mapping → textual ETL → standard database → analytic tool → dashboard

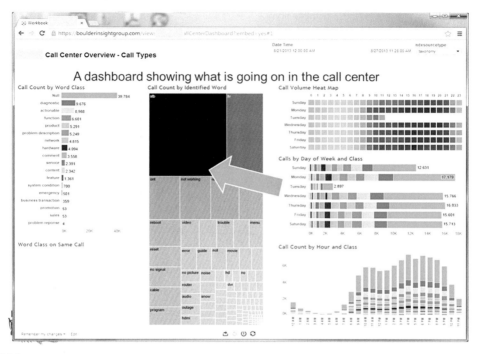

FIG. 10.3.12
A histogram showing the subjects discussed during call center processing.

MEDICAL RECORDS

Call center records are important and are at the center of business value. But call center records are hardly the only form of nonrepetitive records that are valuable. Another form of valuable nonrepetitive data is medical records. Medical records are written usually as a patient goes through a procedure or some event of medical care. The records—once written—are valuable to many people and organizations, to the physician, to the patient, to the hospital or provider, to research organizations, and more.

The challenge with medical records is that they contain narrative information. Narrative information is necessary and useful to the physician. But narrative information is not useful to the computer. In order to be used in analytic processing, the narrative information must be put into the form of a database in a standard database format.

This is a classical case of nonrepetitive data being placed in the form of a database. What is needed is textual ETL.

In order to see how textual ETL is used, consider a medical record. (NOTE: the medical record being shown is a real record. However, it is from a country other than the United States and is not subject to the regulations of HIPAA.)

When looking at medical records, the records start to take a recognizable pattern. The first part of the medical record is the identification part. In this part of the record, one or more identifying criteria are found (Fig. 10.3.13).

SES Number: 000178701
Name: Chica Maria Francesca de Almeida
Dt. Born:. 27/09/1930
Age: 78
Gender: Female
Address: 511 QR SET 04 28 Home
City: FERN
03/06/2009
10:02
Patient with good diet acceptance.
CD: maintained
RODELUZI LUCAS DE ANDRADE nutritionist
03/06/2009
08:10
ICU - HRSam
Medical developments
- 42 days in the ICU
- Pneumonia - treated
- Prolonged MV - difficult weaning
- Eye Conjunctivitis in D - treated
- Monilia intertriginous below the breast D (Started nystatin + zinc oxide topical, topical nystatin but missing)
- ATB: Unasyn 20/04 to 04/05; Azithromycin 21/04 to 04/05.
Patient hemodynamically stable, afebrile, with good diuresis.
Under VM, AC, FiO ^{2} 35%, PEEP 5, FR 14/20 ipm, VC 450/430 ml, 97% SpO ^{2}. Modify for PSV.
Accepting oral diet.
Diuresis 24h 2300 24h ml BH: - 680 ml
-Ap.resp: MVBD with scattered rhonchi
-Ap.CV: BRNF in 2Q no murmurs

FIG. 10.3.13
A medical record.

In the second part of the medical record, there is narrative information. In the narrative section, some doctor or nurse has written down some characterization of a medical event—a diagnosis, a procedure, an observation, and so forth.

In the third section of the medical record are lab results that are relevant to the reason why the patient is in medical care.

Fig. 10.3.14 shows a typical medical record.

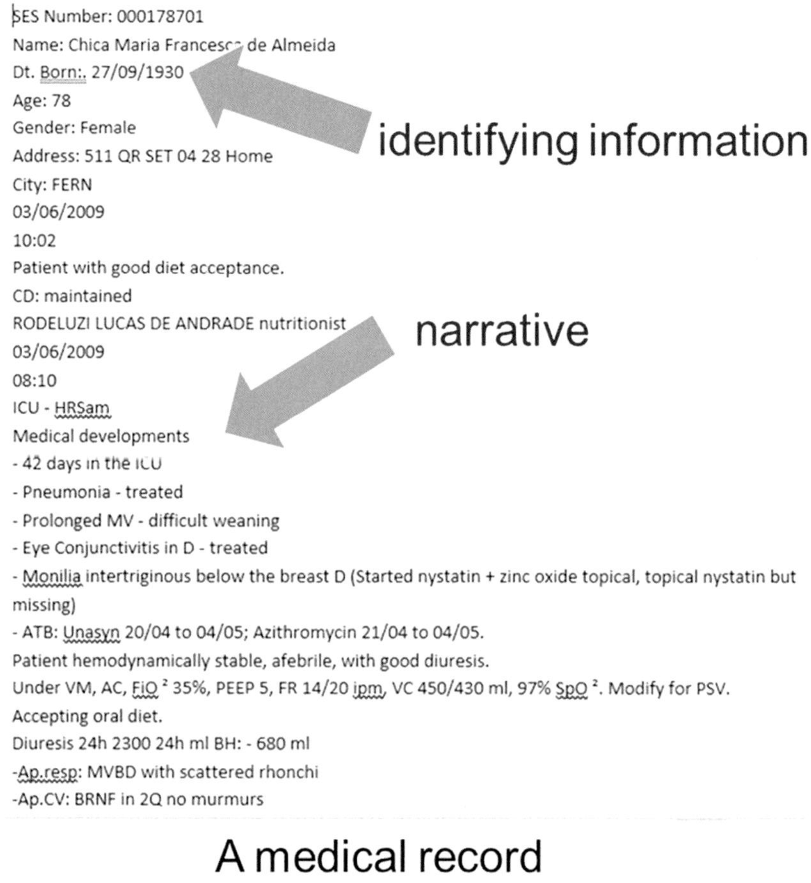

SES Number: 000178701
Name: Chica Maria Francesc- de Almeida
Dt. Born:. 27/09/1930
Age: 78
Gender: Female
Address: 511 QR SET 04 28 Home
City: FERN

identifying information

03/06/2009
10:02
Patient with good diet acceptance.
CD: maintained
RODELUZI LUCAS DE ANDRADE nutritionist

narrative

03/06/2009
08:10
ICU - HRSam
Medical developments
- 42 days in the ICU
- Pneumonia - treated
- Prolonged MV - difficult weaning
- Eye Conjunctivitis in D - treated
- Monilia intertriginous below the breast D (Started nystatin + zinc oxide topical, topical nystatin but missing)
- ATB: Unasyn 20/04 to 04/05; Azithromycin 21/04 to 04/05.
Patient hemodynamically stable, afebrile, with good diuresis.
Under VM, AC, FiO_2 35%, PEEP 5, FR 14/20 ipm, VC 450/430 ml, 97% SpO_2. Modify for PSV.
Accepting oral diet.
Diuresis 24h 2300 24h ml BH: - 680 ml
-Ap.resp: MVBD with scattered rhonchi
-Ap.CV: BRNF in 2Q no murmurs

A medical record

FIG. 10.3.14
Narrative in the medical record.

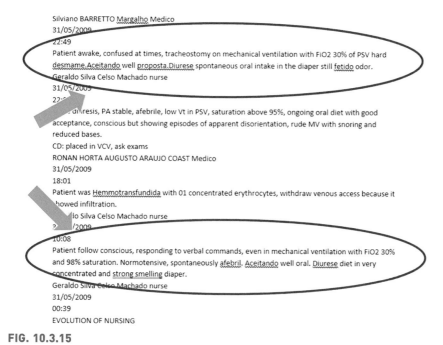

Silviano BARRETTO Margalho Medico
31/05/2009
22:49
Patient awake, confused at times, tracheostomy on mechanical ventilation with FiO2 30% of PSV hard desmame.Aceitando well proposta.Diurese spontaneous oral intake in the diaper still fetido odor.
Geraldo Silva Celso Machado nurse
31/05/2009
22:
diuresis, PA stable, afebrile, low Vt in PSV, saturation above 95%, ongoing oral diet with good acceptance, conscious but showing episodes of apparent disorientation, rude MV with snoring and reduced bases.
CD: placed in VCV, ask exams
RONAN HORTA AUGUSTO ARAUJO COAST Medico
31/05/2009
18:01
Patient was Hemmotransfundida with 01 concentrated erythrocytes, withdraw venous access because it howed infiltration.
lo Silva Celso Machado nurse
/2009
10:08
Patient follow conscious, responding to verbal commands, even in mechanical ventilation with FiO2 30% and 98% saturation. Normotensive, spontaneously afebril. Aceitando well oral. Diurese diet in very concentrated and strong smelling diaper.
Geraldo Silva Celso Machado nurse
31/05/2009
00:39
EVOLUTION OF NURSING

FIG. 10.3.15
Each episode of care has its own narrative.

In a medical record, there is a narrative every time a medical event occurs. Fig. 10.3.15 shows that there is more than one narrative section relating to a patient's visit in the hospital.

The techniques used in processing the medical record include all the ways that textual ETL can process text.

Fig. 10.3.16 shows some of the ways that medical records are processed.

The result of textual ETL processing the medical record is a normalized database.

Fig. 10.3.17 shows the normalized textual-based database that has resulted from textual ETL processing a medical record.

Once the text has been placed in a standard relational database, it is useful for analytic processing. Now, millions of medical records can be analyzed.

Silviano BARRETTO Margalho Medico

31/05/2009

22:49

Patient awake, confused at times, tracheostomy on mechanical ventilation with FiO2 30% of PSV hard desmame.Aceitando well proposta.Diurese spontaneous oral intake in the diaper still fetido odor.

Geraldo Silva Celso Machado nurse

31/05/2009

22:04

Good diuresis, PA stable, afebrile, low Vt in PSV, saturation above 95%, ongoing oral diet with good acceptance, conscious but showing episodes of apparent disorientation, rude MV with snoring and reduced bases.

CD: placed in VCV, ask exams

RONAN HORTA AUGUSTO ARAUJO COAST Medico

31/05/2009

18:01

Patient was Hemmotransfundida with 01 concentrated erythrocytes, withdraw venous access because it showed infiltration.

Geraldo Silva Celso Machado nurse

31/05/2009

10:08

Patient follow conscious, responding to verbal commands, even in mechanical ventilation with FiO2 30% and 98% saturation Normotensive spontaneously afebril. Aceitando well oral. Diurese diet in very concentrated and strong smelling diaper.

Geraldo Silva Celso Machado nurse

31/05/2009

00:39

EVOLUTION OF NURSING

FIG. 10.3.16

Different words are treated differently by textual ETL.

:\proof of concept - credit bureau\equifax\Equi...	Consumer Affairs	7	null	named	2018-04-03 13:42:18.000	site
:\proof of concept - credit bureau\equifax\Equi...	Equifax	33	null	named	2018-04-03 13:42:18.000	company
:\proof of concept - credit bureau\equifax\Equi...	OH	51	null	named	2018-04-03 13:42:18.000	location001
:\proof of concept - credit bureau\equifax\Equi...	word	62	internal source	custom form	2018-04-03 13:42:18.000	context
:\proof of concept - credit bureau\equifax\Equi...	1.0	62	internal source	named	2018-04-03 13:42:18.000	rating
:\proof of concept - credit bureau\equifax\Equi...	2018-02-20 00:00:00	72	internal source	named	2018-04-03 13:42:18.000	date
:\proof of concept - credit bureau\equifax\Equi...	2018-02-20 00:00:00	71	internal source	named	2018-04-03 13:42:18.000	date001
:\proof of concept - credit bureau\equifax\Equi...	.	218	internal source	custom form	2018-04-03 13:42:18.000	eos
:\proof of concept - credit bureau\equifax\Equi...	.	339	internal source	custom form	2018-04-03 13:42:18.000	eos
:\proof of concept - credit bureau\equifax\Equi...	.	461	internal source	custom form	2018-04-03 13:42:18.000	eos
:\proof of concept - credit bureau\equifax\Equi...	.	561	internal source	custom form	2018-04-03 13:42:18.000	eos

FIG. 10.3.17

A word and its context.

Operational Analytics: Response Time

Analytics can be used throughout the computing environment. Indeed, one of the values of even computerizing a system is to be able to do analytics.

One of the most important environments in corporate computing is that of the operational environment. The operational environment is one that is the place where detailed, up to the second decisions are made. The operational environment is used primarily by the clerical community. The operational environment is where the business of the corporation is transacted.

Fig. 11.1.1 shows that there are two primary processing and decision-making environments in most corporations. There is the operational environment, and there is the management decision environment.

There are several criteria that enhance the success of the operational environment. Some of those criteria include the following:

- The ability to create, update, and delete individual transactions
- The ability to have access to data
- The ability to have integrity of transaction processing
- The ability to handle large volumes of data
- The ability to handle data systematically
- The ability to execute quickly

Of all of these factors, the ability to access and process data quickly is the most important in operational systems.

Fig. 11.1.2 shows that performance—the ability to execute transactions quickly—is the most important criteria in the operational environment.

There are many reasons why performance—speed of execution—is so important in the operational environment. The main reason why performance is so important is that the computer has been integrated into the day-to-day business of the running of the corporation. When there is a problem with performance, the day-to-day business of the corporation grinds to a halt.

In order to understand the importance of speed of transaction execution, consider the following circumstances:

309

Data Architecture. https://doi.org/10.1016/B978-0-12-816916-2.00036-X

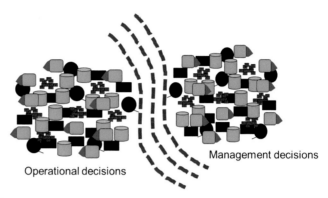

FIG. 11.1.1
Difference between operational decisions and managerial decisions.

FIG. 11.1.2
Operational decisions.

- In a bank, a bank teller must wait 60 seconds for a transaction to process. The bank teller and the customer being served are both irritated.
- In an airline reservation, the airline clerk must wait 60 seconds to conduct business across the network. Long queues of angry travelers build up waiting for the system to finish processing.
- In an ATM environment, customers drive away—angry—when the ATM machine takes 60 seconds to complete a transaction.
- On the Internet, when using a site, viewers go away when the site takes a long time in order to complete a transaction.

And there are many, many other circumstances where transaction response time affects the business of the corporation.

Fig. 11.1.3 shows that transaction response time is essential to the satisfactory running of the business.

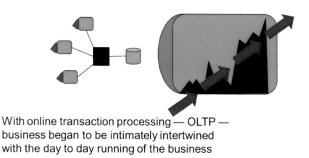

With online transaction processing — OLTP —
business began to be intimately intertwined
with the day to day running of the business

FIG. 11.1.3
OLTP.

TRANSACTION RESPONSE TIME

Transaction response time is the most important element of the operational environment. What then are the elements of response time? Fig. 11.1.4 shows the elements of transaction response time.

At step (1), a transaction is initiated. A customer wants to see how much is in his/her account. A shelf stocker wants to place an item on the shelf of a store. A clerk wants to mark the successful manufacture of an order. An airline wants to upgrade a customer. These are all forms of initiating a transaction.

At step (2), the transaction arrives at the computer. The program goes into execution. Variables are initialized. Calculations are made. Algorithms are executed. Then, somewhere along the line of doing its processing, the computer program discovers that it needs to go to a database and find some data in order to execute.

At step (3), a request is made to the DBMS in order to find data. The DBMS honors the request and goes off to search for some data. Upon finding the data, the DBMS packages the data and sends it back to the computer.

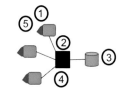

The elements of response time:
(1) – the transaction is initiated
(2) – the application is run
(3) – data is gathered
(4) – the output is prepared
(5) – the output results are displayed

FIG. 11.1.4
The elements of response time.

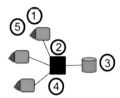

Response time is measured in the time it takes
to go from (1) to (5)

FIG. 11.1.5
Measuring response time.

The program commences processing again. The program discovers that it needs more data so the program issues another request for data to the DBMS. Data are returned to the program.

Finally, upon conclusion of the program—at step (4)—the program inside the computer is ready to return results to the user making the request.

The results are returned to the user at step (5).

Response time inside the computer is measured from the length of time it takes for steps (2), (3), and (4) to execute. On the average response, time is typically between 1 and 2 seconds. Given all the computer had to go through, it is amazing that response time is as fast as it is.

Fig. 11.1.5 shows how response time is measured.

Far and away, the biggest element of response time (i.e., steps (2), (3), and (4)) is the amount of time needed to search for and retrieve data. The processing inside the computer—steps (2) and (4)—occurs very quickly. It is step (3) that chews up the most amount of time.

There is a term for step (3). That term is an "I/O" operation (or an "input/output" operation). An I/O refers to the work done by the system in making either an input or an output to the database managed by the system.

Fig. 11.1.6 depicts an I/O operation.

There are two kinds of speeds found in a computer—electronic speeds and mechanical speeds. Electronic speeds are measured typically in nanoseconds. Mechanical speeds are measured in terms of milliseconds. The difference in speeds is akin to flying on a jet airplane and riding a bicycle. There is that much difference between the two types of speeds.

The internal operations of a computer operate in electronic speeds. The I/O operations of reading or writing to the database operate at mechanical speeds.

In order to get a program to operate quickly, the analyst needs to minimize the number of I/Os that are being done.

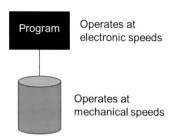

FIG. 11.1.6
An I/O operation.

Minimizing the number of I/Os being done has the effect of speeding a program in its execution. But minimizing I/Os also has the effect of reducing the speed of every other transaction that is awaiting execution.

In a computer, a single program executes one at a time. The other programs that need to execute wait while the one program that is in execution finishes. The time the other programs have to wait is called "queue" time.

Fig. 11.1.7 illustrates queue time.

There are two primary ways that queue time can build inside a computer—either a single program takes a long time to execute or the rate at which transactions arrive at the queue exceeds the average execution time.

In any case in many computers, it is queue time that significantly causes slowdowns in processing.

Another way of looking at the phenomenon of performance is in terms of the number of I/Os being done by a transaction.

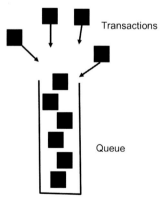

FIG. 11.1.7
Queue time can become a factor.

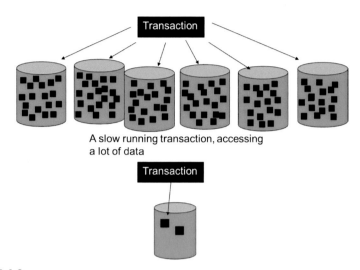

A slow running transaction, accessing a lot of data

FIG. 11.1.8
A fast running transaction accessing a small amount of data.

Fig. 11.1.8 shows two different kinds of transactions.

The transaction on the top is not going to be a fast-running transaction. It has too many I/Os that it has to do. The transaction on the bottom has a much better chance of being a fast-running transaction. It has only 1 or 2 I/Os that it must do.

Therefore, looking at the number of I/Os that a transaction must do is a good way to look at the performance characteristics of a transaction.

There is a way to reduce the amount of I/Os that a transaction has to do.

Consider the transaction shown in Fig. 11.1.9.

In Fig. 11.1.9, it is seen that lots of different kinds of data are needed in order to execute the transaction. If the transaction goes and looks on disk storage for all the different places where the data reside, the transaction will not be a fast-running transaction.

What the database designer could do is to combine all or some of the data into a single database design. There is nothing that says that data of different types must be placed in different databases. In order to enhance performance, the analyst could combine all the data (or even some of the data) into a single database.

This type of design is referred to as a "denormalized" design. Fig. 11.1.10 shows that data can be denormalized.

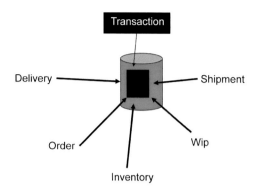

FIG. 11.1.9
Different types of data are grouped together to improve performance.

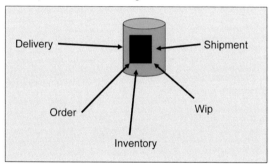

FIG. 11.1.10
Denormalized data.

Once the data are denormalized, the number of I/Os needed to execute the transaction is reduced. The transaction now becomes a fast-running transaction.

Every now and then, it happens that a transaction needs to look at a lot of data, regardless of how the data are organized. Such programs are typical of report programs that look at the day's activities or the month's activities.

Fig. 11.1.11 shows one of these long-running programs.

What happens if one of these long-running programs is mixed with a lot of short-running programs, as seen in Fig. 11.1.12?

The answer is performance for the entire system comes to a halt. The minute the long-running program goes into execution, the queue builds behind the long-running program. And that defeats the purpose of the operational environment.

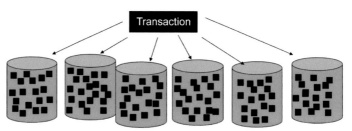

Every now and then it is necessary to access
a lot of data in a single transaction

FIG. 11.1.11
Accessing a lot of data in a single transaction.

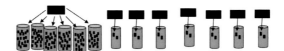

FIG. 11.1.12
Having one transaction that looks at a lot of data disrupts response time for everyone else.

So what can the analyst do if it is necessary to run a long-running program (which is a fact of life)?

Fig. 11.1.13 shows some solutions to allowing the system to run long-running programs and to have online transaction response time.

One solution to resolving the conflict between long-running programs and the need for consistent response time is to partition off the time slots for running

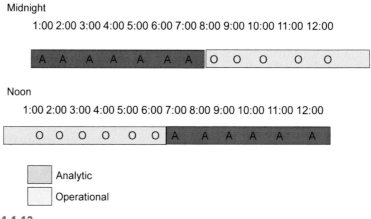

FIG. 11.1.13
Dividing the day into different types of processing hours.

on the computer. All fast-running transactions run during the daytime when business needs for there to be good response time, and long-running programs are able to be executed in the wee hours of the morning, when no one else is using the machine.

An alternative is to execute long-running programs on a different machine on a different DBMS than the database and machine that the transactions are operating on. This alternative works whenever there is no need for the long-running program to access the actual data that are being transacted against.

Operational Analytics

The operational environment is one where the day-to-day activities of the corporation take place. Sales are made. Bank deposits are made. Insurance policies are sold. Grocery shelves are stocked.

In short, the world operates in a modern efficient manner when the operational world runs properly.

The data that are generated by operational processing are of enormous value to the world.

Fig. 12.1.1 depicts the operational environment.

Operational analytics consist of the decisions that are made as a result of the execution of transactions in the operational environment. Those points of data that are at the heart of operational analytics are generated by operational systems. Operational systems are those systems that run transactions and manage data inside a database management system.

There are many characteristics of operational systems. The essence of operational applications is depicted in Fig. 12.1.2.

Operational systems have the mission of being speedy execution, operation against data at a detailed level, and bound together in applications.

Because of the need for speedy execution of transaction, data are often denormalized. Denormalization is the design technique that the designer needs to use in order to enhance performance. But because data are denormalized, they are "pulled apart." One unit of data is found in one database, and the same unit of data is found in another database. The fragmentation of data into separate databases is a natural result of the need for denormalization of data in a high-performance environment. Denormalization of data in the high-performance transaction processing environment is a normal, natural phenomenon.

But there is a side effect of denormalization of data. Because data are denormalized in the operational environment, data are not integrated. The same unit of data often exists in several places. (Or in the worst case, the same unit of data exists in many, many, many places.) The net effect of the same data existing in many places is that the data lose their integrity. One user accesses the data in

319

Data Architecture. https://doi.org/10.1016/B978-0-12-816916-2.00037-1

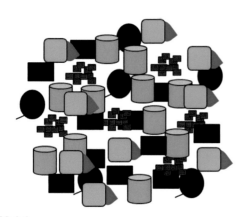

FIG. 12.1.1
Operational environment.

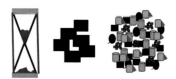

The essence of operational applications
(1) – speed of processing
(2) – operations at the detailed level
(3) – applications

FIG. 12.1.2
The essence of operational processing.

one place and gets one value. Another user accesses the same data in another place and gets a very different value.

Both users think they have the correct value of data. And both users have very different values.

This lack of integrity of data is seen in Fig. 12.1.3.

One can see the frustration across the organization. How in the world can decisions be made when no one knows what the correct value of data is?

But the lack of integrity is not the only problem with operational applications. Another problem with operational applications is that there is only a minimal amount of historical data to be found in operational applications.

There is a good reason for there being minimal history in operational applications. The reason for the minimal amount of historical data is that the need for high-performance trumps all other operational objectives. System tuners

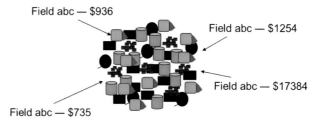

Field abc — $936

Field abc — $1254

Field abc — $17384

Field abc — $735

FIG. 12.1.3
The lack of integrity of data.

Operational
environment
There is very little historical data
in the operational environment

Data warehouse

Single version of the truth

Subject oriented, integrated, non volatile,
time variant collection of data for the purpose
of making management decisions

FIG. 12.1.4
Very little historical data found in the operational environment.

FIG. 12.1.5
The data warehouse—the single version of the truth.

long ago discovered that the more data there are in a system, the slower the system runs. Therefore, in order to have optimal performance, system tuners jettisoned historical data. Because operational systems have a need for high performance, of necessity, there is little historical data found in the operational environment.

Fig. 12.1.4 shows that there is minimal historical data found in the operational environment.

But there is a problem with jettisoning historical data. That problem is that historical data are useful for many purposes. Historical data are useful in the following:

Spotting and measuring trends
Understanding the long-term habits of customers
Looking at developing patterns
And so forth

Because of the lack of integrity of data and because of the need to have a place to house historical data, there arose a need for a different kind of architectural structure than the operational application. Because of the need to do analytic processing (as opposed to transactional processing), there appeared in the world a structure called the "data warehouse."

Fig. 12.1.5 shows the emergence of the data warehouse.

The definition of a data warehouse has been around since the beginning of data warehousing. A data warehouse is a subject-oriented, integrated, nonvolatile, time-variant collection of data in support of management's decisions. A data warehouse contains detailed, integrated data that are historical.

Another way of thinking about a data warehouse is that a data warehouse is a "single version of the truth." The data warehouse is the detailed, integrated bedrock data that can be used for decision-making purposes throughout the organization.

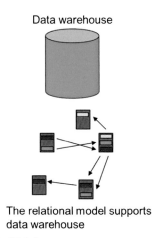

Data warehouse

The relational model supports
data warehouse

FIG. 12.1.6

The relational model and the data warehouse.

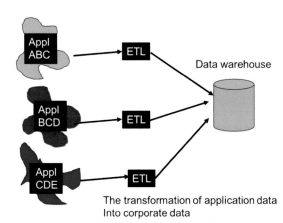

The transformation of application data
Into corporate data

FIG. 12.1.7

Transforming application data into corporate data.

The data model that best serves as a basis for the data warehouse is the relational model. The relational model is normalized data and is good for representing data at its most granular level.

Fig. 12.1.6 shows the relational model that serves as a design foundation for the data warehouse.

Data are loaded into the data warehouse from the operational applications. Data in the operational applications reside in the applications in a denormalized state. Data are loaded into the data warehouse through technology known as "ETL" ("extract/transform/load") technology.

Fig. 12.1.7 shows the loading of data into the data warehouse from the operational environment, passing through technology known as ETL technology.

In fact, data are not "loaded" into the data warehouse at all. The reality is that data are transformed as they pass from the operational environment to the data warehouse environment. In the operational environment, data are designed into a denormalized state. In the data warehouse, data are designed into the normalized state. The purpose of ETL processing is to transform application data into corporate data. To the uninitiated, this transformation doesn't seem to be a difficult process. But in fact, it is.

In order to understand the transformation accomplished by textual ETL, refer to the transformation depicted in Fig. 12.1.8.

In Fig. 12.1.8, application data hold different renditions of data for gender and measurement. In one application, gender is indicated by the values—male and female. In another application, gender is indicated by 1 and 0. In one

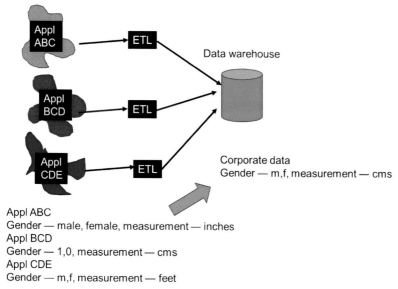

Appl ABC
Gender — male, female, measurement — inches
Appl BCD
Gender — 1,0, measurement — cms
Appl CDE
Gender — m,f, measurement — feet

FIG. 12.1.8
Transformations.

application, measurement is made in inches. In another application, measurement is made in centimeters.

In the data warehouse, there is one indicator for gender—m and f. In the data warehouse, there is one unit of measurement—centimeters. The transformation from application data to corporate data is made during the ETL process.

The diagram in Fig. 12.1.8 is a good illustration of what is meant by the difference between application data and corporate data.

A fundamental concept to the integrity of data and the establishment of corporate data is the "system of record." The system of record is the definitive data of the corporation. In the operational environment, the system of record is the data that feed values to the data warehouse.

Fig. 12.1.9 illustrates the system of record in the operational environment.

It is worthwhile noting that the system of record moves from one environment to the next. The system of record for operational data resides in the operational environment. But as data pass into the data warehouse, the system of record also passes into the data warehouse. The difference is the timeliness of the data. Data in the operational environment are accurate as of the moment of access. Stated differently, data in the operational environment are up to the second accurate data. But when the system of record data moves to the data warehouse, the system of record data becomes accurate as to the moment in history that is reflected in the data warehouse. The system of record is historically accurate in the data warehouse.

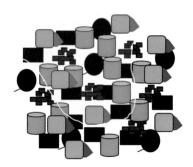

FIG. 12.1.9
The system of record in the operational environment.

DIFFERENT PERSPECTIVES OF DATA

One of the most important functions of the data warehouse is the ability to serve as a foundation for different organizations to look at the same data differently and still have the same foundation of data.

Fig. 12.1.10 shows this capability.

The reason the data warehouse can serve as a foundation of data for different organizations is that the data in the data warehouse are granular and integrated. You can think of the data in the data warehouse as grains of sand. Sand can be shaped

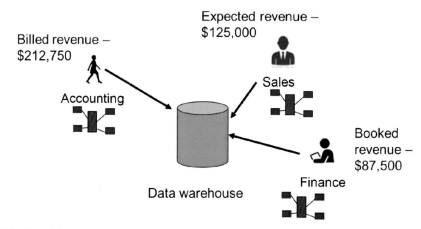

FIG. 12.1.10
Different departments look at the same data differently.

into many different final goods—silicon chips, wine glasses, automobile head-lights, body parts, and so forth. And by the same token, marketing can look at data in the data warehouse one way, finance can look at data in the data warehouse another way, and sales can look at data in the data warehouse yet another way. And yet, all of the organizations are looking at the same data, and there is reconcilability of data.

The ability to serve different communities is one of the most important characteristics of the data warehouse.

DATA MARTS

The way that the data warehouse serves the different communities is through the creation of data marts. Fig. 12.1.11 shows that the data warehouse serves as a basis for data in the data marts.

In Fig. 12.1.11, it is seen that there are different data marts for different organizations. The data warehouse and its granular data serve as a basis for the data found in the data marts. The granular data in the data warehouse are summarized and otherwise aggregated into the form that each data mart requires. Note that each data mart and each organization will have their own way of summarizing and aggregating data. Stated differently, the data mart for finance will be different from the data mart for marketing.

Data marts are best based on the dimensional model, as seen in Fig. 12.1.12.

In the dimensional model are found fact tables and dimension tables. Tables and dimension tables are attached together to form what is known as the "star" join. The star join is designed to be optimal for the informational needs of a department.

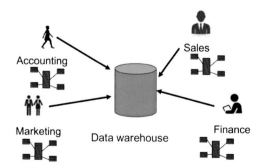

Customized data marts serve the needs of the different departments. The data marts are fed from the data warehouse

FIG. 12.1.11
Data marts are fed from the data warehouse.

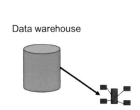

Data warehouse

Data marts are built from the dimensional model and are called star joins. Data from the data warehouse feeds the data marts

FIG. 12.1.12
Star joins.

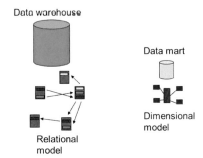

Data warehouses are built on the basis of the relational model. Data marts are built on the basis of the dimensional model

FIG. 12.1.13
Data marts and the dimensional model.

The data marts and the data warehouse combine to form an architecture, as seen in Fig. 12.1.13.

In Fig. 12.1.13, it is seen that the integration of data occurs as data are placed in an integrated, historical fashion in the data warehouse. Once the foundation of data is built, the data are passed into the different data marts. As data are passed into the data marts, data are summarized or otherwise aggregated.

THE OPERATIONAL DATA STORE—ODS

There is another data structure that sometimes appears in data architecture, and that structure is one known as the ODS, or "operational data store."

Fig. 12.1.14 depicts an ODS.

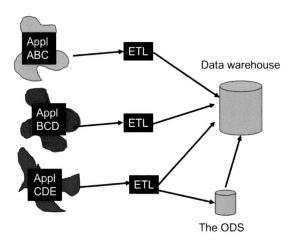

FIG. 12.1.14
The ODS.

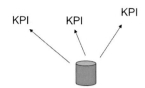

Data marts typically contain multiple KPIs

FIG. 12.1.15
The ODS.

FIG. 12.1.16
Data marts and KPIs.

The ODS has some characteristics of the data warehouse and some characteristics of the operational environment. The ODS can be updated in real time, and the ODS can support high-performance transaction processing. But the ODS also contains integrated data.

In many ways, the ODS is a "halfway" store for data.

Fig. 12.1.15 shows the ODS.

The ODS is an optional data structure for corporations. Some corporations have need of an ODS; other corporations do not need the ODS. As a rule, if an organization does significant amounts of transaction processing, it will need an ODS.

The type of data that is found in the data marts usually includes what is known as a KPI. A KPI stands for a "key performance indicator."

Fig. 12.1.16 illustrates that data marts usually contain one or more KPIs.

Every corporation has its own set of KPIs. Some typical KPIs might include the following:

    Cash on hand
    Number of employees
    Product order backlog
    The sales pipeline
    New product acceptance
    Inventory for sale

KPIs are typically measured on a monthly basis. Fig. 12.1.17 shows such a periodic measurement of KPIs.

There are lots of reasons to measure KPIs on a monthly basis. One value is the ability to spot trends as the trends are happening.

There is a problem with spotting trends on KPIs on a monthly basis, and that problem is that many KPIs are seasonal. By looking at a month-by-month trend line, the trend may not be accurate. To spot seasonal trends, it is necessary to have a measurement of KPIs over multiple years, as seen in Fig. 12.1.18.

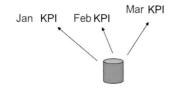

FIG. 12.1.17
Data marts typically contain multiple KPIs.

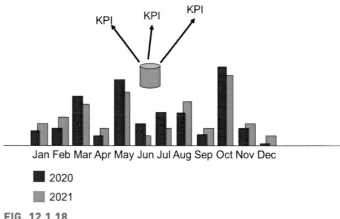

FIG. 12.1.18
Many KPIs are seasonal.

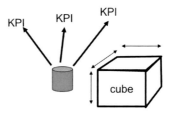

Data marts can also be cast in the form of OLAP or cube technology

FIG. 12.1.19
OLAP technology.

In addition to having KPIs, data marts oftentimes housed in what are termed "cubes." Fig. 12.1.19 shows that cubes often appear in data marts or in conjunction with data marts.

A cube is an arrangement of data that allows data to be examined from different perspectives.

One of the characteristics of data marts is that they are relatively easy and fast to create. Because of the ease of creation, most organizations build new data marts rather than do maintenance to existing data marts.

Fig. 12.1.20 shows that data marts are created rather than maintaining older data marts that need to have a reflection of new requirements.

The long-term effect of constantly creating new data marts is that after a while, the organization is supporting many data marts that aren't being used.

Because data marts contain KPIs, there is great propensity for change. That is because KPIs are constantly changing. Every time the focus of a business

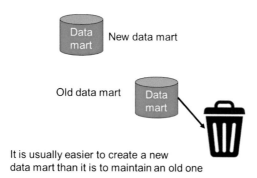

It is usually easier to create a new
data mart than it is to maintain an old one

FIG. 12.1.20
Throwing data marts away.

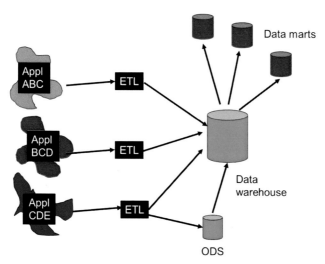

FIG. 12.1.21
Modern operational architecture.

changes, so do its KPIs. One day, the business is interested in profitability. In this case, KPIs focus on revenue and expenses. The next day, the business focuses on market share. The KPIs now relate to new customers and customer retention. The next day, the focus changes to meeting competition. The KPIs now change to looking at product acceptance and product differentiation.

As long as the business changes (and business change is simply a fact of life), KPIs also change. And as long as KPIs change, data marts change.

The generic architecture for the data architecture component of the operational environment is depicted in Fig. 12.1.21.

Personal Analytics

In every corporation, there are two levels of decision-making—the corporate level of decision-making and the personal level of decision-making. The corporate level of decision-making is a formal and even regulated environment. The personal level of decision-making is informal.

There is a big difference between the corporate level of decision-making and the personal level of decision-making. The corporate level of decision-making is where there are contracts, management decisions, and even compliance regulations. There is responsibility to the shareholders at this level of decision-making.

The other level of decision-making is the personal level of decision-making. The personal level of decision-making is off the cuff, individual, and informal. There usually is not any audit trail here. Personal decisions are made spontaneously and the needs for personal decision-making as fluid, changing as often as every minute.

The personal analyst can look at data—any data—through the facilities of the personal analytic environment. The analyst can look at corporate data or personal data. The analyst can look at data in his/her time frame. There is no time constraint on doing personal analysis.

Fig. 13.1.1 shows the two kinds of decision-making.

Personal decision-making is fluid and dynamic. The ideal tool for personal decision-making is the personal computer. The personal computer is affordable, able to be relocated, and versatile. The personal computer is able to be refocused at the drop of a hat.

There is little or no need for formal system analysis or development of the personal computer. The analyst just sits down and jots down what is useful and relevant about what needs to be analyzed.

Of course, the personal computer does not have the speed and capacity of the larger corporate computers. The personal computer is not capable of processing the amount of data that a corporate computer can process. But that is of little concern to the individual analyst.

Fig. 13.1.2 shows that the personal computer is the best tool available for the individual doing personal analysis.

331

Data Architecture. https://doi.org/10.1016/B978-0-12-816916-2.00038-3

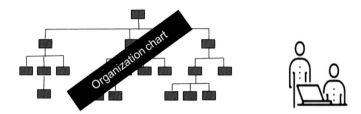

Decisions are made at two different levels—
the corporate level and the individual level

FIG. 13.1.1
Different levels of decisions.

The personal computer is ideally suited for
helping to make personal decisions

FIG. 13.1.2
The personal computer.

The most popular tool available to the personal analyst is the spreadsheet. The spreadsheet—as measured by a number of licenses—has to be the most ubiquitous tool for analysis that there is. There are millions and millions of spreadsheets on personal computers around the world.

At a Midwest bank recently, it was estimated that for the 2000 employees at the bank's one site, there were 4,000,000 spreadsheets that had been created in order to make banking decisions.

Fig. 13.1.3 shows that the spreadsheet is the analytic tool most used on the personal computer.

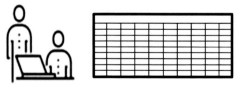

The ubiquitous tool for making decisions on the
personal computer is the spreadsheet

FIG. 13.1.3
The spreadsheet.

There are great advantages to the spreadsheet. The largest advantage is the autonomy the spreadsheet provides the individual analyst. The analyst can do anything he/she wants with the spreadsheet. The analyst can enter any formula, can enter any data, and can change any data that he/she wishes to. There is no one telling the analyst what to do or how to do it.

A second advantage of the spreadsheet is that the spreadsheet is immediate. The analyst needs no special preparation time in order to start using the tool. The analyst just sits down and starts to use the spreadsheet. The analyst can use the spreadsheet to help formulate and structure what needs to be analyzed.

A third advantage of the spreadsheet is its ability to be flexible. The spreadsheet can be changed to suit almost any kind of analysis.

Another advantage of the spreadsheet is its cost. Oftentimes, the cost of the spreadsheet is born when the personal computer is purchased and there is no further charge for the usage of the spreadsheet.

For these reasons and many more, the spreadsheet has found its way into many different environments.

Fig. 13.1.4 shows the advantages of the spreadsheet.

But there are some disadvantages to the spreadsheet. The first disadvantage is that the spreadsheet can be changed at will. Anyone building and managing a spreadsheet can place any value at any time into the spreadsheet, and the spreadsheet won't complain. This means that the source of data going into the spreadsheet is not able to be audited. If an analyst wishes to give himself/herself a raise, as far as the spreadsheet is concerned, the raise has been granted. This of course may not be a reflection of reality. But the spreadsheet does not know or care. Making corporate decisions that are governed by management, contracts, legislature, and shareholders is not advisable when the source of data is a spreadsheet because of this lack of integrity of data.

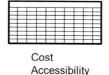

Cost
Accessibility
Ease of use
Flexibility
Adaptability
....

FIG. 13.1.4
There are many reasons why the spreadsheet is widely used.

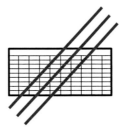

But there are some restrictive disadvantages
To the spreadsheet as well

FIG. 13.1.5
Some restrictive disadvantages.

Another disadvantage of the spreadsheet is that the systems that are created on the spreadsheet are not created with the discipline and the rigor of the corporate-based systems. It is always easy to change a system created on a spreadsheet. But where rigor and discipline of processing are required, that ease of a change in functionality is a liability, not an asset.

Fig. 13.1.5 shows that there are some drawbacks with the spreadsheet.

Decisions are made at both the corporate level and the personal level. But the impact of the decisions is very different. Decisions made at the corporate level affect the budget and the policy of the corporation. Personal decisions influence how an individual does his/her job. But when the day comes where corporate decisions are being made using personal tools, there is a fundamental problem. Fig. 13.1.6 shows that personal decisions should only indirectly influence corporate decisions.

Stated differently, when an individual uses his/her tools on a personal basis and convinces himself/herself and perhaps others of a course of action or a change

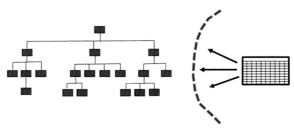

As long as the decisions made at the personal level
do not find their way into the corporation, there is no problem

FIG. 13.1.6
The separation of personal data and corporate data.

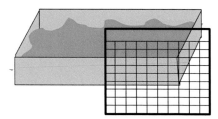

There is a very good fit between the sandbox and
the spreadsheet

FIG. 13.1.7
The fit between the sandbox and the spreadsheet.

in policy, the individual then must convince the corporation. But the person
doing the individual analysis is not in a position to directly interface the corporate data and systems with the personal data and systems.

In a way, the personal analytic systems become an analytic "sandbox."

Fig. 13.1.7 shows that the personal analytic environment is another form of a
sandbox.

In the sandbox, the personal analyst can do anything—can use any data, can
use any algorithm, and can process with no fear of impacting others. But at
the end, when the analyst has gained insights from the sandbox experience,
the analyst must then institutionalize the results and insight into the corporate
system infrastructure.

So, there is a very real and very beneficial impact on corporate system from
personal analytic decisions. However, the impact is indirect not direct.

Data Models Across the End-State Architecture

There are different kinds of data models that are found throughout the end-state architecture. The data models provide an "intellectual road map" as to what data are to be found in the end-state architecture. The value of an intellectual road map is shown by going on a road trip across the United States. Suppose you set out from the East Coast. You drive to places you have never been before—New Mexico, the Grand Canyon, Yellowstone, Santa Fe, Denver, and other places. How do you navigate from one location to the next? You use a road map. The road map tells you where you are right now and how to get to where you are going next.

The data models of the end-state architecture provide the same function. They tell you what to expect to find and how to get to where you will find something else.

THE DIFFERENT DATA MODELS

The different types of data models found in the end-state architecture are shown in Fig. 14.1.1.

The end-state architecture data models include the following:

>   The application functional decomposition and data flow diagram
>   The corporate data model
>   Taxonomies for text
>   The dimensional data model for data marts
>   The selective subdivision of the data lake

Each of these data models and their relation to each other will be discussed.

FUNCTIONAL DECOMPOSITION AND DATA FLOW DIAGRAMS

In the world of applications, there are the functional decomposition and the data flow diagram.

337

Data Architecture. https://doi.org/10.1016/B978-0-12-816916-2.00039-5

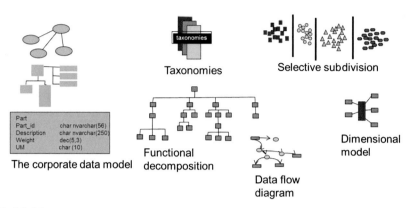

FIG. 14.1.1
Data models across the architecture.

Fig. 14.1.2 depicts these constructs,

The functional decomposition is the depiction of the functions that will be achieved by a system. The functional decomposition is laid out in a hierarchical fashion. At the top of the decomposition is the general function of what is to be accomplished by the system. At the second level are the main functions of what is to be accomplished. Then, each second level function is broken down into its subfunctions, until the point of basic functionality is reached.

The functional decomposition is useful to see what the different activities of a system will be. It is useful for organizing the functions, identifying overlap, and checking to see if anything is left out. When you are setting out on a long trip, it

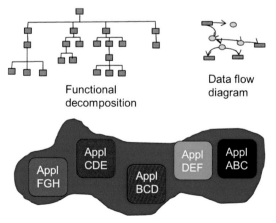

FIG. 14.1.2
The application environment.

Process and data are in lock step
with each other when it comes to
definition of applications

FIG. 14.1.3
Process and data are in lock step.

is useful for looking at a map of the United States to see what states you will visit and the order in which the states will be traveled.

After the functional decomposition is completed, the next step is to create data flow diagrams for each of the functions. The data flow diagram starts with the input to the module and shows how the input data will be processed to achieve the output data. The three major components of a data flow diagram are an identification of the input, a description of the logic that will occur in the module, and a description of the output.

If the functional decomposition is like a map of the United States, the data flow diagram is like a detailed map of a state. The data flow diagram tells you how to get across Texas. You start at El Paso, you head east, past McKittrick Canyon, go to Van Horn and Sierra Blanca, go through Pecos, then on to Midland and Odessa, and so forth. The map of Texas shows details that the map of the United States cannot show. By the same token, the map of Texas does not show you how to get from Los Angeles to San Jose or from Chicago to Naperville.

The nature of functional decomposition and data flow diagrams are such that process and data are intimately intertwined. Both process and data are needed in order to build a functional decomposition and data flow diagrams.

Fig. 14.1.3 shows the tight interrelationship of data and process in the functional decomposition.

The building of functional decompositions and data flow diagrams are used to define and build applications. As a rule, these constructs can be very complex. One of the tools that are used in order to manage the complexity is that of the definition of the scope of development. At the very beginning, there is an exercise that requires that the scope of the application be defined. The scope definition is necessary in order to keep the size of the development reasonable. If a designer is not careful, the scope will become so large that the system will never

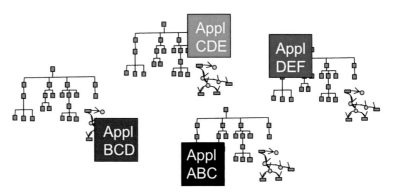

FIG. 14.1.4
Each application has its own functional decomposition and set of data flow diagrams.

be built. Therefore, it is necessary to rigorously define the scope before the development effort ever begins.

The result of the definition of the scope is that—over time—the organization ends up with multiple applications, each of which have their own functional decompositions and data flow diagrams.

Fig. 14.1.4 shows that over time, each application has its own set of definitions.

While the development process that has been described is normal for almost every shop, there is a problem. Over time, a serious amount of overlap between different applications starts to emerge. Because of the need to define and enforce the definition of the scope of an application rigorously, the same or similar functionality starts to appear across multiple applications. When this happens, there start to appear redundant data. The same or similar data element appears in multiple applications.

THE CORPORATE DATA MODEL

When redundant data start to appear, the very integrity of the data comes into question. It is because of this method of developing systems and the inevitable lack of integrity of data across applications that there is recognition of the need for corporate data, not application data.

Fig. 14.1.5 shows the corporate data model.

The corporate data model applies to and is useful for everyone at the company. The different organizations that make use of the corporate data model are shown in Fig. 14.1.6.

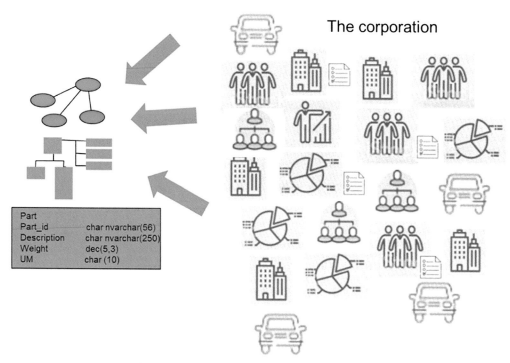

FIG. 14.1.5
The corporate data model.

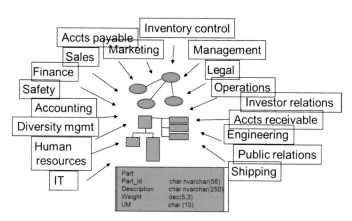

FIG. 14.1.6
The corporate data model represents all the corporation.

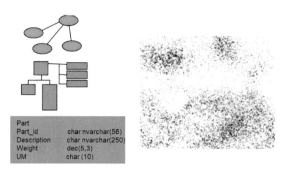

FIG. 14.1.7
The corporate data model represents granular data only.

At first glance, the thought of a corporate data model may seem overwhelming. However, the good news is that most corporate data models do not have to be built from scratch. Consider the fact that within the same companies in an industry, there is a high degree of duplication of a data model. The data model for a bank will be very similar to the data model for other banks. The data model for a public utility will be very similar to other data models for other public utilities. The data model for a manufacturer will be very similar to other data models for other manufacturers, and so forth.

Because of the great similarity of data models within the same industry, there are what are called generic data models. It is easy enough and inexpensive enough to simply buy a generic data model and to customize that data model for a particular company.

Further simplifying the matter is the fact that the data model is built for only the primitive data in the corporation. Summarized, aggregated, or derived data do not belong in the data model.

Fig. 14.1.7 shows that only granular data belong in the corporate data model.

The corporate data model represents the single version of the truth data in the corporation. Corporate data are the place where everyone turns when they have to have a reliable accurate answer.

One of the challenges is the fact that corporate data are usually fed by application data. And application data are decidedly not the single version of the truth in the corporation.

For this reason, the interface between the application data model and the corporate data model is important and needs to be carefully defined. The interface between the application data model and the corporate data model defines an important transformation of data. Once the interface has been rigorously defined, it is easy enough for the programmer to write a program to accomplish the transformation.

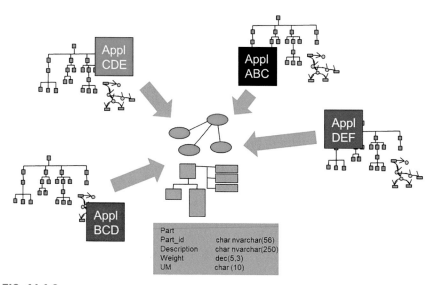

FIG. 14.1.8
Each application has its own interface to the corporate data model.

Fig. 14.1.8 shows that multiple application models connect to the corporate data model.

There are many uses for the corporate data model. But the primary use of the model is to form the basis of database design for the data warehouse.

Fig. 14.1.9 shows that the corporate data model is the basic specification of the data warehouse.

THE STAR JOIN/DIMENSIONAL DATA MODEL

Another type of data model found in the end-state architecture is the dimensional model. The dimensional model consists of a fact table and multiple connected dimensions. The result is what is termed a "star join."

Fig. 14.1.10 depicts a star join.

The star join reflects the needs of the different departments that will be using the data influenced by the star join. Stated differently, there will be a star join for marketing. There will be a different star join for sales. There will be another star join for finance, one for marketing, and so forth.

The reason why there will be a different star join is that the different departments look at data differently. The star join for a department reflects the customized view of data for the department.

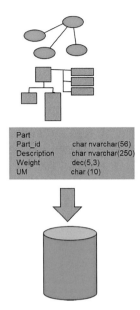

Part
Part_id   char nvarchar(56)
Description   char nvarchar(250)
Weight   dec(5,3)
UM   char (10)

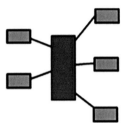

The dimensional model consists of a fact table and dimensions. the dimensional model is often called a "star join"

FIG. 14.1.9
The corporate data model forms the basis for the design of the data warehouse.

FIG. 14.1.10
A star join.

Fig. 14.1.11 shows that there are different star joins for each department.

The source of data for the star join is the corporate data model. Even though the star join reflects a particular customized view of data, the source of the data is uniform. The source of the data is still the single source of truth for the corporation.

It is noteworthy that it is possible to build a data mart whose source of data is not the data warehouse. While such a structure can be built, it is outside the boundaries of the end-state architecture. Building a data mart whose source

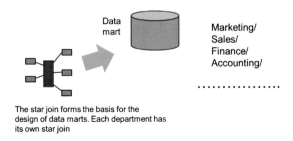

Data mart

Marketing/
Sales/
Finance/
Accounting/
....

The star join forms the basis for the design of data marts. Each department has its own star join

FIG. 14.1.11
The star join and data marts.

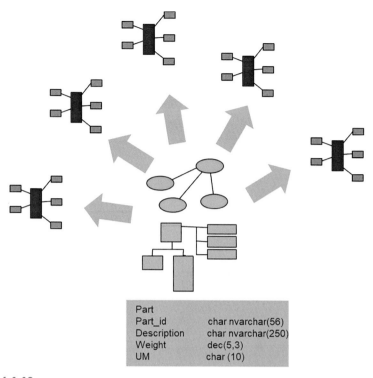

Part
Part_id   char nvarchar(56)
Description   char nvarchar(250)
Weight   dec(5,3)
UM   char (10)

FIG. 14.1.12
The corporate data model forms the basis for the design of the different, customized data marts.

of data is not the data warehouse is like violating the zoning codes of a city. You could build a hovel next to a large office building. But if you do, you will have a poorly planned city. And there are a whole host of other problems that come with having a poorly planned city.

Fig. 14.1.12 shows that star join environment is fed from the corporate data model.

TAXONOMIES/ONTOLOGIES

Another important form of a data model is the taxonomy. The taxonomy is the form of a data model used to shape and manage text. Text is free form. When an author sits down to write a document, the author can compose the document however he/she wishes. Writing—for the most part—is free form.

The data models that fit elsewhere in the end-state architecture simply do not fit text. A wholly different approach is needed for examining and using text in the decision-making infrastructure.

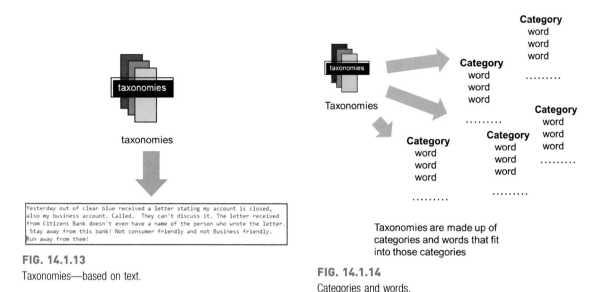

FIG. 14.1.13
Taxonomies—based on text.

Taxonomies are made up of categories and words that fit into those categories

FIG. 14.1.14
Categories and words.

Fig. 14.1.13 depicts the taxonomy that is used to integrate text into the end-state architecture.

The taxonomy—strictly speaking—can take the form of a taxonomy or an ontology. In its simplest form, the taxonomy is merely a collection of classifications. The classification consists of a classification and a list of words that populate that classification. The categories found in the taxonomy reflect the viewpoint of the author.

Fig. 14.1.14 shows that taxonomies are made up of categories and words.

The taxonomies used to understand a document are relevant to the business being discussed in the document. The taxonomies are used to determine the context of the words that are being written. In fairness, there is a lot more to understanding context than merely using a taxonomy on a document. However, the taxonomy is the starting point.

Once the taxonomy is used and once contextualization is done, the text is turned into a database. In essence, the text found in the document being processed is "normalized."

Fig. 14.1.15 shows that a database is created from the document using taxonomies.

The categories found in the taxonomy are dependent on the writer of the document. The designer uses the appropriate set of taxonomies to relate the document to the data that are going to be analyzed.

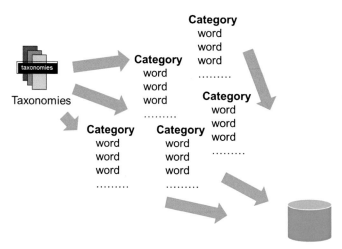

FIG. 14.1.15
Taxonomies—used to shape the data base into which the text is normalized.

In actuality, there are almost infinite numbers of taxonomies. The analyst chooses which taxonomies are the most appropriate to the data that will go into the database.

It is very normal for there to be overlap between words found in different taxonomies.

The categories of the taxonomy ROUGHLY are equivalent to the entities found in the corporate data model. It is noted that the correlation between the categories of the taxonomy and the entities of the corporate data model is NOT an exact match. There can be many differences between the two, so that the correlation is an imperfect match.

Nevertheless, there is a ROUGH approximation between the two types of elements.

Fig. 14.1.16 shows the rough approximation between the two types of data model.

THE SELECTIVE SUBDIVISION OF DATA

The final form of data modeling found in the end-state architecture is the selective subdivision of data found in the data lake. It can be argued that the selective subdivision of data in the data lake is not a data model at all. Indeed, all the selective subdivision of data in the data lake is determined by the organization of data according to certain characteristics of the data. There may be an archival

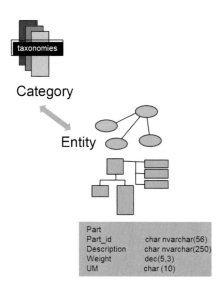

Category

Entity

Part	
Part_id	char nvarchar(56)
Description	char nvarchar(250)
Weight	dec(5,3)
UM	char (10)

The categories of the taxonomy have a high degree of correlation to the entities of the corporate data model

FIG. 14.1.16

Categories and entities.

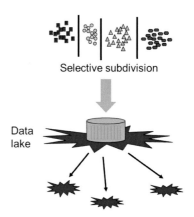

Selective subdivision

Data lake

Selective subdivision determines how the data lake Is to be subdivided

FIG. 14.1.17

Subdividing the data lake.

subdivision of data; a litigation support subdivision of data; an extended, bulk data warehouse subdivision of data; and so forth in the data lake.

Fig. 14.1.17 shows the selective subdivision of data in the data lake.

The selective subdivision of data really does not affect the content or design of data in the data lake. Instead, the selective subdivision merely influences the placement of data in the data lake.

When it comes to the shaping of data found in the data lake, the single largest factor in the shaping of data is the corporate data model, as seen in Fig. 14.1.18.

The preceding discussion has included all the forms of data modeling found in the end-state architecture. The functional decomposition and the data flow diagrams apply to applications. The taxonomy/ontology applies to text. The corporate data model applies to the data warehouse. The dimensional model applies to data marts. And the selective subdivision of data applies to the data lake.

Each of these forms of data modeling has their own idiosyncrasies. Each form of data modeling has a certain similarity to the other forms of data modeling. And each form of data modeling is required in order to build an effective end-state architecture.

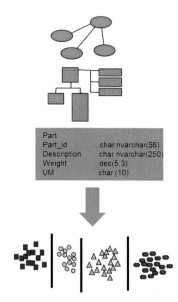

The data model holds its basic shape
throughout the process of subdivision

FIG. 14.1.18
The basic shape of the data model.

PROACTIVE/REACTIVE DATA MODELS

One of the interesting features of the end-state architecture is the ability of the analyst to traverse and communicate from one form of data modeling to another. In other words, when an analyst is working on the corporate data model, the analyst can go look at what the data flow diagrams look like. Or when an analyst is working on a taxonomy, the analyst can look at the corporate data model. Or when an analyst is assigning the selective subdivision of data, the analyst can go look at the functional decomposition of data.

The ability to traverse the network of information of data formed by the different forms of data modeling in the end-state architecture is a very important feature. By being able to traverse the network formed by the different forms of data modeling, the analyst can find and examine the lineage of the data. By examining the lineage of data, the analyst can understand such things as the following:

Where did the data come from?
What data were chosen?
What data were not chosen?
What calculations were made on the data?
When were the calculations applied?

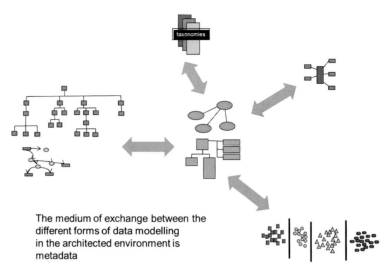

The medium of exchange between the
different forms of data modelling
in the architected environment is
metadata

FIG. 14.1.19
The role of metadata.

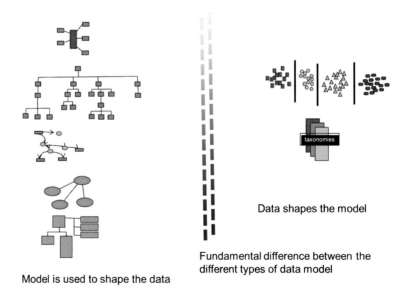

Data shapes the model

Fundamental difference between the
different types of data model

Model is used to shape the data

FIG. 14.1.20
Fundamental differences in models.

In a word, the ability to be able to traverse the network of the different forms of data models in the end-state architecture is one of the more important features of the end-state architecture.

Fig. 14.1.19 shows the network.

There is one important difference between the different forms of data models that must be noted. That difference is that some forms of data models shape the data. But other forms of data models are shaped by the data. Stated differently, some forms of data modeling are proactive and caused the data to be shaped after the model. But other forms of data modeling are reactive and are shaped by the data.

The corporate data model, functional decomposition and data flow diagrams, and the dimensional data model are proactive. The taxonomy/ontology data model and the selective subdivision of data are reactive.

Fig. 14.1.20 shows this property of the different forms of data modeling in the end-state architecture.

The System of Record

End users throughout time have gone through a predictable cycle when it comes to the awareness of the end user to the computer. This cycle of end user awareness is as old as the day the first computer was built, and this cycle appears and reappears in many forms. The first part of the cycle starts when the end user first encounters the computer, saying "I want my data."

THE END USER CYCLE OF AWARENESS

Fig. 15.1.1 shows the first thing the end user wants.

The end user's instincts tell him/her that the most important thing is to get the data for whatever application the end user is building. But it takes a long time to get the data. So, the end user says wait a minute. I don't just want my data; I want it now. I don't want to have to wait all day for my data. Give them to me quickly.

Fig. 15.1.2 shows this next step in the end user cycle.

So, not only does the second step get the end user his/her data, but also the second step in the cycle speeds up the amount of time it takes to get the data to the end user. So now, the end user gets the data quickly.

As soon as the end user discovers that it is possible to get the data quickly, the end user now looks at the data. The end user decides the data can be simplified and organized differently. The data can be visualized. So now, the end user wants the data to be convenient to get and organized and visualized.

Step 3 shows this part of the end user awareness cycle (Fig. 15.1.3).

After the end user starts to get their data quickly and conveniently and simplified and organized, the end user then starts to pay attention to the accuracy and believability of the data. At this point, the end user discovers that he/she has been given incorrect data. The data are worthless because they are wrong. In a way, the data at this point are a liability. It LOOKS LIKE the right data; it is just incorrect. If one were to believe the data, the wrong business decision could be made. And it takes a concerted effort to find out that the data are incorrect.

353

Data Architecture. https://doi.org/10.1016/B978-0-12-816916-2.00040-1

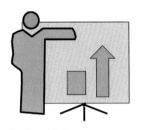

Step 1—"I want my data"

FIG. 15.1.1
Step 1—end user cycle of awareness.

Step 2 —"I want my data now"

FIG. 15.1.2
Step 2—end user cycle of awareness.

Step 3
"I want my data in a convenient, easy to understand manner"

FIG. 15.1.3
Step 3—end user cycle of awareness.

Step 4
"I want accurate data that I can believe"

FIG. 15.1.4
Step 4—end user cycle of awareness.

Now, the end user adds one more parameter to his/her awareness. Now, the end user wants accurate, believable data. Step 4 in the end user awareness cycle looks like (Fig. 15.1.4).

THE SYSTEM OF RECORD

In order to illustrate the insidious nature of step 4, suppose a spreadsheet is created with people's salaries on it. Anyone can create a spreadsheet, and you can put any data you want into the spreadsheet. Now, on the spreadsheet I put an entry for Bill Inmon's salary. I put into the spreadsheet that Bill Inmon makes $1,000,000 a month.

The spreadsheet looks good. It comes from the computer. It has a lot of information on the spreadsheet. The salaries all look to be OK. However, when we come to Bill Inmon, the spreadsheet says that Bill Inmon makes $1,000,000 a month. That information is inaccurate. If management were to act on this information, they might make some very incorrect conclusions about Bill Inmon, because in fact, Bill Inmon DOES NOT make a million dollars a month.

When the discovery is made that the data are incorrect, the end user has just discovered the need for what is known as the *"system of record."*

The system of record in computer systems is the designated guarantee that the data that have been accessed are certified—guaranteed—to be accurate. It is possible for there to be errors in the data found in the system of record. But if there are errors in the system of record, the errors have arrived there by means of passing through rigorous audits and checks. Stated differently, the system of record is the best data that are available, and every effort possible has been made to insure the accuracy of the data. If there are errors in the system of record, there aren't many, and those errors that are found are subject to correction when found to be inaccurate.

Fig. 15.1.5 shows the system of record data.

THE SYSTEM OF RECORD IN THE END STATE ARCHITECTURE

The system of record is a living organism that is found in different places in the end-state architecture. Fig. 15.1.6 shows a simplified version of the end-state architecture.

While there are more components to the end-state architecture than those shown in Fig. 15.1.6, the major components of the architecture are depicted. The system of record exists throughout the different places in the end-state architecture.

Fig. 15.1.7 shows the system of record in the different components of the end-state architecture.

Fig. 15.1.7 shows that part of the system of record exists in the application environment, part of the system of record exists in the data warehouse, part of the system of record exists in the data marts, and part of the system of record exists in the big data environment.

Data integrity

The system of record has the highest data integrity in the corporation

FIG. 15.1.5

Data integrity.

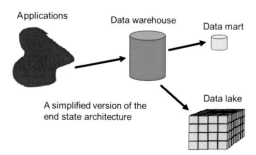

Applications   Data warehouse   Data mart

A simplified version of the end state architecture

Data lake

FIG. 15.1.6

Simplified end state architecture.

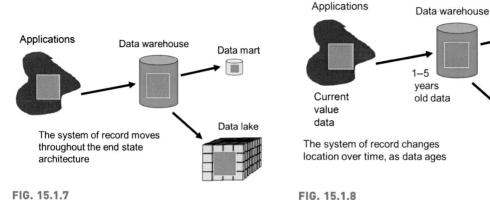

FIG. 15.1.7
Different structures of data.

FIG. 15.1.8
The system of record changes location as data ages.

THE ROLE OF AGE IN THE SYSTEM OF RECORD

The type of data in the system of record that exist in the different environments depends entirely on the age of the data in the system of record.

Fig. 15.1.8 shows the different types of data that exist in the different places.

In the application environment are found the current value data. In current value data, data are accurate as of the moment of access. Only a limited amount of history is found in the application environment.

In the data warehouse are found *early historic data*. For most organizations, early historic data are data that are from 1 to 5 years old.

In the data mart environment is found *departmental customized system of record data*. In the departmental customized data are found data that are customized for each department, such as marketing, sales, and finance.

In the big data environment are found *deep historic data*. Deep historic data are system of record data that is 6 years and older data.

A SIMPLE EXAMPLE

As a simple example of system of record data, suppose you want to find out what your account balance is right now. You go to the application environment to find out what your account balance is. Now, you are doing your income taxes, and you need to find a check that you wrote 13 months ago. You go to the data warehouse to find that check.

Now, suppose you want to find a marketing analysis of your account along with other similar accounts. You look to the system of record in the marketing data mart. Now, suppose you are being audited by the IRS and you need to go find a check that was written 10 years ago. You go to the system of record in big data.

At every point along the line, you can find reliable, accurate data by looking in the system of record.

THE FLOW OF DATA IN THE SYSTEM OF RECORD

When looking at the mapping of the system of record to the end-state architecture, it is seen that there is a flow of data from one component to another. In some cases, the data simply flow from one component to another. For example, data flow from the data warehouse to big data. But in other cases, the flow of data takes place in the form of a transformation. Data within the system of record are transformed as they move from the application component to the data warehouse component, and data are transformed as they move from the data warehouse to the data mart.

Fig. 15.1.9 shows that transformation takes place.

The transformation of data as they move from the application environment to the data warehouse environment is one where the measurement and definitions of data are altered. As a simple example, data in the application environment are measured in inches, while data in the data warehouse are measured in centimeters. As data pass from the application environment to the data warehouse, the calculation of converting data from inches to centimeters is made.

The transformation of data from the data warehouse to the data mart is a different kind of transformation. Typically, this transformation is made in the selection and calculation of data. As a simple example, the data warehouse holds data about all customers. Only the customers from Missouri are selected and then only customers who have spent more than $1000 a month. Then, data about these selected customers are then added together and placed in the data mart.

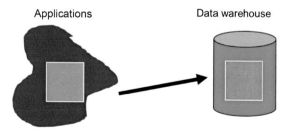

FIG. 15.1.9
Transformation.

OTHER DATA THAN THE SYSTEM OF RECORD

Another interesting point is as follows: is there data in the application environment or the data warehouse or the big data environment that is not part of the system of record? The answer is absolutely yes—there are data in those places that are not part of the system of record. And it is perfectly all right to access and use that data. However, for extreme confidence in the data, data from the system of record should be chosen.

To use an analogy. Suppose you wanted to enter a car race. You have two choices—drive a Porsche or drive a Volkswagen. Your chances at winning the race are probably improved by choosing the Porsche. But you can choose the Volkswagen and enter the race. And who is to say that you might not win with the Volkswagen. However, to improve your odds of success, you probably would be better off choosing the Porsche.

Fig. 15.1.10 shows the data outside the system of record.

IS DATA UPDATED IN THE SYSTEM OF RECORD?

Another interesting issue arises—can data inside the system of record be updated? The answer is yes—of course, it can. However, there are some considerations when it comes to the issue of update.

Suppose you have a bank account. Suppose you go and look at your bank account balance as of 10:13 am. Then suppose at 10:45 am, you make a withdrawal from the bank account. The withdrawal is transacted immediately. When you reference the amount of money you have in your bank account, the value can change on a moment by moment basis. Therefore, you have to reference not only the amount of money in the bank account but also the moment in time the amount was accurate at.

So, update can be done in the application environment.

The data warehouse environment is different. New records can be placed in the data warehouse. For example, there may be a record of your daily activity. As of

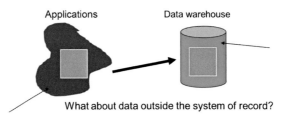

Applications   Data warehouse

What about data outside the system of record?

FIG. 15.1.10
Data outside the system of record.

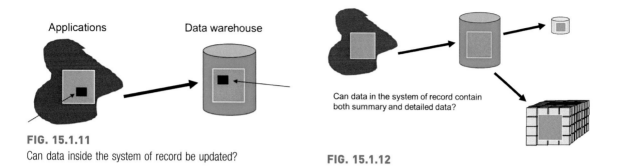

Applications

Data warehouse

FIG. 15.1.11
Can data inside the system of record be updated?

Can data in the system of record contain both summary and detailed data?

FIG. 15.1.12
What about detailed and summary data?

July 15, you had $nnnn dollars in your account.
And as of August 3, you had $yyyy dollars in your account. So, data in the data warehouse are constantly being updated. However, a historical record is kept in the data warehouse as of the changing values over time.

Fig. 15.1.11 shows that data in the system of record can certainly be updated.

DETAILED AND SUMMARY DATA IN THE SYSTEM OF RECORD

Another important issue is whether the system of record can hold both detailed and summary data. Of course, the system of record can hold primitive, detailed data. There is no question about that. But the real question is whether the system of record can hold summary data.

The answer is yes—of course, the system of record can hold summary data, as seen in Fig. 15.1.12.

However, when summary data are held in the system of record, there is an extra, compulsory component not seen elsewhere. When summary data are held in the system of record, documentation of how the summary was made must be included as well. The documentation of the summarization needs to include at least the following:

What data were included in the summarization?
What data were excluded from the summarization?
When was the summarization made?
What formula was used for the summarization?
What program(s) made the summarization?
Where were the results of the summarization sent?

Fig. 15.1.13 shows that summarization in the system of record requires special documentation.

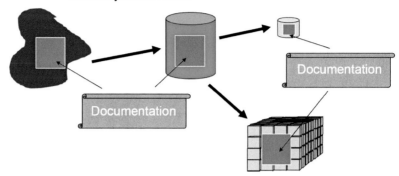

Once summary data is put into the system of record, so must documentation about the summary be put into the system of record

FIG. 15.1.13
The role of documentation.

AUDITING DATA AND THE SYSTEM OF RECORD

The system of record is useful for many purposes. The primary purpose of the system of record is to establish a foundation for the making of business decisions with confidence.

It goes without saying that data found in the system of record are ideal for the purpose of auditing. Conversely, it would be very dangerous (and probably misleading) to conduct an audit of data outside the system of record.

Fig. 15.1.14 shows that the system of record supports auditing.

TEXT AND THE SYSTEM OF RECORD

An interesting issue is as follows: where does text fit into the system of record? The answer is that any text used for entry into the corporate decision-making environment becomes part of the system of record. Text is a special case of data.

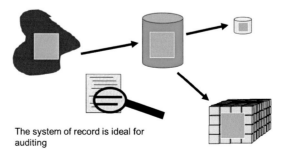

The system of record is ideal for auditing

FIG. 15.1.14
Auditing.

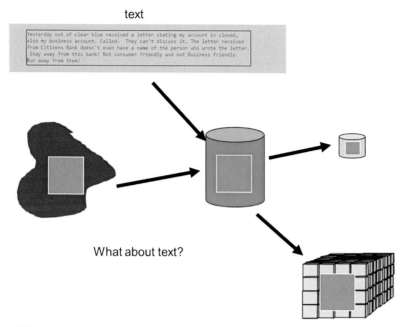

text

Yesterday out of clear blue received a letter stating my account is closed, also my business account. Called. They can't discuss it. The letter received from Citizens Bank doesn't even have a name of the person who wrote the letter. Stay away from this bank! Not consumer friendly and not Business friendly. Run away from them!

What about text?

FIG. 15.1.15
Where does text fit?

Text cannot be changed once the author has written the text. It is legally and ethically improper to take a written document and alter the document. For that reason, text that is used in decision-making becomes an essential part of the system of record.

This applies EVEN IF THE TEXT IS NOT CORRECT. Suppose someone writes "Bill Inmon makes a million dollars a month." Certainly, the information portrayed in the text is incorrect. But of that is what the author wrote, then the text cannot be changed, even though the text conveys an incorrect idea.

Of course, there is all sorts of text that is written that is never used in the corporate decision-making process. This text is NOT part of the system of record. Only text used for inclusion into the database infrastructure is used for the system of record.

Fig. 15.1.15 shows the relationship of text in the system of record.

Business Value and the End-State Architecture

THE EVOLUTION OF THE END STATE ARCHITECTURE

The story of business value across the end-state architecture begins with an understanding of the evolution of the architecture across the history of the organization. The following describes the typical evolution of the architecture. (NOTE: the depiction is for a hypothetical "typical" corporation. There is absolutely nothing to say that the evolution of the end-state architecture will be different in some organizations.)

The typical evolution is shown in Fig. 16.1.1.

The first part of the end-state architecture to be built is the applications. After the applications have matured and the siloed effect of the applications is noticed, a corporate data warehouse is built. The corporate data warehouse integrates the application data and provides a place for historical data to gather. After the data warehouse is built, the different data marts begin to spring up.

Data start to accumulate in the data warehouse. Then after a while, the data lake/big data environment is built. The data lake/big data environment is also used to collect data from external and extraneous sources.

Finally, textual data are gathered from raw text and are incorporated into the infrastructure.

In such a fashion, the corporation gathers data and organizes it according to the end-state architecture.

WHAT IS MEANT BY "BUSINESS VALUE"

In order to understand how the end-state architecture relates to business value, it is worthwhile to examine what is meant by "having business value."

363

Data Architecture. https://doi.org/10.1016/B978-0-12-816916-2.00041-3

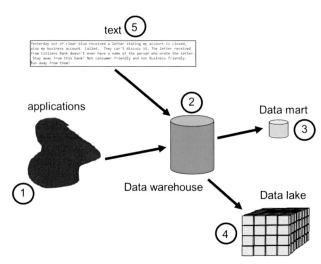

FIG. 16.1.1
A typical order in which the end state architecture is built.

There are actually many interpretations of having business value. The interpretation used here is a classic interpretation of business value. Enhancing business value means the following:

Growing the revenue of the corporation
Growing the customer base of the organization
Increasing the profitability of the corporation
Increasing the product and packaging mix of the corporation

All of these factors lead to the enhancement of the business health of the corporation.

Fig. 16.1.2 shows this interpretation of business value.

TACTICAL BUSINESS VALUE/STRATEGIC BUSINESS VALUE

In general, there are two approaches to address business value. Business value can be addressed at the tactical level, and business value can be addressed at the strategic level. Successful businesses address business value at both of these levels.

As an example of the tactical level of business value, the business considers the activity of the prospect/customer at the point of purchase. Typical tactical considerations are such things as follows:

Can the purchase be made conveniently?

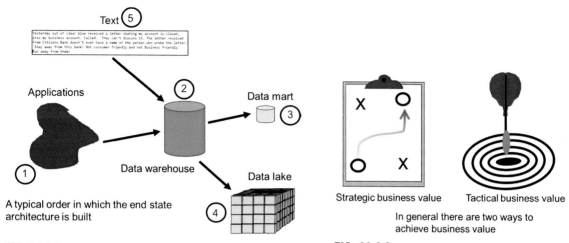

FIG. 16.1.2
The business value is different at each stage of development.

FIG. 16.1.3
In general there are two ways to achieve business value.

Can the purchase be made quickly?
Is the process of making a purchase simple?
What does the customer need in order to make the actual selection?

These are but a few of the tactical considerations.

Strategic decisions are far-reaching, long-term decisions.

Typical of strategic decisions are as follows:

Should the corporation open up business in a new territory?
Should the corporation acquire another company?
Should the corporation start to develop a new product line?

These are the kinds of decisions that are typical of strategic thinking.

Fig. 16.1.3 depicts the difference between tactical and strategic decision-making.

VOLUME OF DATA VERSUS BUSINESS VALUE

There is a relevant interesting graph that depicts something very unintuitive. The graph shows that as the volume of data increases, the business value of data across the corporation decreases. Stated differently, when the corporation is first gathering data and using the computer, the business value achieved is quite high. But as time passes and the volume of data in the corporation grows, the business value of the data in the corporation decreases.

Fig. 16.1.4 shows this relationship.

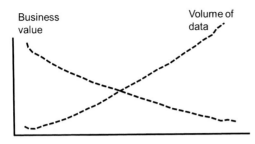

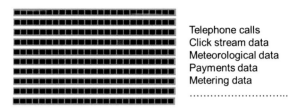

Telephone calls
Click stream data
Meteorological data
Payments data
Metering data
....

FIG. 16.1.5
Nearly every occurrence is bereft of business value.

FIG. 16.1.4
Business value versus the volumes of data.

THE "MILLION IN ONE" SYNDROME

There are several reasons for the phenomenon shown in Fig. 16.1.4. The first of these reasons can be called the "million in one" syndrome.

Consider the diagram shown in Fig. 16.1.5.

Fig. 16.1.5 shows that there is a lot of data. And only one occurrence out of all the data is of interest. That one unit of data is shown in a different color. The red unit becomes lost in all the other data.

In order to illustrate the million in one syndrome, consider this. A record is made of every phone call in the United States every day. In a day's time, there will be hundreds of millions of phone calls for which a record is made. Every time a dial tone is made, a new record is recorded.

Now, suppose an analyst is looking for phone calls made by a terrorist. In a day's time out of hundreds of millions of records, the analyst may find two or three calls. The probability of a phone call being of interest approximates $1/100,000,000$. The odds are infinitesimal that any phone call may have a legitimate business interest. And finding that one or two phone calls out of all the phone calls is a really complex and expensive thing to do.

There is a tremendous amount of data that is stored in order to find a paucity of business value

That is one reason for the equations shown in Fig. 16.1.4.

WHERE BUSINESS VALUE OCCURS

But there is another reason for the relationship shown in Fig. 16.1.4. That reason is that the preponderance of business value occurs where there is the least data. Fig. 16.1.6 shows this phenomenon.

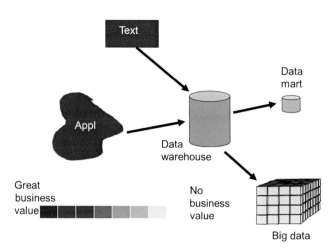

FIG. 16.1.6
The scale of business value across the end state architecture.

In Fig. 16.1.6, it is seen that different environments have different amounts of business value. The scale goes from dark to light, where the darker the color, the greater the business value.

The darkest color is in the application environment. There is a great deal of business value there. There also is a great deal of business value in text. There is still a lot of business value in the data warehouse and in the data marts. And there is only a scant amount of business value in the big data environment.

Yet proportionately, there are much more data in the big data/data lake environment. This is another reason for the relationship shown in Fig. 16.1.4.

DATA RELEVANCY OVER TIME

There is yet another reason for the relationship seen in Fig. 16.1.4. That reason is that as data age, over time, the data lose its relevancy.

Fig. 16.1.7 shows this phenomenon.

In Fig. 16.1.7, it is seen that as data age, the data lose relevancy. Stated differently, the fresher the data are, the greater the chance that the data are relevant to today's world.

Over time, business conditions, technical conditions, market conditions, product conditions, and government conditions all change so much that looking at data from an earlier day and age is simply meaningless. The data grow so old that any conclusions are simply not relevant to today's world.

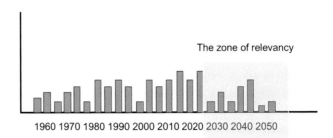

FIG. 16.1.7
Over time older data loses its relevancy to the business of today.

Yet, that older data are held within the system—usually in the data lake environment.

There are then a whole host of reasons for the truth shown in the Fig. 16.1.4.

WHERE TACTICAL DECISIONS ARE MADE

When considering business value, it is worthwhile noting that there is a symbiotic relationship between tactical decisions and strategic decisions. Fig. 16.1.8 depicts this relationship.

Fig. 16.1.8 shows that—for the most part—tactical activities and transactions occur in the application environment. And strategic activities and decisions occur in the data warehouse and the data mart environment. A cycle of processing occurs between the two.

Transactions are run in the application environment. Data are produced as a by-product of those transactions. The data find its way into the data warehouse.

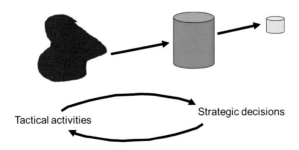

The applications environment is where tactical activities occur.
The data warehouse and the data mart environment is the place
where strategic decisions are made

FIG. 16.1.8
Where different activities occur.

The data in the data warehouse and the data mart are studied, and new decisions are made. The new decisions have an impact on the transactions that are run. In turn, a new set of transactions are run, and their data are stored in the data warehouse.

This cycle of data has a profound impact on the business of the corporation.

Managing Text

Text is the Wednesday's child of technology. It has been forgotten and abandoned, to the point that organizations act as if they don't have any text, much less text that contains important data. Yet in most corporations, some of the most important information is bound up in text.

For years, it was not possible to read text automatically and use it in the decision-making process. But that has changed. Today, it is possible to read text and to include it in standard databases. In doing so, text has become an important source of data in the corporate decision-making process.

THE CHALLENGE OF TEXT

There are many very valid reasons why text is so difficult to work with and manage. The primary reason has to be that text does not fit well into a standard database management system. Stated differently, the fit between text and a database management system is awkward at best and a total mismatch at worst.

A standard database management system requires data to be tightly structured. The DBMS requires that fields of data be uniform in size, that the attributes are able to be defined, and that keys be readily available in order to store the data. The very essence of a DBMS is uniformity in the units of data held in the database. Text meets none of those requirements.

DBMS requirements are rigid. DBMS requirements are nonnegotiable. You either arrange data the way the DBMS wants you to or you don't use a database.

And text is free form. No one tells the author of words or the speaker of words what to say. The very essence of communication with language is the freedom to express one's self as one desires. Every person expresses differently.

Fig. 17.1.1 shows that the nonuniform nature of text does not fit with a standard database management system.

The misfit between a DBMS and text has been noticed for a long time. Indeed, there have evolved over a long time a series of solutions (or attempts at solutions) over the years. There has been a progression over time that tries to

371

Data Architecture. https://doi.org/10.1016/B978-0-12-816916-2.00042-5

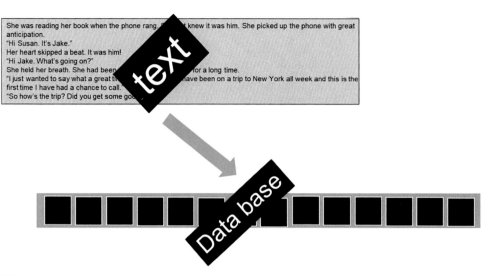

FIG. 17.1.1
Fitting text into a standard data base is an awkward thing, at best.

address the different problems that arise when trying to place text into a database.

Fig. 17.1.2 depicts the evolution.

The first attempt to manage text was to create a standard field definition and to stuff text into the definition. Structural definitions such as text field char (1000) were created. While it is possible to place text in a field such as the one described, there were lots of problems. Some text entries were much shorter

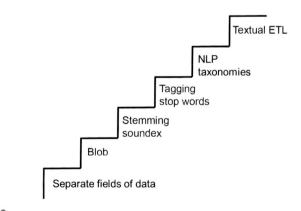

FIG. 17.1.2
The evolution of textual integration into data base technology.

than 1000 bytes (thus wasting space), and some text entries were much larger than 1000 bytes (creating a complexity). From a size standpoint alone, merely defining a field of data was not an effective solution. The length of the field was always either too long or too short (or both).

The next approach by the DBMS vendors was to allow a field called a "blob" to be defined. The blob would allow any length of text to be entered, thus solving the problem of defining the length of a field properly. But merely placing text into a blob only solved one problem of placing text into a database. Once text was placed into a blob, there was nothing real that could be done with it other than the mere placement of the data into a database. Trying to do any meaningful analysis on text inside a blob was extremely difficult to do.

The next step in the solution to dealing with text that needed to go into a database was to employ the practice of "stemming." Stemming was the practice of defining words that are related at the root stem. For example, the word move has a relation to the words moving, mover, moved, mover, and so forth. The word move is the stem of the other words. Stemming was the first real step toward the systemic analysis of words. However, stemming had little practical value. Stemming was an interesting exercise, but stemming had little practical use.

Along with stemming came the practice of soundex. In soundex, words are spelled and classified according to their sound. Like stemming, soundex had few practical applications. However, both stemming and soundex were the first steps in starting to deal with text systemically.

The next step was the practice of identification and the removal of stop words. Stop words are extraneous words that are needed for proper communication but which are extraneous to the meaning of what is being said. Typical stop words are words such as "a," "and," "the," and "to."

In a way, stop word removal was the first significant practical step to starting to deal with text. Stop word removal erased words that "got in the way" and removed unnecessary text for further consideration.

After stop word removal came tagging. Tagging is the practice of examining a document and finding and identifying desired words found in the document. Tagging words inside a document is a good and effective way to start to understand what is inside a document. However, tagging had several drawbacks. The first drawback of tagging is that in order to know how to tag a document, you had to know what words you were looking for before you ever did the tagging. This presupposes that you know what the person is going to say before they say it. And in most circumstances, that is a fallacious assumption. The second drawback of tagging is that there is a lot more to understand about text than the mere identification of words.

Nevertheless, tagging was a real step forward in the management of text.

The next step in the progression to putting text into a database was that of using taxonomies in order to analyze sentences. Taxonomic resolution occurs when a taxonomy is created, and the taxonomy is matched against the raw text. In matching the text, words could be classified. In many regards, the use of taxonomies was the secret that began to unlock the process of textual analysis. There are MANY things that can be done with text when the text is matched against a taxonomy.

Following taxonomic analysis, there came NLP—natural language processing. Natural language processing took all the previous techniques and built on them in order to produce an effective way to examine and analyze text.

In the final phase of the evolution, there is textual ETL (or textual disambiguation). Textual ETL does everything that NLP does and adds a lot of other functionality. The emphasis of textual ETL is on the identification of the context of text, not the text itself. In addition, textual ETL specifically builds databases. And textual ETL also does in-line contextualization.

Today, with textual ETL, you can read text and turn it into useful databases. Once you have constructed the databases, you can then use standard visualization tools to analyze the data.

THE CHALLENGE OF CONTEXT

The first and biggest problem with trying to incorporate text into a database environment is that text does not fit comfortably inside a database. But that is not the only problem. The second major problem is that in order to deal with text, you have to deal with context as well. Stated differently, dealing with text is one problem. Dealing with the context of text is an entirely different problem. But in order to put text meaningfully into an environment where it can be analyzed, you MUST deal with both text and context.

Fig. 17.1.3 shows that text and context must be considered.

So, why is context so difficult to deal with? Consider the word "ship." When you read a sentence and you see the word ship, what do you think of? Do you think of a large boat on the ocean? Do you think of an airliner? Do you think of a package that needs to be sent somewhere? Do you think of soldiers that are about to be transported somewhere? Do you think of someone being fired? Do you think of something else? The truth is that the word ship can mean lots of things, most of which are very different from each other.

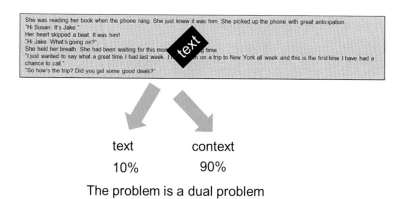

The problem is a dual problem

FIG. 17.1.3
Both text and context must be taken into account.

The way you know what is meant by "ship" is to understand the context in which the word is used. Stated differently, the context of a word is usually EXTERNAL to the word. And the external nature of context is true of EVERY word and EVERY conversation.

And that is the hard part of understanding context. Context exists EXTERNALLY to the words that it applies to (for the most part). Occasionally, context is found within the sentences themselves. But far and away, the much more normal case is for context to be found external to the words being analyzed.

Fig. 17.1.4 shows that context exists external to the words that are being analyzed.

That is why context is 90% of the work done by textual ETL in order to read and prepare text for inclusion into a database.

Despite the fact that context is so difficult to identify and manage, it is MAN-DATORY that context be included with EVERY word put into a database. If a word was to be put by itself into a database, the word would be naked. A word without context would be lost and almost useless for the purpose of being analyzed.

Textual ETL then is the technology that allows text to be read and meaningfully placed into a database. Textual ETL ALWAYS—in every case—considers both the word and its context.

Fig. 17.1.5 shows textual ETL.

Textual ETL reads as input raw text, taxonomies, and other input and deter-mines what text is important and how the text is to be processed. The output is a standard database.

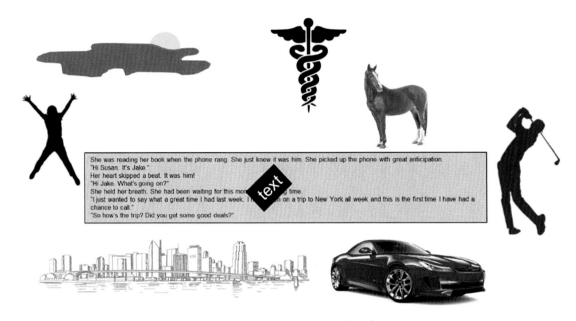

The challenge with context is that 99% of context
exists outside of the text itself

FIG. 17.1.4
Nearly all context exists outside the text itself.

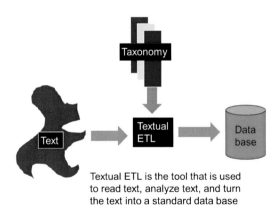

Textual ETL is the tool that is used
to read text, analyze text, and turn
the text into a standard data base

FIG. 17.1.5
Textual ETL.

THE PROCESSING COMPONENTS OF TEXTUAL ETL

From a processing standpoint, there are two major processing sections of textual ETL. There is document fracturing, and there is named value processing (sometimes called "in-line contextualization").

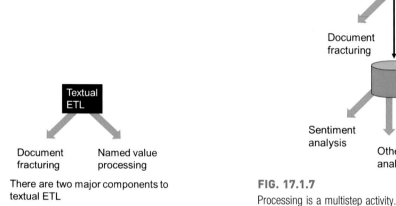

FIG. 17.1.7
Processing is a multistep activity.

There are two major components to
textual ETL

FIG. 17.1.6
The components of textual ETL.

Fig. 17.1.6 shows these two major divisions of the processing that occur within textual ETL.

In document fracturing, a document is processed in such a way that—upon being processed—the document remains in a recognizable state. In named value processing, the document is processed, but the document itself is not recognizable at the end of processing.

SECONDARY ANALYSIS

Textual ETL is really only the first step in the analysis of text. Textual ETL produces a simple file that is then further analyzed. The first step gathers the information and contextualizes it. However, to do textual analysis, further processing is necessary.

Fig. 17.1.7 shows that the output from textual ETL goes through a secondary analysis. Typical secondary processing includes such activities as sentiment analysis, medical record analysis and reconstruction, call center analysis, and other types of analysis.

For example, sentiment analysis includes such activities as scope of inference analysis, connector analysis, and predicate location.

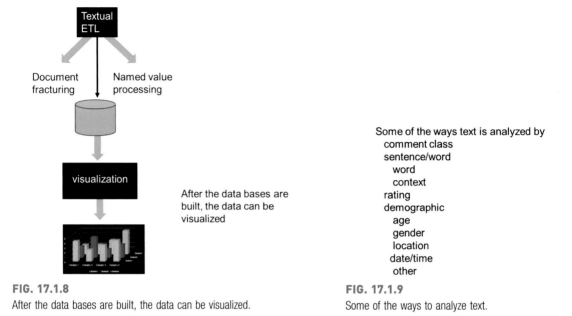

FIG. 17.1.8
After the data bases are built, the data can be visualized.

FIG. 17.1.9
Some of the ways to analyze text.

Fig. 17.1.8 shows the secondary processing that occurs after textual ETL is done.

VISUALIZATION

After secondary analysis is done, the results can then be visualized. The output of the secondary analysis is a simple database that can easily be used by an analytic visualizer.

Fig. 17.1.8 shows that visualization is the best way to show the results of analytic processing.

The visualization that is done can be customized to suit the application. There are MANY ways the analyst can shape the visualization. Fig. 17.1.9 shows some of the typical parameters that can be used to shape the visualization.

MERGING TEXT BASED DATA AND STRUCTURED DATA

The primary value in being able to meaningfully put textual data into a database is to analyze the data. And there is great value in being able to do just that. However, there are some other really important benefits. One of those benefits is to be able to intermix textual data and standard structured data.

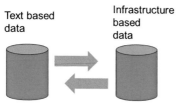

FIG. 17.1.10
Intermixing data.

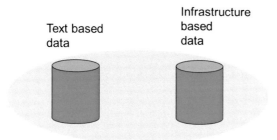

FIG. 17.1.11
Analytical possibilities.

Fig. 17.1.10 shows that once textual data are captured inside a standard database, it can be freely mixed with classical structured data.

And once text-based data and classical structured data can be mixed together, they can be analyzed together. Fig. 17.1.11 shows the ability of the analyst to do investigation into intermixed data.

The mixing of the two types of data together sets the stage for analytic possibilities that were once only a dream of the analyst.

An Introduction to Data Visualizations

INTRODUCTION TO DATA VISUALIZATIONS—OVERVIEW

Data is necessary for business. When data is put into a visualization, they can be used to tell a story. Telling a story is a sequence of events that can show past, present, and future. Using visualizations to tell a story about data can show patterns, trends, and relationships to focus on what is important. A visualization can also be used to enable discovery of new information by making it easier to understand the data and the different dimensions hidden in the data. Visualizations are changing the way we tell a story about the data to provide better information, knowledge, and insights.

■ Example

A hotel collects a large amount of data through guest surveys. By combining guest survey data with review data from the Internet, a visualization is created to better understand where hotel improvements are needed. By observing trends or patterns in all the data collected from the hotel guest surveys over time, additional insights about the hotel operations may be gained. Using visualizations allow the hotel manager to explore the data and show collectively insights across all data that tell a story where the hotel may have some strategic opportunities before business is lost to competitors. ■

Fig. 18.1.1 shows where a visualization can help along the path to gaining deeper insights in the data for decisions and actions that provide business value.

Data can take opinions and turn them into facts. Fact-based decision-making requires not only good data but also the ability to turn the data into useful information and knowledge through analysis. Many decision-makers are not in the role of analyzing or working with data; they require data to be presented in a format for them to make decisions. Visualizations allow data to be explored easily or to be presented in a way where they can be better understood for

Data Architecture. https://doi.org/10.1016/B978-0-12-816916-2.00052-8

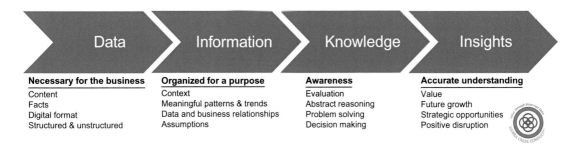

FIG. 18.1.1
Using visualizations for data to insights.

decisions to be made. When visualizations are created correctly, good decisions can be made that provide business value.

PURPOSE AND CONTEXT

A good visualization is one that is understood by the audience and meets the purpose for creating the visualization. The purpose may be to show analytic results to executive management, to show social media trends to educate the public, or to show findings in the data to improve business performance. If the purpose is to improve business performance, a dashboard can be created through the use of visualizations. The outcome of a good visualization will be improved collaboration, decisions, and actionable insights.

Visualizations can be used to explore the data or to tell a story. They can be simple or more complex depending on the story to be told and the data available. Selecting the appropriate forms for the story to be told is important to make it easy to understand by the audience. It is also important to add additional details to the visualization such as labels to ensure it is interpreted correctly by the audience and the proper context is understood. Fig. 18.1.2 is an example of a bad visualization due to missing titles. Although this visualization includes a scale, it is not clear what is being compared and can be misinterpreted or misleading.

VISUALIZATION—A SCIENCE AND AN ART

Telling a story about the data is both a science and an art. Selecting the right colors in the visualization can have an impact on how the story is interpreted. Certain colors such as reds and greens should be avoided as indicators as readers who are color-blind may not tell the difference in the colors. Both shapes and colors should be used. Colors may relate directly to a business, or certain colors can trigger different emotions in a visualization. Blues can have

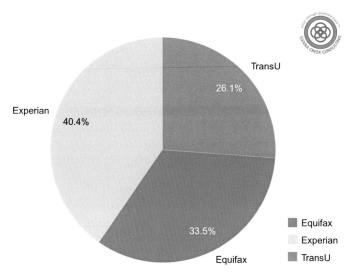

FIG. 18.1.2
Bad visualization showing missing titles.

a calming effect and greens can have a feeling of safety, where reds can generate danger or energy and purple can generate feelings of power or luxury. Shapes, colors, different color hues, and appropriate font sizes should be considered to present the story in a way that the audience can easily understand it in the right context. Too much information should also be avoided, so the story presented in the visualization is clear and not cluttered as shown in Fig. 18.1.3.

VISUALIZATION FRAMEWORK

A framework or methodology should be used to create a visualization that is interpreted in a way that brings value to the audience. Too often, a developer has a story in mind, but without using a clear methodology, the solution is not interpreted in a meaningful way or with the right context. Poor decisions can be made if the context is not clear or if the purpose for the visualization was not well defined in the beginning. Fig. 18.1.4 shows a framework that is easy and effective to use when creating a visualization.

STEP 1: DEFINE

The first step to create a good visualization is to define what problem needs to be better understood through analyzing and presenting the data in a visualization solution. This step involves understanding the purpose for the visualization, and who will have access to view or interact with the visualization

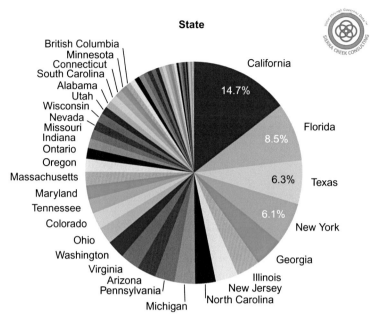

FIG. 18.1.3
Bad visualization example showing clutter.

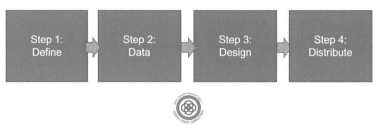

FIG. 18.1.4
Visualization framework.

when it is complete. Different roles in the organization may understand or use the results in different ways. Table 18.1.1 shows some examples of different roles to consider before creating a visualization to understand the business need or purpose.

The define step also considers the purpose for the visualization to meet the needs of the audience. Will the visualization be used to inform or educate the audience, or will it be used to influence a decision? Is there an immediate problem to be solved, or is the purpose to explore the data to provide more insights for strategic decisions? To answer these questions, it will be important

Table 18.1.1 Example Visualization Audience Roles and Actions

Role	Purpose or Action
Executive	Corporate strategy decisions
Chief data officer (CDO)	Influence corporate strategy and define data management strategy
Business manager	Understand performance
Data analyst	Immediate response
Customers or prospects	Inform or educate

for the visualization designer to meet with the audience to understand the business need or purpose at the beginning.

■ Example

Hotel staff tells management new mattresses are needed because of guest feedback. The hotel manager needs to decide where to invest in hotel improvements. The visualization designer meets with the hotel manager to understand the business problem. Data are collected from guest surveys and online comments, and a visualization is designed to look at guest sentiment over time. The visualization is used to explore the data and to determine if bed comfort or mattress complaints are a problem compared with other issues. The visualization designer presents the story by showing different visualizations with a recommendation to the hotel manager who can see clearly where funding is needed to improve guest feedback and reduce loss of business.   ■

STEP 2: DATA

The second step to create a good visualization is to understand the data to be used for the visualization. Creating a visualization should be relative to the purpose as defined in the first step. Understanding what type of data is available, how much data are available, and if the data available can tell the right story through a visualization is also important.

Types of Data

When it comes to visualizations, data can be categorized into different types. The most common groupings are known as *structured* or *unstructured*. When data are put into a workable format, such as a table with rows and columns or a database, it is considered structured. Unstructured data include data that do not fit into a standard workable format and may include data such as text or comments. When working with unstructured data to create a visualization, additional work may be needed first to put the data into a workable format.

Data Sources

Too often, companies are *data-rich but information-poor*. This is usually the case when there are a lot of data, but they reside in many different places and don't integrate well to be useful. For example, data may be in a spreadsheet, text file, or database. To create a visualization, data can be gathered from many different sources, but it's important to understand how the different data sets may be related. Not all data gathered may be used or important that can be determined when creating the visualization. Data sources may be internal to the company or external, such as publicly available data. Depending on the visualization software used, there might be additional data provided to enrich the visualization such as maps. An example of using public review data from the Internet and combining it with Maps using Qlik Sense[1] is shown in Fig. 18.1.5. This example shows higher volumes of data by location on a map using bubble size.

Other examples of data sources include the following:

- Operational applications
- Cloud systems
- Files (such as Excel and comma-separated values (CSV))
- Time-tracking systems
- Scanning systems
- E-mails

FIG. 18.1.5
Data visualized using Qlik Sense map feature.

---

[1]Qlik Sense is an analytic tool that can be used for creating visualizations. https://www.qlik.com/us/products/qlik-sense

- Customer call centers
- Surveys
- Internet

Data Organization

The data must be organized to create a visualization. This means data must be put into a workable format. Most tools for creating a visualization provide detailed information how to manage data in the application or how to connect different data sources. Best practice will require the data to be organized into a rows and column or table format. Each value in the table should be the same unit of measure. For example, Table 18.1.2 shows airline flight data in a row and column format and having the same unit of measure. When dealing with time data, the time format must also be consistent. For example, dates should be in a consistent format such as MMDDYYYY to be visualized correctly.

Table 18.1.2 Airline Flight Data Organized in a Row and Column Format

Year	Airline	Domestic Flights	International Flights	Total Flights
2017	Southwest	1,313,573	34,308	1,347,881
2017	American Airlines	886,803	193,145	1,079,948
2017	Delta	917,231	144,295	1,061,526
2017	United	580,293	167,578	747,871
2017	JetBlue	291,995	62,369	354,364

Depending on the story to tell, skills and knowledge in statistics may be needed. More complicated visualizations can use calculations to show the results of the analysis. Although visualizations can tell a story using good data, they can also be used to distort reality by presenting the data in different ways. When using line or bar charts, use caution not to distort the data by truncating the bottom of the line or bar chart where differences between the data points appear larger. Also, use caution with scales, such as different size bubbles to ensure they are at the correct scale for comparisons.

Data Quality

Data quality is important for a good visualization. Good data include data that are complete, clean, not questionable or conflicting, and valid. Quality data can lead to better decisions and better visualizations. There are different dimensions of data quality to be considered including the following:

- Accuracy—correct values
- Completeness—no missing values
- Consistency—same unit of measures or time format
- Integrity—data that are reliable
- Timeliness—data relevant to the time period
- Uniqueness—removal of duplicates

- Validity—data that are valid and not made up
- Accessibility—data that are accessible with permissible use

Data can be collected from many different places. Before designing a visualization, it's important to understand the data that will be used. Data can be structured, such as a customer name and location, or unstructured, such as a customer comment or phone call transcribed to text. When collecting the data, it's important to understand how different data sets are related. For example, if structured customer data and unstructured customer comments are going to be used, then how are they related? What will be communicated through a visualization and what kind of story will be told? By understanding these questions, then the right type of visualization can be used.

STEP 3: DESIGN

The concept of using a visualization to represent data has been around for hundreds of years. Today, with the advancements in technology and business intelligence (BI) technology capabilities, there are many tools available to help create a visualization. Technology has made it possible to process high amounts of data quickly. Technology may continue to advance capabilities to create a visualization—perhaps through audio describing what a user wants to see or through machine learning. No matter where we are going with the creation of a visualization, there are fundamentals that are important to understand. When it comes to design, the most important fundamental is to ensure the context of the visualization is understood by the user. Before the *design* step, it's important to have followed the methodology and have the *define* and the *data* steps understood. Choosing the appropriate chart requires an understanding of the data properties and purpose for the visualization.

Forms of Visualizations

When the business need or problem is understood and the data have been gathered, the visualization can be designed. There are many different forms of visualizations that can be used depending on the data, but choosing the right visualization to improve the user experience in telling the story is important. All visualizations should include not only the visual that represents the data but also additional information such as labels and text so the audience can understand the content and the context. Table 18.1.3 shows some basic forms of visualizations that can be used. Some of these charts can be enhanced; for example, a time element can be used for a bubble chart to show changes over time. Examples for some common basic charts will be discussed. However, there are many different forms of visualizations that should be reviewed before designing a visualization.

Table 18.1.3 Forms of Visualizations

Visualization Form	Number of Categories	Number of Numerical Variables	Purpose	Audience Ease of Interpretation	Example
Number chart		1	Display	Easy	Average rating or score
Pie chart	1	1	Proportion comparison	Easy	% of negative sentiment by company
Bar chart (basic)	1	1	Showing exact values	Easy	Top consumer complaints about Equifax in a given period of time
Bar chart (grouped side by side)	Multiple	1 or 2	Compare categories	Easy	Compare hotels grouped by hotel ratings
Bar chart (Stacked)	Multiple	1	Compare categories	Easy	Compare hotels by on line customer review sentiment
Line (single)	1	1 + Date variable	Trends over time	Easy	Sales over time
Line (multiple)	Multiple	1 + Date variable	Compare multiple categories over time	Difficult	Consumer sentiment over time for each credit bureau
Maps	Multiple	Multiple	Comparing variables and geospatial analytics	Difficult	Location and volume of customer complaints
Scatter chart	0 or 1	2	Relationships and correlations between numerical values	Difficult	Relationship between cancer rates and country
Bubble chart	0 or 1	3	Relationships and correlations between numerical values	Difficult	Comparing airlines by assets, revenue, and profit

Number Charts

The most common visualization is a simple number chart. A number chart as shown in Fig. 18.1.6 is a good visual for a dashboard to easily communicate any total such as a count, a percentage, an average, or a dollar amount. Trend indicators can also be used in a number chart but should represent the same period of time (such as annual, quarterly, daily, or monthly).

FIG. 18.1.6
Number chart.

Pie Charts

Pie charts have been around for hundreds of years to show parts of a total relationship over a static period of time (such as a slice of the pie vs. the whole pie).
Pie charts are a simple way to visualize simple comparisons for a single category; however, they do not work well to compare the size or segment across
multiple pie charts. A pie chart splits a population of data for a single category
into segments, and the total of all the segments equals 100%. If there are too
many segments, then pie charts do not work well as they can be difficult to label
or to show the difference in proportions. Also, a pie chart can take a lot of space
on a dashboard or report. Fig. 18.1.7 shows an example of a pie chart where the
category is ratings for a hotel. Ratings are segmented 1 through 5, and the pie
chart shows the percentage of each segment.

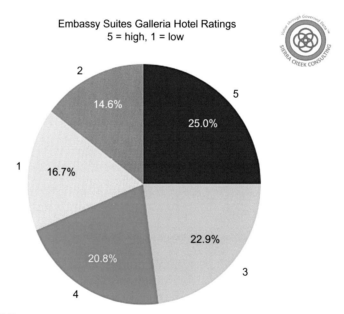

FIG. 18.1.7
Pie chart.

Bar Chart

A bar chart is used for comparison ranking across one or multiple categories.
There are different types of bar charts, and choosing the best one will depend
on the data available. A simple bar chart is easy to interpret and can be used to
show totals or trends for a single category. Fig. 18.1.8 shows an example of a
simple bar chart.

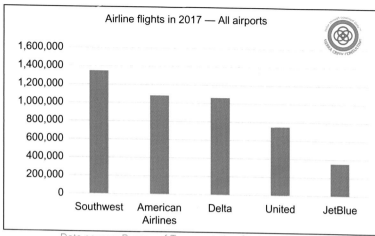

FIG. 18.1.8
Bar chart.

Stacked Bar Chart

A stacked bar chart can be used to show totals for a single category or to compare categories when there is more than one. For example, Fig. 18.1.9 shows the

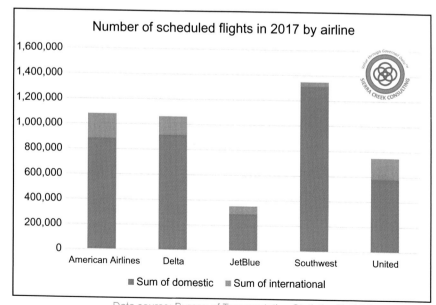

FIG. 18.1.9
Stacked bar chart example.

number of scheduled flights in 2017 for US airlines by domestic and international in one stacked bar chart using public. Stacked bar charts are great to show survey responses or any type of data that has multiple categories.

Horizontal Bar Chart

A horizontal bar chart works well if the category labels are long. Although the data presented are similar to the simple or stacked bar chart, using the horizontal bar chart may be selected to better display the labels or for sizing depending on where it will be displayed. A horizontal bar chart may be chosen over the other types of bar charts to better tell the story with the data available (Fig. 18.1.10).

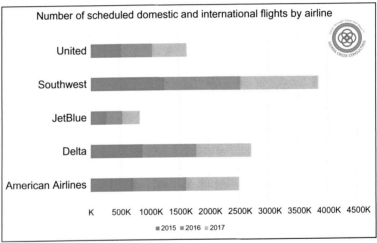

Data source: Bureau of Transportation Statistics T-100 Segment data

FIG. 18.1.10
Horizontal bar chart.

Line Chart

Another basic form of visualizing data is using a line chart. Line charts require time data in consistent intervals. Fig. 18.1.11 shows an example of a multiple line chart where there are multiple categories plotted over time. The variable being plotted is customer sentiment for three different companies. This type of chart is not good for a static visualization, such as a PowerPoint presentation as it can be too cluttered. However, using a visualization tool such as Qlik Sense, the audience can interact and select a custom time range that will allow the user to drill down to see more details. This chart combined with others in an interactive visualization can be very powerful for exploring the data to tell a story.

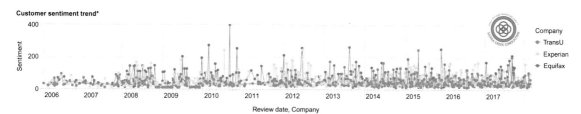

FIG. 18.1.11
Line chart showing multiple categories.

Bubble chart

Another type of chart to compare different variables is a bubble chart or scatterplot. A bubble chart is a good visualization to show in a 3-D format, but it is more complicated and requires more skill to create. Different colors or bubble sizes can be used to show a lot of information in a single chart. A bubble chart looks at data in a snapshot of time. However, by plotting different snapshots of data over different periods of time, this chart can become animated to show changes through data in an interesting form.

STEP 4: DISTRIBUTE

A data visualization is a way to tell a story through a graphic representation of the data and a way to share the story among both technical and nontechnical people. The last step when the visualization is complete is to *distribute* the visualization. There are many ways a visualization can be shared or distributed. It's important to consider this step before you design your visualization as the purpose will define how it should be distributed. Is the purpose for the visualization to inform or to allow data discovery? Will your audience view only or interact with the visualization to discover insights?

Purpose: To Inform or Educate

To inform or educate the audience, the story should unfold by showing the data and visualizations in an order that tells the story. For example, if data are collected to understand customer sentiment about their hotel stay, a visualization can be created to show the customer sentiment over time and put into a story format. Consider using data from the past, present, and predicted future to tell stories for the best outcome or decisions.

Visualizations can be shared or distributed to inform or educate the audience in different ways that may include the following.

> *PowerPoint:* Visualization charts may be copied and pasted to a PowerPoint slide with additional details added to tell the highlight what is being told.

Dashboard: A dashboard is a collection of visualizations aligned to the business goals to be used as a management report. A dashboard can provide an at-a-glance view of key performance indicators (KPIs) and measures to drive action for improvements.

Infographic: An infographic is similar to a visualization as it is a visual representation of the data. However, an infographic may contain more images, pictures, and words that are conceptual in addition to data in a visual form. Infographics are usually very focused and used to captivate an audience. They can be a single page or multiple pages in length. Infographics can be a great tool to use for marketing campaigns or to summarize a study to include visualizations.

Purpose: To Interact or Explore

If the purpose for the visualization is to explore the data, then an interactive visualization can be valuable. To distribute an interactive visualization will depend on the software used. Most visualization tools have the capability to publish the visualization to the Internet (cloud) so the user can interact and explore the data. With defined user permissions, the user can change different variables, while all charts in the story update. Interactive visualizations are great for the user to do "what if" questions and to see the outcome visually.

DATA VISUALIZATION TOOLS AND SOFTWARE

The practice of creating visualizations is rapidly growing just as machine learning, digital facial recognition, unstructured data analytics, and data science are growing. There are many smart and user-friendly tools available for creating visualizations. Selecting the appropriate tool will depend on many factors, including the knowledge, skills, and abilities of the visualization producer. Some features to consider when selecting a tool include the following:

- Ease of use
- Drag and drop capability
- Ability to connect to multiple data sources
- Ability to manage the data
- Open and standard APIs
- User-friendly development environment
- Ability to share and collaborate
- Interactive capability
- Features that are up to date
- Scalable
- Manageable security
- Nice-looking visual results to fit the purpose

Here are some of the leading tools on the market today for creating visualizations without requiring detailed programming skills:

- Qlik
- Tableau
- Microsoft Power BI
- Sisense

SUMMARY

There is great value in the process of creating and telling a story through visualizations. The visualization framework is the best methodology to use to ensure visualizations are created with the right content and can be understood in the right context. The process of *defining* the purpose and talking with the audience, collecting the *data*, *designing* the visualization in a story format, and *distributing* the visualization allows data to be more easily understood for the audience to focus on what is important. Using visualizations to tell a story through data is a great way to provide better information, knowledge, and insights. Telling a story through visualizations will continue to be necessary moving forward to enable data to be better understood for more accurate outcomes and decisions.

Glossary

6 sigma Six standard deviations used to describe a level of quality in which six standard deviations of the population fall within the upper and lower limits of quality

Access The operation of seeking, reading, or writing data on a storage unit

Accuracy to reality A characteristic of information quality measuring the degree to which a data value correctly represents the attributes of the real-world object or event

Accuracy to surrogate source A measure of the degree to which data agree with the original, acknowledged authoritative source of data about a real-world object or event

Acronym resolution The process of expanding acronyms into their literal meaning

Accuracy A qualitative assessment of freedom from error or a quantitative measurement of the magnitude of error

Active data dictionary An automated metadata management facility that is tightly and interactively woven into the development and analysis process

Actuary A professional mathematician trained in the art of studying life expectancy and accident probabilities

Ad hoc processing One time only casual access and manipulation of data never used before, usually done in a heuristic, iterative manner

Address The location of a unit of data

After image A snapshot of data placed on a log after the conclusion of a transaction

Agent of change A motivating force large enough not to be denied

Algorithm The instructions that govern the flow of activity in a procedure

Alternate spelling A different way of forming a word pattern

Amazon.com A successful dot.com retailer company

Analog A type of computing driven by sensory perceptions and signals, as opposed to a digital computer

Anchor data in a dis The key attribute(s) of a dis

API Application programming interface

Application A computerized system dedicated to solving or empowering a specific business function

Application blocking of data The grouping of different occurrences of data into a single unit of storage controlled by the application programmer

Application database A collection of data organized in support of a specific function

Archival database A collection of data containing information of a historical nature

Archival processing The activities surrounding older and/or inactive data

Array of data A data structure that holds multiple occurrences of data

Artifact A design technique used to support referential integrity in a decision support system (DSS) environment

ATM Automated teller machine—a "money machine"

Attribute A value of data that is distinguishable from other values

Audit trail Data that are useful in tracing the activity of one or more transactions

Availability The measurement of time for the online system to be up and running

Backup A file serving the purpose of allowing an online file to be restored as of some moment in time

Batch Computer environment in which long running sequential programs can run where there is no conflict with the online transaction environment

Batch processing The collection of transaction into "batches" that are processed collectively

BCD Binary-coded decimal

BI Business intelligence

Bias The condition in sampling where the sample contains data that are not representative of the whole

Bill of materials A listing of the components of an assembly

Blather Email message generated internally that have no business relevance

Block of data A large physical unit of data that can contain records of data

Blog A personal diary that is open for the public to scrutinize

Boiler plate Text that is copied verbatim for the purpose of serving as a general template

Browser A program executing on a client to interpret a Web page (usually in HTML) and render a proper image of that page

Buffer A work space, usually in memory

Business process A synonym for value chain, the term used to differentiate a value chain of activities from a functional process or functional set of activities

Business rule A statement expressing a policy, guideline, or condition that governs business activities and/or business decisions

Byte A basic unit of storage, usually 8 bits in length

C Name of a programming language first developed as part of the UNIX project at AT&T but now widely used by personal computer software developers

Cache A buffer inside the computer built and maintained at the device level. Retrieval of data stored in cache is accomplished in terms of electronic speeds

Call center A facility of the organization where an agent of the organization can engage in conversation with other people

CASE Computer-aided software engineering—generally refers to a class of software products that are used to partially automate the design and development of other software

CDC Change data capture—the incremental changes to a database are captured and stored and then retransacted or logged onto another database

Cell of a spreadsheet A basic unit of data found in a spreadsheet

Change data capture (CDC) The data that are gathered incrementally as a result of transaction processing in order to form the basis of update to a data warehouse

Class I ODS An ODS whose latency is measured in 1 second or less

Class II ODS An ODS whose latency is measured in 4 hours or less

Class III ODS An ODS whose latency is measured in 24 hours or less

Client The node in a client-server architecture that initiates a request to a server and processes the results

Click stream data Automated measurements of the activity occurring on a web site

Cluster A means of storing date from multiple tables based on a common key value

COBOL Common business-oriented language—an early popular computer language, designed for the business user (see Grace Hopper)

Code (1) A symbolic value or (2) instructions written in a language directing the computer how to proceed

Collision The mapping of two or more records to the same location by the hasher

Column A vertical table in which values are selected from the same domain

Comments A field of data containing free-form text

Compliance Business rules enforced by legislation or some other governing body

Connector A symbol used to indicate that one logical grouping of data has a relationship with another logical grouping of data

Constraint The business rule that places a restriction on business actions and/or decisions

Content enriched Big data whose content has been contextualized

Context The surrounding environment that gives definition to a word

Contextualization The process of identifying the context of a word

Core An early form of storage for storing data available to the CPU. Core operated under the principles governed by the hysteresis curve

Corporate data The entire body of data of the corporation

CRM Customer relationship management—a popular DSS application used to streamline customer relationships

CRT Cathode-ray tube—a display device; a screen

Cullinet An early DBMS vendor selling a networked database management system

Current valued data Data whose accuracy is as of the moment of access; online data

Curve of usefulness The curve that indicates that the fresher data are, the more likely they are to be useful

Customer The user or consumer of a product or a service

Cycle The complete steps required to execute a process

Cycle time The measurement of cycle time

Data analyst An individual who gathers and analyzes the results of the execution of a process

Database A structured collection of units of data organized around some topic or theme

Data definition The process of defining the semantics of data

Data element An attribute belonging to an entity

Data flow diagram (DFD) A schematic indicating the direction of the movement of data

Data governance The activities necessary to the management of integrity of data

Data integrity The assurance of the timeliness and the accuracy of data in a database system

Data item set (DIS) The midlevel data model

Data mart A subset of a data warehouse that's usually oriented to a business group or team

Data mining Analysis of large quantities of data to find patterns such as groups of records, unusual records, and dependencies

Data model An abstraction of data

Data quality The properties of data embodied by the "five Cs": clean, consistent, conformed, current, and comprehensive

Data scientist An individual dedicated to the study of patterns found in data

Data store (1) A component of a DFD in which data are shown to be collected outside of a process or (2) a place where data are kept

Data structure A logical relationship among data elements designed to support specific data manipulation functions

Data virtualization The process of retrieving and manipulating data without requiring details of how the data formatted or where the data are located

Data visualization Presenting data in a visual way, such as with graphs and charts, helps business people glean insights they might not otherwise see. Dashboards use the concept of data visualization to present data for analysis. IT is often a part of self-service BI but is only as effective as the quality of the data it draws upon

Data warehouse A subject-oriented, integrated, nonvolatile, time-variant collection of data in support of management's decisions

DB2/UDB Database management system by IBM

DBMS Database management system—system software that manages the storage and access of data on disk storage

DC Data communications—technology that manages messages generated as part of transaction processing

Decryption The process of returning text to its original state after that text has been encrypted

Defect An item that does not conform to expected quality standards

Denormalization The design technique of placing normalized data in a structure so that access to the data is optimized

Dependent data mart A data mart whose sole source of data is the data warehouse; a dependent data mart is a component of the corporate information factory

Derived data Data whose value is achieved as the result of a calculation

Dimension A category for summarizing or viewing data (e.g., a time period, product, product line, and geographic region)

Dimensional modeling A generally accepted practice in the data warehouse industry to structure data intended for user access, analysis, and reporting in dimensional data models

Dimension table The place where extraneous data that relate to a fact table inside a start join are placed

Direct access of data The ability of a database management system to directly find data, as opposed to having to sequentially search for data

Directory A table, block, folder, or database containing indexes and their interpretation

Dis Data item set—the midlevel of a data model

Disk storage Physical media used for storing values of data

Distillation The process of analyzing a large number of records (usually big data records) and producing a single result

Document A basic unit of textual data

Documentation Verbiage describing a system, application, database, procedure, etc.

Document fracturing In textual disambiguation, the process of sequentially processing text looking for text that satisfies such criteria as stop word processing, stemming, homographic resolution, and so forth

Download The movement of a bulk amount of data from one environment to another

Drill down processing The analytic activity of examining an element of data at a lower level of detail after examining the value of data at a higher level

Ed Yourdon An information technology pioneer who started the "structured" movement

Electronic text Text in a form where the words of the text are recognized by the computer

ELT Extract/load/transform—the process of extracting, loading, and transforming data. The problem with ELT is that many organizations only extract and load the data but fail to transform the data

E-mail Messages from one party to another carried on an electronic medium

Encoding The process of encryption of text into a form unrecognizable by an outsider

Encryption The process of scrambling data into a form that is not recognizable

Entity A broad classification of data; a subject area

ERD Entity relationship diagram—a logical description of how the major subject areas of the corporation fit together

ERP Enterprise resource planning—the name given to technology where applications are written by a vendor where there are multiple users of the software

ETL Extract, transform, and load—the process in which data are taken from the source system, configured, and stored in a data warehouse or database. ETL tools automate data integration tasks

Event The demarcation or recording made of the passage of some activity

External data Data whose source is outside of the system of the organization

Export The process of moving data from one environment to another

Fact table The data structure where basic facts in a star join are stored

Farmer A person in the organization who does analytic work that is repetitive and predictable

Feedback loop A procedure where the results of one iteration of processing are made available for the next iteration of processing

Field An element of data and attribute

File A collection of records

File structure The organization of the collection of records

Filter The process of removing data from a set of data based on the value of one or more fields of data

Flat file A collection of records where the structure of each record is identical

Foreign key An attribute used for distinguishing a record that participates in a relationship with another table

Format The arrangement of data onto a data structure

Functional decomposition The process of reducing a large function or process into smaller finer functions

Generic data model A data model of an industry, rather than of a specific company. A generic data model can be used as a template that can be customized for a given company within the industry that has been modeled

Granularity The level of detail found in a record of data

Great divide The division of big data between repetitive data and nonrepetitive data

GUI Graphical user interface

Hadoop, technology designed to house big data A framework for managing data

Hashing algorithm An algorithm converts data values into an address

Heuristic process An iterative process, where the next step of analysis depends on the results attained in the current level of analysis

HIPAA The law protecting medical privacy

Hit An occurrence of data that satisfies one or more search criteria

Hollerith punched cards An early means of storing data, typically containing 80 columns

Homograph A word or phrase whose interpretation depends on the person who originally wrote the word or phrase

Homographic resolution The process of contextualizing data based on the identity of the person who uttered the text

Host The processor receiving and processing a transaction

HTML Hypertext markup language

IBM A large computer manufacturer

IBM 360 A machine that standardized operating systems. With the IBM 360 line, there was compatibility of processing across different machine types. A revolutionary technology that changed the face of computing

Identifier An attribute used to pick out a row of data from a collection of rows of data

IDMS A network DBMS by Cullinet

Image A picture, such as a real estate photo of a house for sale or an x-ray

IMS Information management system—a hierarchical DBMS by IBM

Index A database shows the address of a database record based on a value found in the record

In-line contextualization The technique of inferring context by establishing a beginning delimiter and an ending delimiter

Inmon, Bill The father of data warehouse and textual disambiguation

Instance A member of a shared partition database system, such as an Oracle cluster

Integrity of data The assurance that data are correct and accurate as stored

Internet The system by which data are stored and are made available to a large audience

Interactive A mode of processing in which the end user directly moves data into and out of a system

Intranet A TCP/IP network that is physically separated from the Internet

Inverted list A data structure in which a flat file is indexed

I/O Input/output operation—the activity or reading or writing a record to disk storage. I/O operations happen in terms of mechanical speeds

ISO International Organization for Standardization

IT The information technology organization—the organizational entity charged with building and managing applications and technology systems

Iterative process A process that is done in short finite steps, where there are many steps, but where each step is taken quickly

Join The process of merging two or more tables on the basis of a common key

Key An identifying attribute of data

KPI Key performance indicator—a measurement made periodically by the organization that examines important variables

Language The text that is used to communicate with the computer. Some languages are optimized for ease of use. Other languages are optimized for speed of processing

Legacy systems The older systems used to run the business of the corporation as it was defined 10 or 20 years ago

Line The hardware by which data flow into or out of a device

Lineage of data The "family tree" of data. Data are transformed in many ways as they pass through a system. The lineage is a record of the transformations of data from the moment they enter a system until they are used in analysis.

Link The mechanism by which two systems or two environments form a common relationship

Linux An operating system

Load utility A utility provided by a DBMS vendor in which data are efficiently loaded into the DBMS

Lock The means by which data are protected from update process while the transaction that is updating the data is in execution

Log A journal of activities

Log tape A sequential record of the activities that have occurred inside a system. Sometimes called a "journal" tape. The primary purpose of a log tape is for backup and recovery of a system

Machine cycle A full cycle of processing inside a computer

Magnetic tape An early sequential storage mechanism

Mainframe The monolithic processors produced by IBM and Amdahl

Mapping The instructions to textual ETL as to how to interpret a document or type of document

MapReduce A language for processing big data

MDM Master data management—the set of processes used to create and maintain a consistent view, also referred to as a master list, of key enterprise reference data. These data include such entities as customers, prospects, suppliers, employees, products, services, assets, and accounts. They also include the groupings and hierarchies associated with these entities

Mean The average value of a set of values

Median value The middle value of a set of values when the values are ranked according to value

Memory The high-speed storage that is available to the computer. Memory is accessed and processed in terms of electronic speeds

Message The data input by the end user in order to initiate a transaction

Metadata The classic definition of metadata as "data about the data."

ODS Operational data store—a type of database often used as an interim area for a data warehouse. Unlike a data warehouse, which contains static data, the contents of the ODS are updated through the course of business operations

Meteorologic data Data downloaded from a satellite regarding weather patterns on earth

Methodology A prescribed way of executing a process

Microsoft A software vendor primarily of desktop technology

MPP Massively parallel processing—a type of operating system capable of handling large volumes of data

Multiplex The ability of a system to share memory

Named value processing One of the two primary processing paths for textual ETL. Named value processing includes standard index processing, in-line contextualization, and custom variable processing

Narrative Prosaic text

Network The means by which electronic communications occurs between two or more nodes

Networked DBMS A DBMS whose primary relationship between records is a networked relationship

NLP Natural language processing—the notion that the context of text can be inferred from the text itself

Node A processing location in a network

Nonlinear format A format of text or reported values where the text or variables are arranged in a nonlinear format

Nonrepetitive data Data whose records have no predictable pattern of structure or content. Typical nonrepetitive records include e-mail, call center data, warranty claim data, and insurance claim data

Nonvolatile data Data that once written cannot be changed. Sometimes called "snapshot" data

Normalization The process of organizing data at its detailed level into according to its existence criteria

Occurrence A specific instance of an entity type

OCR Optical character recognition

ODS Operational data store—a data structure that contains some of the properties of the data warehouse and some of the properties of the operational system. As a rule, the ODS is an optional structure that is found at some companies and not at others

OLAP Online analytical processing—this technique for analyzing business data uses cubes, which are like multidimensional pivot tables in spreadsheets. OLAP tools can perform trend analysis and enable drilling down into data. They enable multidimensional analysis such as analyzing by time, product, and geography. The major types of OLAP processing are MOLAP (multidimensional) and ROLAP (relational). HOLAP (hybrid) processing combines them.

OLTP Online transaction processing—the environment where online transaction processing is executed

Online response time The length of time from the moment an operator initiates a transaction until that transaction returns output to the user

Online storage Storage devices that can be accessed directly and interactively

Ontology A logical relationship of elements participating in a taxonomy

Operating system The technology that controls the computer and all its operations

Operational BI Analytic processing based on data generated by operational processing

Operational environment The processing center where day-to-day transactional processing is supported

Operational system A system that manages and executes the transactions used in the day-to-day operations of the organization

Operations The department charged with running the computer environment

Optical disk A storage medium using lasers rather than magnetic devices

Oracle A large database vendor

Oxide The surface of the storage medium where bits are stored

Page A basic unit of storage in DASD

Paper tape A very early form of storage

Parallel I/O In a nonmainframe environment, when more than one processor does I/O at the same time, it is called parallel I/O

Parallel management of data The processing approach where multiple machines are run in tandem with each other so that the elapsed processing time is reduced

Parameter An elementary data value used as a criterion for qualification of data

Parent/child relationship A hierarchical relationship of data for every parent node, there can be from 0 to n children nodes.

Pareto chart A method of displaying data values over time and classification

Parity check A means of ensuring the quality of data at the lowest level of storage

Parsing The process of reading text and finding contextualized value that resides in the text

Partition A segmentation technique in which data are divided into physically different units

Passive data dictionary A repository of data where the storage of metadata may or may not be used in the development and analytic process

Pattern analysis The analysis that seeks to find recognizable patterns in the occurrence of points of data

PC Personal computer—a laptop/desktop device for personal computing

PDF Portable document format by Adobe

Peak period processing The time of day when the most activities are passing through the system

Performance The measurement of system response time

Physical characteristics of data The physical dimension and configuration of a unit of data or data structure

Physical model The physical definition of the shape and structure of data (as defined to the DBMS)

Poisson distribution The right-hand side of a bell curve as measured from the zero axis

Populate To load data into a previously unpopulated database

Population The totality of the sets of data constituting a database or a group of entities being analyzed

Post processing The processing that optionally can occur after text has passed through textual ETL

Prefix space The overhead space that every occurrence of data has that allows the system to form a structure of data

Preprocessing The editing that can precede textual processing

Primary key Unique identifying information for a unit of data

Primitive data Data whose existence depends on only a single occurrence of a major subject area of the enterprise

Probability of access The mathematical statement of the likelihood that a unit of data will be accessed

Processor The hardware at the center of the execution of a computer program

Program A procedure embodied in code

Proper text Formal text as taught by a teacher of language (as opposed to slang, shorthand, notes, comments, etc.)

Proximity analysis An analysis based on the closeness of words or taxonomies to each other

Public accounting firm An organization charged with commenting on the compliance of a publicly traded corporation to accounting standards and rules

Punched cards An early form of storage that had many disadvantages

Queue time The length of time a transaction waits in the processing queue before the transaction is processed

Query A procedure executed by a computer program in search of qualified data

Query language A computer language designed to support end user queries

Random access The ability of the system to directly access data

Random-access storage A storage technique where the time required to obtain information is independent of the location of the information most recently obtained

Random number generator An algorithm that is capable of generating numbers in a seemingly random sequence

Random sampling The process of selecting a subset of a large population for analysis

Record A unit of data that typically contains keys and attributes

Record locking A means of ensuring transaction integrity during update processing

Recovery The restoration of a system (usually an online system) to an earlier moment in time

Redundancy Multiple occurrences of the same unit of data

Referential integrity The process of relating data together in a disciplined manner

Relational model A form of data where data are normalized

Repeating groups A collection of data that occurs multiple times within a given record of data

Repetitive data Data whose units repeat in terms of structure and even content

Report decompilation The process of reading a report and reducing the report to a normalized database. In general report, decompilation is a nonlinear process because of the complexity of the format of the report

Reporting The process of collecting data from various sources and presenting it to business people in an understandable way

Repository A place where important corporate metadata are stored

Requirements A statement of what is needed in the functionality of a system

Reservations systems A system where corporation makes general reservations for services and products, such as an airline, hotel chain, or car rental organization

Response time The measurement of time from when a transaction is initiated until the first of the transaction output is returned to the user

ROI Return on investment

Rolling summary data A technique of archiving data where the most recent data are the most detailed stored and where over time the detailed data are rolled up into a summary-level data

Roman census approach The method of moving processing to the data rather than moving data to the processor

Root segment The base occurrence of data for an entity; the data to which all other data relate

Row A basic unit of storage; a record of data

SAP An ERP application software company

Sarbanes-Oxley Act A law requiring information compliance for publicly traded corporations. Sarbanes-Oxley was passed because of the misdeeds of Enron corporation

SAS A company specializing in statistical analysis software

Schema The means by which a pattern of data is identified

SDLC System development life cycle—the waterfall approach to the development of systems (see Ed Yourdon)

Security The protection of data and transactions

Select The identification of a set of data that meet specified criteria

Sequential analysis of data A process in which data are accessed sequentially

Sequential file A file of data that has been organized where one unit of data is accessed in a linear fashion

Scope of integration A statement of the limits of integration

SDLC System development life cycle—the development life cycle based on the contributions of Ed Yourdon and Tom Dimarco

Security The means by which data are protected

Self-service BI An infrastructure that allows BI consumers to get the information they need without the help of the IT group

Session The work or activities accomplished in one sitting by the end user

Shared memory An arrangement of processors in which up to four processors share the same memory (see multiplexing)

Shorthand The practice in transcription of not writing down actual words but writing down shortened symbols for those words

Silicon A raw material much like sand that can be shaped into many different end products, such as semiconductors, beer bottles, and body parts

Silicon Valley The location where original technological innovation starts, in the Northern California, San Jose, Santa Clara, Mountain View vicinity

Siloed systems The practice of building application system that has no interface or exchange of other application systems, where there are common data between those systems

Skip sequential The more of accessing data where data are accessed directly, followed by long periods of sequential access

SKU Stock keeping unit—in retailing, the practice of tracking a record of each unit of inventory

SLA Service-level agreement—the agreement within the corporation governing response time of transaction systems and "up time," the amount of time the system is up and available

Slang Improper language—language that is used improperly, such as the word "ain't"

Sort To arrange data in a sequence based on values found in the data

Snapshot record A record of data taken at a moment in time that cannot be updated

Snowflake structure The dimensional modeling approach where more than one star schema are joined together

Source code The uncompiled version of code

Spam Unwanted, unsolicited e-mail generated outside the corporation

Sparse index An index that contains only selected entries of data

Spider web systems The early architecture where applications grew in a siloed manner

Spreadsheet The primary tool found in the personal computing environment

SQL The language interface for relational systems

SQL Server The DBMS built and managed by Microsoft

Staging area A location where data that are to be transformed are held in abeyance waiting for other events to occur

Standard work unit (SWU) The process of creating small modules that can flow efficiently and without bottlenecks

Star schema (or "star join") A fact table and its related dimension tables

Statistical analysis The process of looking at a large number of values and evaluating the values mathematically

Stemming The reduction of words to their root. For example, the stem of moving, moved, mover, and move is the stem "mov"

Stop word A word in a language that is needed for communication but not needed to convey information. In English, there are stop words such as "a," "and," "the," "to," and "from"

Storage hierarchy Storage units linked to form a storage subsystem in which some units are small and fast to access and other units are larger and slower to access

State A stage in a life cycle

Structured data Data that are managed by a database management system

Subdoc processing The recognition by textual ETL of the logical grouping of sections of text

Subject-oriented database A database organized around the major entities of the corporation

Synonym In grammar, a word that is a substitute for another word

System of record (or "single version of the truth") The building of systems where there is integrity of data; there is one and only one location where any given unit of data is created, updated, and deleted from

Table A relation that consists of a set of columns with a heading and a set of rows (tuples)

Taxonomy A classification of text

TCP/IP Transmission control protocol/Internet protocol—networking protocol developed initially for DARPA widely used on UNIX networks

Teradata A database software company

Text Words; language

Textual disambiguation The process of reading text and formatting text into a standard database format

Textual ETL See textual disambiguation

Time stamping The practice of adding an element of time to a given row of data

Time variant Data that cannot be updated and whose value is accurate as of some one moment in time

Tom Demarco An early pioneer along with Ed Yourdon specializing in structured systems development

Transaction A computerized process that conducts business, usually updating or creating values

Transaction processing environment The location and equipment where transaction processing for a corporation takes place

Transparency The property of a structure of data to be able to be examined synthetically

Trend analysis The analysis of data over a period of time

Trigger The tripping of a condition that causes another event to occur

Uniprocessor A computer that has only one processor

Unstructured data Data whose logical organization is not apparent to the computer

Unstructured data warehouse A data warehouse whose source of data is unstructured data

Update To change or alter the value of data in a database

User The individual engaging in computation

Variable fields Fields that may or may not occur in a data structure

Variable length fields Fields of data that are not fixed in length

VDU Video display unit—a terminal

Video Media where there is moving action and accompanying audio

Voice recognition The technology that allows voice to be converted to an electronic format

Waterfall development The SDLC, so called because any one development activity must be done before the next activity can begin and because the output from any one level of activity becomes the input into the next level

Zachman, John A thought leader and pioneer in computer science

Zachman framework The development framework built by John Zachman where engineering principles are applied to the information systems development process

Index

Note: Page numbers followed by *f* indicate figures and *t* indicate tables.

Printed in the United States
By Bookmasters